Ecocriticism Unbound : Mapping Common Ground

Editors

Sarita Chanwaria   Sarita Jain

Pustak Bharati
Toronto Canada

Book Title : Ecocriticism Unbound : Mapping Common
Ground

Editors : Sarita Chanwaria and Sarita Jain

Published by :
Pustak Bharati (Books-India)
180 Torresdale Ave, Toronto Canada M2R 3E4
email : pustak.bharati.canada@gmail.com

Copyright ©2024

ISBN : 978-1-998027-04-0

ISBN 978-1-998027-04-0

9 781998 027040

Contents

PREFACE

Sustainable development - development that does not destroy or undermine the ecological, economic, or social basis on which continued development depends - is the only viable pathway to a more secure and hopeful future for rich and poor alike.

- **Maurice Strong** (1925-2015)
Opening Statement to the Rio Summit, 1992.
(www.mauricestrong.net)

The world today is facing ecological imbalance due to excessive modernization, urbanization and industrialization. During the last few decades, the expanding footprints of development and urbanization have posed a great threat to human society as well as the mother earth. The extensive misuse of natural resources has left us at the brink of ditch. The rainforests are cut down, the fossil fuel is fast decreasing, the cycle of season is at disorder, ecological disaster is frequent now round the globe and our environment is at margin. Under these circumstances, there arose a new theory of reading nature writing during the last decade of the previous century called Ecocriticism. It is a worldwide emergent movement, which came into existence as a reaction to man's anthropocentric attitude of dominating nature (Mishra, Sandip Kumar. (*Ecocriticism: A Study of Environmental Issues in Literature. BRICS Journal of Educational Research*, 6 (4), 168-170, 2016). The word 'Ecocriticism' came to light for the first time in William Ruckert's essay "Literature and Ecology: An Experiment in Ecocriticism" in 1978. He defines the term as the "application of ecology and ecological concepts to the study of literature because ecology (as a science, as a discipline, as the basis for human vision) has the greatest relevance to the present and the future of the world" (107). The word remained dormant until Cheryll Glotfelty popularized it in the critical field in 1990's. In the Introduction to her book

The Ecocriticism Reader she defines the term as:

…the study of the relationship between literature and the physical environment. Just as feminist criticism examines language and literature from a gender-conscious perspective, and Marxist criticism brings an awareness of modes of production and economic class to its reading of texts, ecocriticism takes an earth centered approach to literary studies"(xix).

Even though knowledge about environmental challenges has been widespread for several years now, but still due to materialistic and consumerist approach of people towards nature, not much success has been gained to address them positively. As far as literary world is concerned, we have many ecological thinkers, critics, poets and authors who have voiced their concern for the depletion of the natural environment through their writings and have created awareness among masses regarding conservation and sustainable use of natural resources and also cautioned man against the wrongs he is committing against nature.

In the words of M.H. Abrams: "Ecocriticism (or by an alternative name, environmental criticism) designates the critical writings which explore the relations between the biological and the physical environment, conducted with an acute awareness of devastation being wrought on that environment by human activities" (*A Glossary of Literary Terms*, 11th edition, e-book, Cengage Learning, 2014, p. 98). Although the term is not easily definable as it is an umbrella term, multidisciplinary in nature and holds various stances, yet the entire Eco critics share the core assumption:

that human culture is connected to the physical world, affecting it and affected by it. Ecocriticism takes as its subject the interconnections between nature and culture, specifically the cultural artifacts of language and literature. As a critical stance, it has one foot in literature and the other on land; as a theoretical discourse, it negotiates between the human and the nonhuman. (Glotfelty xix)

A broad area of study, ecocriticism incorporate within its domain elements of different subjects like geography, economics, biology, physics, chemistry, history, health, technology, sociology, culture and ecology. It deals with how environmental issues, cultural issues concerning the environment and attitudes towards nature are presented and analyzed. One of the main goals in ecocriticism is to study how individuals in society behave and react in relation to nature and ecological aspects. This form of criticism has gained a lot of attention during recent years due to higher social emphasis on environmental destruction and increased technology. It is hence a fresh way of analyzing and interpreting literary texts, which brings new dimensions to the field of literary and theoretical studies. Ecocriticism is an intentionally broad approach that is known by a number of other designations, including "green (cultural) studies", "ecopoetics", and "environmental literary criticism." Ecocriticism is informed by many other fields, including ecology, environmental history, and social ecology (literariness.org).

This book offers a compendious and global understanding of a dynamic and complex problem by considering its diverse aspects, effects and dimensions through various angles. The book discusses current environmental issues and draws our attention towards environmental liability. The research papers in this volume deal with both fictional texts and other written forms to reflect on the ecological concerns and discuss human and 'other' relationship in a comprehensive way. It help apprise and make us understand the interconnectedness of all living and non-living entities like human, animal, birds, insects, rivers, mountains, flora and fauna. It draws our attention to establish a holistic relationship with nature and celebrate the beauty and power of nature. Also, it caution against the impending environmental threats that need immediate attention. This anthology is a valuable addition to the ecocritical studies. It would be pragmatically beneficial for the teachers, professors, research scholars and all those who are interested in the theory of Ecocriticism and Green Studies.

Sarita Chanwaria
Sarita Jain

Re-*Greening the Earth* : Locating the Eco-poetic in Select Translations from Malayalam Poetry

Vrinda. R. Chanth

Abstract

Kerala, a land of hills, forests, backwaters, and beaches boasts of a variety of endemic species of plants and animals. The culture has always been closely aligned with practices that nurture and preserve the biodiversity of the region. The literature from the region also reflects an eco-consciousness embedded in the sensibility of the people. The changing weather patterns and the unprecedented floods of 2018 had an adverse impact on the lives of the people and the natural environment. This led to a renewed focus on writings that are both "environmental" and "environmentalist." In 2023, *Greening the Earth: A Global Anthology of Poetry* edited by K. Satchidanandan and Nishi Chawla was published. It brought together voices from different parts of the world which urged a re-greening of the earth and envisioned a future when man lives in harmony with nature. This paper attempts a close reading of select writings from Kerala, included in this anthology, to understand the eco-consciousness in contemporary Malayalam literature. The definitions of Eco poetry or "green poetry" that emerges from these writings will be analyzed to understand the diverse ways of being Eco poetic.

Keywords: Eco poetry, re-greening, Malayalam, environment, biodiversity.

The South Indian state of Kerala, known by the epithet "God's Own Country," is renowned for its rich and varied flora and fauna. Nestled between the Western Ghatson the east and the Arabian Sea on thewest, Keralais one of the most biodiverse statesinIndia. A land of hills, forests, backwaters, lagoons and beaches, Kerala boasts of a variety of endemic species of plants and animals. With various indigenous tribes of Kerala that live in close proximity to nature and religious practices such as *nāga* worship (worship of snakes) that centres around *kavum-kulavum* (sacred groves and ponds) associated with temples and traditional households, the culture has always been closely aligned with practices that nurture and preserve the biodiversity of the region. The literature from the region also reflects an eco-consciousness embedded in the sensibility of the people.

Vernacular literature from Kerala has its origins intraditional folksongs and ballads replete with native elementssung by rustic musicianswho travelled from place to place. Malayalam literature before the 15th century renders itself to a tripartite classification, namely, pure Malayalam literature, Tamil-Malayalam literature and Sanskritised Malayalam literature. The writings of Cherusseri Namboodiri, Thunchathu Ramanujan Ezhuthachan and Kunjan Nambiar are considered to be the beginnings of Modern Malayalam Literature. Amongst this great trio of Modern literature in Malayalam, Thunchathu Ezhuthachan is "regarded as maker of Modern Malayalam and the father of Malayalam Poetry" (Paniker 31). It is significant that heinvented and perfected a new genre of poetry known as *Kilipattu* (parrot song). The poetic rendering of the epic *Adhyatma Ramayana*in Malayalamby Thunchathu Ezhuthachan follows the structure in which a parrot is called upon to narrate the different episodes of the epic. The work is often praised for its "use of language" (Paniker 35). Dr. K. Ayyappa Paniker, in *AShort History of Malayalam Literature* hails Ezhuthachan as the "greatest synthesizer" Kerala has ever produced and extols his ability to judiciously fuse together "disparate elements" (31). The *Kilipattu*can be considered a type of nature poetry emblematic of a culture in which the humans, plants, animals, and the other elements of nature co-exist with mutual respect and harmony.

Kerala, as a land of spices, also had a significant place in the trade map. It attracted foreign powers such as the Portuguese, Dutch and others for trade. The colonisation of India, for the first time, resulted in a shift from the rustic lifestyle based on the principal of oneness with nature to a society based on capitalist principles. The post-colonial era was characterised by a shift from the agrarian way of life to an urban way of life. It also witnessed an increase in migration of Malayali population to different parts of the world in search of livelihood. The close ties with nature were loosened and it resulted in a decrease in ecological consciousness and subsequent environmental degradation. Fuelled by the capitalist ideas ofdevelopment, activities such as forest land encroachment, sand mining, quarrying, land excavation, irreversible conversion of wet-land eco-systems of paddy fields and many more have resulted in degradation of the environmentand an increased incidence of natural calamities in the region.The changing weather patterns and the unprecedented floods of 2018 had an adverse effect on the lives of the people and the natural environment. This led to a renewed focus on environmentalist and ecological writings in Malayalam.

However, the Save Silent Valley Campaign, which began in 1966, to protect the rain forests of the Silent Valley Region in Palakkad district of Kerala was one of the earliest environmental protection movements in India. As G. Madhusoodanan rightly states in his introduction to the edited volume *Ecocriticism in Malayalam* (2022), "ecological awareness in Malayalam literature emerged as a movement in parallel with the Silent Valley movement to protect the pristine rain forest of Western Ghats from submergence, in a proposed hydroelectric project" (xiii).

3

Many writers of the period such as Sugathakumari, O. N. V. Kurup, Ayyappa Paniker, Vishnunarayanan Namboothiri, and the critic K. Velayudhan Nair joined together under the leadership of renowned writer N.V. Krishna Warrier to form a Nature Protection Committee. Many writers, naturalists and scientists became part of this "environmental resistance movement against the project"and "thus emerged a new phase of writers" activism and, through their writings, a new literary sensibility was formed" (xiv).Thirty poems written by twenty poets who were part of the movement were collected and published as the "first anthology of eco-poetry in Malayalam called *Vanaparvam* [Forest Chronicles] in November 1983" (xiv). Though these poets were dubbed as "tree poets," their writings heralded a phase of environment-tally conscious literature in Malayalam (xiv).

The devastating floods of August 2018 marked another watershed moment in the history of Kerala. The torrential downpour and the resultant floods, which caused landslides, altered the course of rivers and caused irreparable damage to the environment, became one of the greatest calamities in terms of loss of lives, livelihoods, homes and habitats. Many eminent scientists and ecologists attributed the disaster to unsustainable development practices in ecologically sensitive areas of the state. This initiated dialogue on the need for holistic developmental ideas and practices that stressed on sustainability. There was an influx of writings that stressed on the interconnection between man and ecology. Not only did these writings have nature as an important theme but they also display an eco-consciousness which is the need of the hour.

Many writers and critics began revisiting the existing literature on ecology. One such attempt was a compendium of ecocritical writings in Malayalam, which were translated into English, and published by Cambridge Scholars Publishing in 2022. The volume titled *Ecocriticism in*

Malayalam, edited by G. Madhusoodanan, includes critical articles on the evolution of environmental aesthetics, studies of ecopoetry, short stories and econovels in Malayalam. In 2023, *Greening the Earth: A Global Anthology of Poetry* edited by K. Satchidanandan and Nishi Chawla was published. It brought together voices from different parts of the world which urged a re-greening of the earth and envisioned a future when man lives in harmony with nature. This paper attempts a close reading of select writings from Kerala, included in this anthology, to understand the eco-consciousness in contemporary Malayalam literature.The definitions of ecopoetry or "green poetry" that emerges from these writings will also be analyzed to understand what it means to "re-green" the earth.

The term "green" in the title of the anthology *Greening the Earth*when translated into Malayalam renders itself to myriad interpretations. As T. Srivatsan states in his essay "Ecoaesthetics and Ecolinguistics" (2022), the word "green" (*pacha*) translates as pure, raw, green colour, undried, uncooked, uncured, unadulterated, emerald, unripe, untainted, one's true nature, and so on (81).He discusses the "need to create a "green" Malayalam that is not anthropocentric, but one which enables a safe passage to the green vistas of a new holistic vision"(81). Ecolinguistic consciousness along with ecological awareness is what many contemporary writings aspire to achieve. Terry Giffordin's *GreenVoices: Understanding Contemporary Nature Poetry* (1995) defines "green poetry" as "nature poems which engage directly with environmental issues" (3). The hues of green painted by the verses of P. N. Gopikrishnan, S. Joseph, M.P.Pratheesh, P. Raman, P.P. Ramachandran, K. Satchida-nandan, Jeet Thayil and Veeran kutty are laudable attempts at creating a world that goes beyond the dualist philosophy based on nature-culture dichotomy.

P. N. Gopikrishnan's "How does an 'Un' Get Added to

Our Ease?" translated by K. Satchidanandan begins by asking pertinent questions such as why ants which carry a dead cockroach don't carry men, or why parrotsdon't "carry men in their beaks like cornstalks" or why goats never eat humans like they chew leaves (119). These questions serve as pointers to how the animal world abides by the laws of nature. The tone soon shifts and the poem goes on to describe how the lens through which humans view the natural environment has a reductive effect. "What we call a tree" is the "mark of a vanished forest,"what we call a cat "is what was left / after the exodus of beasts" and what we call a pool is "a drop that fell" when the "wild stream fled the land" (119). These descriptions are startling revelations of how the humans have contributed to the destruction of the natural world around them. The anthropocentric world view, coupled with unsustainable forms of development point to a history of human evolution marred by exploitation of nature. The marks of aggression behind every human freedom, the figures and philosophies of Buddha and Gandhi, the thought process of Karl Marx and the dying words of Socrates that he owes a rooster to the Roman God are all presented as interspersed with nature and natural phenomena. The citational and palimpsest nature of postmodern poetry augments the critique of ecologically ruinous tendencies. The poem concludes with the lines:

> Plants are studying us
> like we study them.
> As we turn the small into big
> with our microscopes,
> they are also turning us small
> with another lens.(120)

Here, we see that the poem envisions a world where plants and humans coexist and share a reciprocal relationship. The poem describes how the natural world and the human world mirror each other's actions. P. N.

Gopikrishnan's writing seamlessly traverses the realms of the artistic, the cultural, the natural and the scientific and amalgamates them into a unified whole.This poem isboth "environmental" and "environmentalist" and hence, ecopoetic. John Shoptaw in his article "Why Ecopoetry?" liststhe prerequisites of an ecopoem as being both "environmental" and "environmentalist." Environmental as in poetry that is "about the nonhuman natural world—wholly or partly" and poetry that is "ecocentric, not anthropo-centric," and environmentalist as in poetry that is rhetorically "urgent" and aims to effect change by "unsettling" the readers through its depiction of "environmental damage or risk" (Shoptaw). It is in line with Forrest Gander's definition of ecopoetry in *Redstart: An Ecological Poetics* as "poetry that investigates—both thematically and formally—the relation-ship between nature and culture, language and perception"(qtd. in Shoptaw).

S. Joseph's "Different Poems" translated by K. Satchidanandan finds poetry in human activities, a rhythm that is inextricably linked to the natural world. The plough-man's poem, the washerwoman's rhythm, the forest-dweller's poem, the boatman's poetry, the beggars' poetry, and the grave-digger's poetry are all found in their chores. The clothes hear while sleeping in the sun, the stone looks at the mason who looks at it, the tin-pot becomes poetry"for one out of sex- work" and so on. All these get cultivated in the field and the poem ends with the lines:

> The field is ripe for harvest
> Reaping is poetry,
> to be sitting, tired from reaping,
> in the shade of the coconut tree,
> to be drinking water. (148)

The ruminations about different kinds of poetry point to the inter-connectedness of the human and natural world. The cycles of nature and the rhythms of human activities are juxtaposed. The writing is both self-aware and self-reflexive and there is a notable shift from the anthropocentric to the ecocentric. S. Joseph, a voice of the underprivileged, the marginalised and the subaltern in Postmodernist Malayalam poetry, tunes into the rhythm of everyday life of "local" people and finds a poetic cadence that reverberates beyond the binaries ofnatural-cultural and essentialist-constructivist

M. P. Pratheesh's "Playing Hide and Seek" translated by K. Satchidanandan is a startling description of how a child playing hide and seek dies of snake bite. The child presses its head on the tree and closes its eyes, while the snake which lives in the hollow of the tree brushes its poison teeth and slithers away. "The tree does not see anyone :/ not even the dead child, not even the curled-up snake" (225). The casual and almost euphemistic tone of the poem and the matter-of-fact presentation of death is unsettling on multiple levels. The snake "brushes" its "poison-teeth" and "slithers away/ without losing her way" and "the tree does not see" the "dead child" or "the curled-up snake"(225). The poem is innovative and is designed to unsettlethe readers. The tree as a metaphor for the world, the child with its eyes covered as a metaphor for the indiscriminate developmental activities unmindful of the consequences and the snake as a metaphor for the resultantdisasters that strike and leave "all changed, changed utterly" is an interesting way of looking at the poem. The dead child, the curled-up snake that slithers away "without losing her way" and the tree not seeing either the child or the snake is the story of progress and development and consequent degradation, death and decay that surrounds us.

P.P. Ramachandran's "O Wind, O Sea!" translated by A. J. Thomasis a commentary on the environmental impact of the construction of the eight-lane Expressway across Kerala. The poem begins with a striking simile which compares the hill that disappeared due to sand mining to a bronze water-jug stolen from the front veranda at night. The rain and sunshine looked for it but the hill was nowhere to be found. The practice of keeping a bronze water-jug in the verandafor people to wash their feet before entering the house was prevalent in traditional households in Kerala. It was considered an indispensable part of everyday life and culture. The hill that is an important part of the natural world disappears just like the "stolen" water-jug. How man steals from nature the source of her sustenance is deplorable. The utilitarianism in our approach to nature is critiqued in the opening lines. The poetic voice states that his house is on the "hip of a hill/ that is still left intact" (234). The poem describes how many hills such as the Pantalam-hill, Pootra-hill, Puliara-hill, Para-hill, Chola-hill, Chanta-hill, Palmyra-hill and so on are now daily-wage workers at the construction site of the Expressway. The image of the hills boarding the lorry as their names are called out, getting down when ordered and remaining standing forever "carrying on their flattened heads/the eight lane Expressway" is a graphic description of how nature, at times, becomes a mere tool to serve our capitalistic and consumerist goals of development (235). The mining of the hills, theirreversible change in topography, the loss of flora and fauna and the displacement of humans are all rolled into one. The poetic voiceexhorts the wind, the sea and the coconut fronds to signal their presence once in a while, for the Expressway will separate them forever. The poem ends with the lines:

We are going to be this side of the Expressway
and you, on that side
Not likely
to see each other again.
Like Narayani in Basheer's story
who threw a dry twig up into the sky
You too must show some sign:
I will wait for it. (235)

Themention of Narayani, the heroine of Vaikom Muhammad Basheer's novelette *Walls*isfascinating. The story of two lovers—theinmate of a women's prison and theinmate of a men's prison—separatedby a huge wall is a potent image of love and separationin the collective Malayali psyche. P.P. Ramachandran's writings in general and this poem in particular espouses the concept of ecopoetry as "nature poetry that has designs on us, that imagines changing the ways we think, feel about, and live and act in the world"(Shoptaw).

K. Satchidanandan's "History" challenges the anthro-pocentric world view that paints history as the history of man on earth. As the elements of nature predate man, and as nature will continue to exist even after humans are long gone, the notions of man as the crown of creation and nature as a passive receptacle are challenged. The poem contrasts the human attitude to other objects, plants and animals and their attitude towards humanity. We consider ourselves "witnesses to the objects, plants and beasts on earth" and think that they were created for us whereas, they who were witnesses to our creation "don't think so" and they have blessed us with "water, shade, flowers, fruits, milk" and so on (259). The evolution of human attitude towards nature is depicted as a journey from fear through reverence to disdain. We worshipped them, and later we "ousted them from history/turned us into our slaves and menials (259)." The poem puts forth many questions that highlight the human exploitation of nature. For instance, the lines

> Have you ever had to watch your brothers
> being axed and sawn into pieces
> to be sold in the timber market?
> Or hanging on a hook, bleeding,
> in a meat shop?. (259)

makes us painfully aware of the inhumanity of human actions often exacerbated by our egotism. The poem, true to its ecopoetic nature, places all objects, plants, animals and humans on par with the other.

The poem foretells the impending doom of humanity asour own inventions will soon "render us redundant" and the objects, plants and animals "who saw our rise / will, in total detachment/watch our fall"(260). History of humanity as a history of exploitation, violence and bloodshed that has caused the depletion, destruction, death and decay of the environment and as something that will cause our own extinction is highlighted in the poem. The poem ends on the note that the objects, plants and animals in nature will survive even after we are gone and they will write a history in which "the tale of our arrival and departure/will be told in just a paragraph" (260). The history of humanity as a paragraph in the history of our planet is staggering and thought provoking. The poem describes the history that will be written by the world of plants, animals and other objects as a history that will be written in a "secret language of the leaf-veins/ and the tortoise-shell" scribbled on rocks and green leaves "by the liquid fingers of the rain" where only "they" and "their God"will feature(260). The realm of language, literature and narratives as exclusively human is challenged.The poem accentuates the need for a shift from anthropocentric to bio-centric with an emphasis on the physical world that sustains life.

The English translation of Veerankutty's "Rain, Wind" describes the elements of nature and the cycles in nature. The metaphor of the rain as "an ocean overturned" and the wind as "cotton soaked in ether/ that God / drops down" are interspersed with questions such as "[w]ho is it that dries it up" and "[w]ill it haveways left/ to travel back"(305). Veerankutty, one of the prominent voices of environmental poetry in Malayalam presents the physical world, man and God as interrelated andinterdependent.

P. Raman's "Mother" describes in ten words the

benevo-lence of Mother Nature. Nature's ability to selflessly nurture is put side by side with the selfish human world in the lines:

> To fill
> My Pitcher
> The river needs
> Just
> A smile. (233)

The possessive determiner "my" and the adverb "just" meaning only or simply explicate the materialistically driven world where the ownership of the pitcher is emphasized and the value of a smile is understated. The generous nature and the precious smile add layers of meaning to the poem.

Jeet Thayil's poems on how to be a leaf, a horse, a crow, a bandicoot and a krait are reprinted from his collection *English Poems* (2003). These poems state how learning from the physical or animal worldcan resolve many of the maladies plaguing the human world. For instance, the lines, "[a]s for a crow, / kill colour, / turn black" is a very potent statement that underminesbinaries such as human-animal, essentialist-constructivist and white-black. The ironic tone of these poems is unmissable and they prompt the readers to re-examineman-nature relationship (296).As Cheryll Glotfelty states in her introduction to *The Ecocriticism Reader: Landmarks in Literary Ecology* (1996), the common strand that binds together all enquiries in the field of ecocriticism is the way in which "human culture is connected to the physical world, affecting it, and affected by it"(xix). According to her, the subject of Ecocriticism is "the interconnections between nature and culture, specifically the cultural artifacts of language and literature" and "[a]s a critical stance it has one foot in literature and the other on land; as a theoretical discourse, it negotiates between the human and the nonhuman" (xix).

The selections from *Greening the Earth*that feature in

the above analysis explore the human-non-human relationships, the ethical aspect of man's exploitation of nature, the impending ecological crisis, and the need for environmental awareness and sustainable development. Through startling tropes and descriptions, these poems call for holistic approaches to re-green the earth through actions driven by awareness, and accountability. In a world marked by incredulity towards totalising stories, these poems are perfect exemplars of diverse ways of being ecocritical and ecopoetic.

Works Cited:
Gifford, Terry. *Green Voices: Understanding Contemporary Nature Poetry*. Manchester UP, 1995.
Glotfelty, Cheryll. "Literary Studies in an Age of Environmental Crisis." Introduction. *The Ecocriticism Reader: Landmarks in Literary Ecology*, edited by Cheryll Glotfelty and Harold Fromm, U of Georgia P, 1996, pp. xv-xxxvii.
Gopikrishnan, P.N. "How Does an 'Un' Get Added to Our Ease?." Satchidanandan and Nishi, *Greening the Earth*, pp. 119-20.
Joseph, S. "Different Poems." Satchidanandan and Nishi, *Greening the Earth*, pp.147-48.
Madhusoodanan, G., editor. *Ecocriticism in Malayalam*. Cambridge Scholars Publishing, 2022.
Paniker, Ayyappa. K. *A Short History of Malayalam Literature*. 6th ed., Information & Public Relations Department, Kerala State, 2006.
Pratheesh, M. P. "Playing Hide and Seek." Satchidanandan and Nishi, *Greening the Earth*, p. 225.
Ramachandran, P. P. "O Wind, O Sea!." Translated by A. J. Thomas. Satchidanandan and Nishi, *Greening the Earth*, pp. 234-35.
Raman, P. "Mother." Satchidanandan and Nishi, *Greening*

the Earth, p. 233.

Satchidanandan. K. "History." Satchidanandan and Nishi, Greening *the Earth*, pp. 259-60.

Satchidanandan, K., and Nishi Chawla, editors. *Greening the Earth: A Global Anthology of Poetry*. Vintage, 2023.

Shoptaw, John. "Why Ecopoetry? There's no Planet B." *Poetry Magazine*, Poetry Foundation, Jan.2016, poetry foundation.org/poetrymagazine/articles/70299/why-ecopoetry.

Srivatsan, T. "Ecoaesthetics and Ecolinguistics." Translated by Rayson K. Alex. Madhusoodanan, *Ecocriticism in Malayalam*,pp. 74-82.

Thayil, Jeet. "How to be a Crow."Satchidanandan and Nishi, *Greening the Earth*,p. 296.

Veerankutty. "Rain, Wind." Satchidanandan and Nishi, *Greening the Earth*,p. 305.

Chapter 2

Kadvi Hawa : The Debt that Humanity is Accruing

Smriti Srivastava

Abstract

India has been fascinated by cinema in all its forms and guises since the first movie was shown in India. Indian Hindi film industry has been prolific and referential. It has continued to evolve with the changing times. Movies pertaining to social causes have always been a part of the rubric but recently the focus has shifted to environmentally aware movies. One such movie, *Kadvi Hawa/Dark Wind* (2017) is the focus of this paper. The movie deals with the plight of debt-ridden farmers in a darkly humorous tone and at the same time indicate that the pain of the farmers is directly related to climate change caused by unbridled exploitation of natural resources.

The chapter proposes to analyse the various elements of a movie– misé en scene, themes, dialogues, characters, tropes, etc. employed by the movie to examine whether the movie transcends anthropocentric concerns to give equal importance to the environment and may be classified as 'Eco-cinema'.

Keywords: Ecocinema, Environment, Agrarian crisis, Climate change, Zoomorphism

"A nation that destroys its soils destroys itself. Forests are the lungs of our land, purifying the air and giving fresh strength to our people."

--Franklin D. Roosevelt

India is one of the biggest producers of movies in multiple languages in the world so much so that movies have become an integral part of human life in India and one of its biggest exports. They depict the social scenario, political beliefs, cultural traditions, and economic changes that are taking place in the country and are one of the biggest influences on the people.However, consciously ecological, and environmentally aware movies have been a rarity in this prolific medium and despite having such a large following due to its accessibility and easy comprehensibility, Indian Hindi movie industry (popularly known as 'Bollywood') has mostly kept silent about the extreme weather events and climate changes occurring on the sub-continent.

For decades verdant landscapes with roaring waterfalls may have formed a romantic backdrop or rural drought prone barren fields may serve as witness to humans' struggle to survive and win over his/her adverse circumstances but till very recently the focus was never on the grandeur and dynamism of nature itself. The camera never focused on the landscape as an entity but rather as a corollary of the scene's requirement. The 'gaze' of the camera has always been anthropocentric, denying any agency to the natural setting. It is a friend or a foe depending on the main character's needs. A young calf elephant can help the hero win over the villain and gain the hand of his ladylove in *Haathi Mere Saathi*(1971) or an earthquake might serve as a cinematic tool to separate a loving and happy family as in *Waqt* (1965). Floods, droughts, earthquakes, etc. being natural phenomenon did not need an explanation; they were to be survived and transcended.

In the last decade, on the one hand commercial cinema has incorporated glimpses of extreme climate phenomenon, nature protecting itself from the juggernaut of progress by 'converting' humans into its own personal bodyguards by infecting the main character with a virus as in*Bhediya* (2022) or depletion of resources as in the water tanker scene in *Fukrey 3* (2023). On the other hand, an environmentally conscious cinematic form is developing amongst parallel cinema in Indian film industry that may fall under the category ofEco-cinema.

Kiu Wai Chu to Roger C Anderson's has traced the coinage of the term 'Ecocinema' "Ecocinema: A Plan for Preserving Nature." Kiu has described the genre as:

Similar to the tradition of nature writing in literary studies, the initial impetus of studying natural environments in film lies in a romantic notion of resisting the destruction andconquest of nature, as a means of raising awareness towards the physical world...Inspired by recent earthquakes, floods and other natural catastrophe, eco-disaster filmsbecome one of the major topics in ecocinema studies over the past decade...In addition to natural phenomena, ecocinema also concerns human-induced problemson ecology and the environment.(2)

On the other hand, Scott Macdonald considers this restrictive and has defined the role of Ecocinema as:

As I see it, the fundamental job of anecocinema is not to produce pro-environmental narratives shot in aconventional Hollywood manner (that is, in a manner that implicitly-promotes consumption) or even in a conventional documentary manner(although, of course, documentaries can alert us to environmental issues).The job of an ecocinema is to provide new kinds of film experience that demonstrate an alternative to conventional media-spectatorship and help tonurture a more environmentally progressive mindset.(20)

In Indian Hindi movie industry, there has been an increase in the number of movies recently that are trying to create environmental consciousness though the audience of such movies is limited most of the time and thus they do not gain as much popularity as commercial cinema. This is evident from the fact that many of the films that were awarded 'Best Film on Environment Conservation,' an award category that was instituted in 1999 under National Film Awards, are not known to the populace. Films like*The*

Bhopal Express (1999), *Peepli Live* (2010), *Jal* (2014), *Kaun Kitne Pani Mein* (2015), *Kadvi Hawa* (2017), *Kedarnath* (2018), etc have focused on various ecological factors that have affected society and life in general in an adverse manner. Sharma and Chaubey have commented on these movies' "utter reluctance to use nature as a decorative background to romantic songs … instead placing it at the centre to highlight the human ignorance and greed that leads to an unstable Ecological environment" in their paper "Climate Change in India: A Wakeup Call from Bollywood" (3)

The focus of this study, *Kadvi Hawa/Dark Wind* is one such movie. Directed by Nila Madhab Panda and produced by Drishyam Films, Panda and Akshay Parija, the film is a commentary on the extreme climate events and the consequences thereof. As is evident from the poster of the movie given below that the movie deals with the plight of farmers trying to survive in a drought ridden land. The cracks of an arid field overlap the face of the main character Hedu (Sanjay Mishra) showing the interconnectedness of humanity and the natural world. The unthinking actions of humankind have brought about this drought that is now in its turn impacting human life. The dull browns of the land and the human face show the desolation and barrenness that both share. The colour brown then darkens into red colour signifying the deaths/suicides that occur due to this barrenness. The poster carries a dire warning, which is meant for all the people sitting, glued to their screens, ignoring the extreme climate events taking place around them – #OPENYOUREYES. It is not only the target audience that has to be aware of their actions and their consequences but also any passer-by who glances at the poster and yet the warning worded in English (even in Hindi poster) is aimed at the educated masses. Sanjay Mishra is blind and is thus unable to see though he can sense the changing times but humanity in general needs to wake up to the fact that they

18

have been blind in their pillaging of nature and its resources.

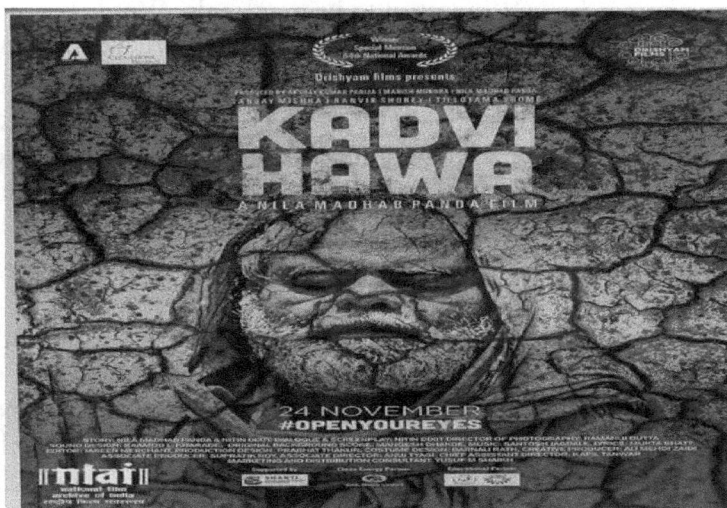

Fig 1: Poster for *Kadvi Hawa* courtesy NFAI

The movie revolves around Hedu, a blind farmer, who is trying to lighten the burden of his farmer son, Mukund, by trying to get rid of his loan and Gunu (Ranvir Shorey), a recovery agent for the bank from where Mukund has taken the loan. Ironically, the movie is set in the fictional village of *Beehad Mahua* as opposed to the *Nadiwala Mahua*. Beehad Mahua has a landscape that is desolate with mostly desert vegetation and asymmetrical sand hills that are devoid of much greenery. The use of 'Mahua' to name the fictional town is itself symbolic as Mahua is a tree that can adapt to arid and semi-arid conditions. Its fruits and flowers have a sweet flavour and fragrance and yet folk wisdom says that an excessive use of its flower or fruit can lead to madness. This might be representative of the fact that the uncaring 'use' of land and water is the reason for this dearth and drought. It references Sanjay Mishra's later dialogue about *hawa* that *"Hawa to baadal laat hai. Hawa to sardi, garmi sab laat hai. Hamar zamaane main char alag alag dishaon se Khushbu le k aat thi wo. Abae na jaane kya ho gaya hai usko, jaise bimar ho gai ho"* (Wind used to bring clouds. Winds brought summers and winters. In my time, it used to bring sweet fragrances from the four corners of the earth. Now, no one knows what has happened to it? It is as if it has fallen sick)(Mishra, Shorey and Shome). This dialogue also gives the movie its title *Kadvi Hawa* as opposed to the fragrant one that earlier used to bring clouds and thus rains and solace.

The scarcity of water due to climate change is so severe that Hedu's daughter-in-law must bring water from a faraway water source and that water is rationed during daily use. There has been no rain for a long time and the spectre of loan is always haunting the farmers and, in some cases, has caused them to commit suicide. This has led to equating the recovery agent Gunu to a *yamdoot*. However, Gunu who belongs to Odisha is a victim of another extreme weather event, cyclones. His one wish is to move away from the shore town of Kendrapadain Odisha that is susceptible to cyclones. They strike a deal according to which Hedu will inform Gunu about which farmer had enough money to pay off his loan but was hiding it and in return, Gunu will pay him a certain amount that will go towards paying off Mukund's loan.

The plight of the farmers is presented through the metaphor of a mouse caught in a trap (the barren hills) which borrows from Zoomorphic critical analogy which "acknowledges the similarities shared across species and brings to the fore questions of a shared animality, thereby posing the question: what does it mean to be human? This technique is inherently political. It elucidates the suffering of animals by comparing human and non-human experiences." (Parr) In the movie, Sanjay Mishra compares the farmers to mice. His dialogue, *"koi fanda laga k mar raha hai, koi zeher kha k"*(Panda) that maybe translated as "some die by hanging, some die by poison" holds true for the farmers of the region who are caught in the trap of loan with ever increasing interest that might be compounded across generations with no reprieve. The farmers very much like the mentioned mice are in hiding and nowhere to be seen. Not a single scene of farming or farms is a part of the movie and yet the pain and sorrow of farmersis expressed and represented self-reflexively in an artful manner by the movie and its protagonist. The audience is never introduced to Janki's father but they hear of his suicide indirectly, see his dead body being carried for cremation and yet any discussion on the cause of his death is muted. Hedu refuses to answer his granddaughter Kuhu's questions about her friend Janki's father. The suffering of mice when they feel trapped is equated with that of the farmers crouching under the weight of their loans in what may be termed "Biospherical egalitarianism" (Næss) which believes in the inherent interconnectedness of life where no one is more important than the other.

The changes in the seasonal cycle have been highlighted through a darkly humorous classroom scene, which is narrated by Kuhu to Hedu at night. Kuhu's teacher after making his students repeat after him that "*Mausam ka chakra chalta hai to chalta hi rehta hai*" (Panda) (seasonal cycle goes on uninterrupted) asks the class to answer the question, "*saal main mausam kitne hote hain?*" (How many seasons are there in a year?). While everyone replies four as they have read in their books, one of the student courageously opposes this by pointing out that he has only experienced summers and winters, and monsoon cannot be a season as it rains only 2 or 3 times in a year. All the students laugh at his logic but the mood turns sober when Janki's uncle comes to pick her up from school.

Later that night Kuhu shares the incident with Hedu and asks him whether that was true expecting him to laugh it off but Hedu replies to her in a grave manner that it used to be so in his time but now it has changed. This simple sharing of day-to-day details between grandfather and granddaughter takes a dire turn with the highlighting of the disruption of the seasonal cycle. Elsewhere while talking to Gunu, Hedu says that earlier farmers could easily grow two crops in a year but things have changed. Hedu despite his blindness has trained his other senses to read his surroundings and being a farmer, his instincts are to read the weather and identify the disruptions. He considers the wind/hawa to be sick/diseased/ill maybe referring to the pollutants that it carries over from the cities. Hedu is also pointing out that not following the seasonal patterns is a symptomatic manifestation of a bigger pathological issue with the wind.

Hedu's blindness thus also works on a symbolic level. He is literally blind but not unaware while others (including the audience) are blind to their surrounding and changing climates and yet survival has taken precedence over everything, even his conscience. Gunu who has lost his father to a cyclone ten years back and loses the rest of his family to cyclone 6B at the end of the movie is only thinking of survival. He is not speculating about the changes in climate patterns or worrying about the incapability of farmers to sow their crops. His only desire is to bring his family safely to Mahua, a landlocked region so that they may stay safe from the frequent cyclones that devastate the shorelines. Aware or ignorant of the changes, both lose their fight to survive in the end and nature collects a heavy toll for running roughshod over it. Panda in a way has commented on the detractors of environmental conservation who deny climate changes, global warming, etc by showing that whether one believes in it or not, nature and its processes and entities will not discriminate between believers and detractors.

Water conservation is another important trope in the movie that serves like a peephole to a not-sodistantdystopian future where water is sold and soon might become too expensive to procure. The camera's gaze that constantly tracks across the barren landscape is never able to find any trace of water except for the one that is carried in pots by Parvati (Tillotama Shome), Hedu's daughter-in-law from a faraway water source. The opening scene where Hedu walks across the landscape is a close up shot where the camera faithfully follows at Hedu's heels while the screen lightens up as daytime arrives and the camera lens transitions to a long shot that gives one a feel of the desolate landscape. The camera records not only the Hedu's movements but it also problematizes the encroachment of humans into this zone of sand and foliage as they try to make their way towards their destination.

Gunu, who is fixated on saving his family by relocating them from a shore town, whichis constantly threatened by cyclones to this landlocked area, always refers to water as a source of his loss but though the narrative focuses on him and his life at intervals, no images of the ocean are shown on screen. Fresh water is fast running out due to the inability of rains to replenish the ground water table while the vast oceans are unable to quench the thirst of people and are a threat to their lives and livelihood due to heavy rain or cyclonic depressions. Hedu constantly reprimands Kuhu not to give him excess water when he goes to freshen up every morning and in turn, he is constantly reminded by her that if the water runs out then he will not be able to find any water nearby. Hedu wishes to teach Kuhu to use natural resources judiciously while she is focusing on him as a person so being more important than the resources. The director thus, lays the responsibility for the lessening of rains and the increase in extreme climate events at the doors of humanity and its anthropocentric tendencies through Hedu and Kuhu's ongoing debate.

For Hedu water is more precious than anything else is,

even God is. When he wishes to thank Gunu for paying him in return for being an informant for loan recovery, Hedu says, "*tum hamare lie baarish ban k ae ho*" (Panda) translated to "you have appeared like the rains in my life". There is nothing better as far as Hedu is concerned to show his respect and thankfulness towards Gunu. He is thankful to Gunu and still unable to understand why Gunu wants to move away from his home in Odisha. For him Odisha seems like a paradise as "*har taraf paani hi paani hai. Suna hai har ghar k peeche ek talaab hot hai? Hawa ki badi kripa hai tum sabo pe*" which translates to "there is water everywhere. I have heard that every house has a small pond in its backyard. You all have been blessed by nature/hawa". However, contrary to his imaginings he gets a very cold and sarcastic response from Gunu, "*Kuch jaada hi*" (it can be too much).

At the end be it drought or cyclones, both claim their dues. Despite their efforts, human protagonists are defeated in the face of natural disasters. Hedu is unable to save his son from disappearing. In an extended shot, he is shown running around looking for him but for once the wind does not bring comfort and the land is as unsympathetically dry as always. He comesback a beaten man who spends his time waiting for his son to turn up and considering his son's disappearance a punishment for informing on other farmers to save his son from the burden of the loan. The family (Hedu, Parvati and Kuhu) continue holding onto the faint hope that Mukund is not dead by continuing with their daily routine; Parvati still wears *sindoor* (visual marker of marital status) and Kuhu still goes to school while Hedu continues waiting. The idea of the group loan is in itself a comment on humanity which has taken a group loan from nature to use its resources and in case of a person's passing away or defaulting on the loan, the rest of the group will have to bear the increased burden of accrued interest. Similarly, though Gunu has been able to recover some portions of the loans with the help of Hedu, he has not been able to recover/retrieve his family from danger and he has to deal with the uncertainty of not being able to get in touch with them due to cyclone.

The movie has only one track *Main Banjar* that plays in the background when Hedu is looking for his son. Santosh Jagdale composes it, the lyrics are written by Mukta Bhatt and Mukesh Kanan sings it. It beautifully exposes the *"mayoosi ka manjar"* (scene of desolation) that lives in the eyes of every farmer that equates himself with the land he tills and his family that bears the brunt of this barrenness. Their despair is tangible in the song and forces us to answer the question of why the people who are deeply connected with land/sea/nature are the ones who pay the biggest price for mankind's oblivion towards the needs of environment. The end credits roll with the voiceover of Gulzar reciting his poem *"Mausam beghar hone lage hain"* which points out human culpability in seasonal cycle's disruption.

> *Banjare lagte hain mausam,*
> *Mausam beghar hone lage hain,*
> *Jungle, ped, pahad, samandar,*
> *Insan sab kuch kaat raha hai,*
> *Cheel cheel k khaal zameen ki,*
> *Tukde tukde baant raha hai,*
> *Aasman se utre mausam,*
> *Saare banjar hone lage hain,*
> *Mausam beghar hone lage hain,*
> *Daryaon pe baandh lage hain,*
> *Phodte hain sar chattaano se,*
> *'Baandi' lagne lagi hai zameen,*
> *Darti hai ab insano se,*
> *Behti hawa pe chalne wale,*
> *Paon patthar hone lage hain.*
> *Mausam beghar hone lage hain.* (Panda)

Paraphrased as: Seasons seem to have become nomadic / seasons have also started becoming homeless. Jungle, trees, ocean, mountains, everything is being indiscriminately cut down and used by humans / humans have scraped together every piece of land and has divided it amongst themselves. Seasonal cycles are disrupted / causing failure of crops. Seasons have also started becoming homeless. Dams have been constructed over rivers / waters strike against their concrete futilely. Earth appears to be a slave / who is scared of humans. Feet that walked over lush fertile lands as if on air / have become hardened by walking over dry barren land. Seasons have also started becoming homeless.

This seems to be a fitting end to a narrative that is inextricably weaving human destiny with the sustenance and continuation of nature. The movie is a cinematic example of camerawork that looks at environment as a character, which will not be ignored. It makes its presence felt in every scene of the movie whether it is through the long shots that pan out to provide the audience with full view of the landscape and give an impression of scorching heat and barrenness. Each and every dialogue of Sanjay Mishra is an eye opener about climate change and its consequences – agrarian crisis, migration, farmer suicide, etc. The characters and the team of the movie are not looking for easy answers; they are waking the audience to the devastating events that are taking place around them. The movie through its one and a half hour run time acts not only as a cinematic marvel but also as a heartrending wake up call to the continuing environmental devastation due to human greed.

Works Cited:

Chu, Kiu Wai. "Ecocinema." Journal of Chinese Cinemas (2016): 1-4.
Kadvi Hawa. National Film Archive of India. Poster for Kadvi Hawa. 2020.

Kadvi Hawa. Dir. NIla Madhab Panda. Perf. Sanjay Mishra, Ranvir Shorey and Tillotama Shome. Drishyam Films. 2017.

Macdonald, Scott. "The Ecocinema Experience." Ecocinema: Theory and Practice. Ed. Rust Stephen, Salma Monani and Sean Cubitt. New York: Routledge, 2013. 17-41.

Næss, Arne. "The Shallow and the Deep, Long-Range Ecology Movements: A Summary." Deep Ecology for the Twenty-First Century. Ed. George Sessions. Boston: Shambhala, 1995. 151-155.

Parr, Aaron. Mapping Contemporary Cinema: Short Guide to Zoomorphism. 2015. 15 July 2024
 <https://mcc.sllf.qmul.ac.uk/?p=1528>.

Sharma, Manvi and Ajay K. Chaubey. "Climate Change in India: A Wakeup Call from Bollywood." Rupkatha Journal on Interdisciplinary Studies in Humanities 12.5 (2020): 1-9.

Chapter 3

Ecocricial Sensibility in the Poetry of Nissim Ezekiel and A. K. Ramanujan

Poonam Rani Gupta

Abstract

"A work of genius must have "spirit" which it gets through its content."

Kant, Immanuel

Indian English poetry is one of the oldest forms of Indian English literature and has been a rich contribution to the world of literature. "Indian poets writing in English have succeeded to nativize or Indianize English in order to reveal typical Indian situations" (Wikipedia). An ecocritical approach entails how one look at the literary works with special reference to the sensibility and depiction of nature and environment. The proposed research paper endeavours to study the ecological implications in the poetry of the most oft quoted Indian poets writing in English Nissim Ezekiel and A. K. Ramanujan. Thus, the chief aim of the proposed article is to assess how their poetry reflects the eco consciousness in broader sense of the term. It is not merely the aesthetic beauty of nature and the landscape the poets are concerned in their poetry, but they are more concerned with the deterioration of ecology due to man's fast-growing actions. The poetry of these two icons serves as an eye-opener to show the man a true picture that he is just a part of his surroundings and not the master of it.

Keywords: Indian English poets, ecology, ecocriticism, environment, eye opener.

The growth of human life on earth is just impossible without the ecological poise, for instance, the importance of trees on the earth for the sustenance of life is well known to everyone. They provide us oxygen to breath, food to satisfy our hunger and shelter to live thus they can make life on the earth fitting to live. Each and every living creature on the earth in the ecosystem is a part of the food chain. The disturbance in the ecosystem by way of overexploitation of nature and the natural resources can lead to the disaster in the entire ecology and ultimately it can raise a question of human existence. In brief, environmental cataclysm is the most imperative concern the globe is facing today. A wide range of environmental tribulations such as climate change, stratospheric ozone depletion, degraded air and water quality, dearth of fresh water, land contamination, deforestation, soil erosion and biodiversity loss have surfaced the entire world. The issue of environmental crisis has become the major concern of environmental science and management unit or departments. They have been playing multifarious roles to tone down this crisis.

Literature develops better ways of understanding nature and more consciousness about the relationship with nature. Today, there is an urgent need that people of all over the globe should be environmentally literate. Literature being the mirror of society could not have failed to reflect all environmental issues. Nature and literature have always shared a close relationship as is evident in the works of poets, writers, historians and philosophers down the ages in almost all cultures and languages of the world. Literature serves as an appropriate tool for the attainment of the poised and sustained society where man and physical environment co-exist in never ending relationship of interdependence. Hemlata Srivastava in her book entitled *Signature of Literature on Society: Society, Culture and Literature* (2013) says, "Literature serves as the determining factor in shaping the character of society...literature should become the guiding source" (Srivastava 13). Literature of today has started addressing the environmental issues with an intension to bring awareness about the environmental damage. Eco-criticism has emerged as a new branch of "the study of relation between literature and physical environment" (Glotfelty Cheryll xviii). The writers of 'Green Studies' dealing with ecological consciousness aim at bring the ecological consciousness among the people regarding the fact that Earth is losing its health because of the abuse of nature by the humans. Literary critics try to study how this close relationship between nature and society has been textualised by the writers in their works. In this context following terms have become very important today – ecology, eco centric and ecocriticism.

Ecocriticism got currency towards the later decades of the 20th century. William Rueckert is regarded as the first being to have used this term, but the consciousness towards environment is apparent in Richard Carson's book, Silent Spring (1962). After him, Raymond Williams' seminal book, *The Country and the City* (1973), can be regarded as a landmark in the history of environmental studies. William Rueckert used the term 'ecocriticism' in 1978 in his essay entitled "Literature and Ecology: An experiment in Ecocriticism". Cheryll Glotfelty and Harold Fromm defined the term 'ecocriticism' in, *The Ecocriticism Reader: Landmarks in Literary Ecology* in the following words, "it is the study of the relationship between literature and the environment" (19). Prof. Gregcomments in this regard, "Ecocriticism is a critical mode that looks at the representation of nature and landscape in cultural texts, paying particular attention to attitudes towards 'nature' and the rhetoric employed when speaking about it. It aligns itself with ecological activism and social theory with the assumption that the rhetoric of cultural texts reflects and inform material practices towards the environment, while seeking to increase awareness about it and linking itself (and literary texts) with other ecological sciences and approaches. (242)

In the Indian ethos, to be in symphony with nature has

always been the accepted way of living. Advaita Vedanta, the primal Hindu philosophy advocated the oneness of all life and considered the world as one family, *'Vasudheva Kutumbhkam'*. Here the entire universe is considered a living being, called —*Viraat*, in the ancient Purusha Sukta. In the Bhagvad Gita, Sri Krishna compares the world to a single Banyan tree with unlimited branches of which all the animate and inanimate beings are a part. (BG 15.1-4), meaning thereby that all life and non-life are infused with individual spirits, the *Jiva*. The Samkhya tradition reveres the five great elements, the *Panchmahabhuta*, i.e. earth, water, fire, air, and space as the building blocks of physical reality. Various manifestations of nature, like mountains (e.g. Goverdhan) and rivers (e.g. The Ganges, the Yamuna, Saraswati even their confluence) trees (e.g. Bodhi tree or Tulsi) and animals (e.g. cow) etc. are either worshipped or form a part of important rituals. The highest ethical standard thus becomes 'Sarva Bhuta Hite', (BG 5.25) meaning welfare of all beings. Atharva Veda too declares, "*Maata bhoomiputroahamprithivyah*" (AV 12.1.12).

Thus, it is obvious that the literary works produced in India have a special place for nature. The literature of ancient times or the religious texts has treated nature whether it be the Biblical Garden of Eden or the forest where Lord Rama was exiled. It is observed that trees and wilderness have played the crucial role of the provider, protector and destroyer. A closer look at the green writing of Indian authors will reveal many hidden aspects of Indian landscape. Apart from delineating the aesthetic beauty and power of nature, many Indian English poets and writers have started depicting the concern for ecology with an alarming threat of disaster due to nature exploitation by the humans. Many ecocritics draw attention to this aspect of environmentalism where the concern for ecology is mentioned in the literature being known as Ecocriticism. But it was Nirmal Selvamony who introduced the course titled "Tamil poetics" at Madras Christian College in 1980 and with his endeavour, the beginning of ecocritical studies in India can be well witnessed.

Indian poets writing in English delineate the aesthetic beauty of nature but they do not miss the opportunity to exhibit the dark reality of the exploitation of nature and animals by the humans. Nearly all Indian English poets like Sri Aurobindo, Sarojini Naidu, Nissim Ezekiel, A. K. Ramanujan, Keki N. Daruwalla, Dilip Chitre, Gieve Patel and many more have delineated nature and environment in their poetry. Natural elements like the rivers, the sky, hills, animals, and other creatures keep coming in their poetry as a form of their poetic experiences. The close study of the contemporary Indian English Poetry brings out the nuance of eco-conscious warning the humans to witness the catastrophes due to annihilation of nature. The proposed articleattempts to explore the ecological implications and environmental sensibility along with a special kind of awareness to protect the environment in the poetry of Nissim Ezekiel and A. K. Ramanujan.

Nissim Ezekiel (1942-2004) is as one of the oft quoted Indian poets writing in English. His first volume of poems appeared in 1952 entitled *A Time to Change*; this was followed by other volumes such as *Sixty Poems* (1953), *The Third* (1959), *The Unfinished Man* (1960), *The Exact Man* (1965), and *Hymns in Darkness* (1976). In All these volumes of poems he has dealt with anextensivevariability of themes such as love, isolation, human flaws, imperfections and superstitions along with his deep-rooted concern with the environment of the globe in general and his native and i.e. India in particular. Ezekiel was quite responsive to his environment as he seems to believe that "India is simply my environment. A man can do something for and in his environment by being fully what he is, by not withdrawing from it" (Introduction CP xxii). The poet seems to have been deeply engrossed in the contemporary environment of India; he cannot part himself from it though at times he is satirical towards the human foibles. He has become at par with the culture, society, geography, polity, language, environment as well as humanity. Ezekiel's biocentric approach is observed in "Foresight", where he says "We shall not find a tragic end beyond the mountains where ancient gods are buried. We could be buried there beneath a landscape brave with life… (CP 51).but at the same time he seems to have biocentric approach and in awareness regarding the contemporary environmental crisis is brought by him in some of his poems such as "Squirrel", "Sparrows", "Poet, Lover, Birdwatcher".

In this contemporary world of Mammon worship, mankind has forgotten the importance of his own environment; he does not carry even in his distant insight, the realization of the veritable fact that after life the dead will be buried in the landscape itself, in turn making the dead as well as the buried full of life. In the landscape, each and every species have to be dependent on each other to rule over the odds and this is what is called ecological consciousness. In this regard Ezekiel's oft remembered poem "Sparrows" serves as an outburst on the human cravings for materials beyond their requirements. Sparrows live a self-sufficient life, they seek minimal requirement such as just to fly freely without any stress of wants, they intend to mate which is quite natural, and then to build a nest. This motive of the sparrow has been used by the poet to satirize the mankind which constructs its manor grandly without requirements and even craves to have few more and thus stands as a hindrance in front of ecological fruitions. The 'nest' stands as a symbol for openness, warmness giving an overall view of things, which is quite against the contemporary human world. Mankind in this so calledmodern world is happy to live in its fake cosset, in its illusory world. Man considers itself to be the superior amongst all living creatures, but it seems that man is breaking human/animal binary opposition by moving against the rule of eco system. The poet rightly mentions in his poem: "and then I face the facts- the mating and the nest Primeval root of all the rest" (CP 104).Again, the poem "Squirrel" brings forth the poet's approbation for the world of non-human world. Here Ezekiel uses the personal pronoun 'he' for the squirrel in order to bring down the binary opposition between human and non-human entity. This poem implies that humanity has been a danger to the animal world - the squirrel does not want to be 'caressed' physically but from a distance. The danger that lurks on the squirrel makes it run away from the human world into its own safety zone.

Thus,both the poems "Squirrel" and "Sparrows" show nature from eco-critical point of view. According to Suresh Fredrick "Both the squirrel and sparrows are animals that live close to human beings.... But human culture devalues these animals, making symbiosis impossible" (Frederick 139).

There is a series of poems that deal with the poet's growing concern for his own environment. The poem "Poet,Lover,Birdwatcher" carries beauty and aesthetic sense within it but at the same time it is blunt enough to criticize the human behaviour towards nature. The language is lucid enough and direct which makes the subject matter stand as a statement without any pretence. "Poet, Lover, Birdwatcher" brings within its purview nature as well as human and non-human entity. According to the poet, birds and women represent nature and that it is not possible to value and identify with them hastily. They cannot be studied under compulsion or even in fretfulness: To force the pace and never to be still Is not the way of those who study birds or women. (CP 135) The poet expresses his longings to have patience so as to comprehend the incomprehensibility of the world. Mutual understanding, compromise and allowing others to the passageway of existence is the crux of ecological stand point. Ezekiel rightly points out in the poem, "The hunt is not an exercise of will But patient love relaxing on a hill To note the movement of a timid wing; Until the one who knows that she is loved No longer waits but risks surrendering" (CP 135).

Nissim Ezekiel seems to be of the view that mankind is destroying the ecological atmosphere and balance in the universe. Man in the blind pursuit of material possessions which is momentary on this earth is annihilating the ever-valuable nature. In this poem, the poet says that it is the poets, lovers and birdwatchers that can annul the disparaging conduct of the contemporary world. The poet brings forth his concern for ecology with a style that is suited for the purpose. His poems are written in lucid language and is full of intellectuality suggesting his great concern for the living as well as non-living community, which is both responsible in their own ways for the environment to be healthy. It seems that he wants to bring self-realization amongst the souls of this contemporary world to perform their due responsibilities to save the biodiversity as we all have to add towards the cycle of life. Through his poems Ezekiel seems to bring consciousness amongst the mankind and this shows his rootedness in nature.

Attipat Krishnaswami Ramanujan was born in Mysore on 16 March 1929 in a Srivaishnava Brahmin family. A.K. Ramanujan was well versed in English, Tamil and Kannad languages. His creative works have been written in English, while Tamil and Kannad became the sources of his translation, though he also wrote some creative works in Kannad too. A. K. Ramanujan was a versatile scholar, poet, and translator whose poetic voice tends to be vigorous and occupies a prominent place in 'new' Indian English poetry. His poetry collections are: *The Striders* (1966), *Relations* (1971), *Selected Poems* (1976), *Second Sight* (1986) and *The Black Hen.Collected Poems* (1994) were published posthumously. The environmental awareness is quite evident in the poetry of A.K. Ramanujan. Sometimes he deals symbolically with physical environment and pays a considerable attention to theconservation of nature. He seems to be against the concept of anthropocentricism. In the very introduction of Ramanujan's *Collected Poems*, Vinay Dharwadker asserts, "One of the recurrent concerns in Ramanujan's poetry as a whole is the nature of the human body and its relation to the natural world" (XVII-XVIII).

Along with a number of poems "The strider" is a poem in which Ramanujan depicts a water insect and reveals his "deep ecological sensibility". The poem is all about the strider which lives on the surface of water. The poem "Snakes" also refutes the idea of anthropocentricism and reflects the poet's awareness of physical environment. Here, poet's mother adores 'Snakes'. The poem ends with the Poet's longing for walking in woods as he writes, "and I can walk through the words". In the poem "Chess Under Trees with an ex-maharajah", the poet paints a beautiful natural picture: The mountain skies were preoccupied by dynasties of the mountain pine, while their tattered banners harped at the drizzling string of rain. (C. P. 27) The poem 'Anxiety' depicts the four necessary elements of the human body which are fire, water, earth, air and these are all the natural objects Vinay Dharwadker is right when he writes that, "From a modern and secular environmentalist viewpoint, the human body appears to be entirely natural is contained in nature, and returns after death, or ought to return, to nature" (viii). The poet deals with this theme thus: Flames have only lungs, water is all eyes. The earth has bone for muscle and is a flock of invisible the air pigeons. But anxiety can find no metaphor to end it. (C. P., 29)

Again, Ramanujan's poem "Christmas" depicts the poet's awareness towards his environment. Though Ramanujan, in this poem, draws the picture of a tree and co-relates it to his real life, his elaboration and nature consciousness deserve specific mention. The poet writes:

"For a moment, I no longer know leaf from parrot or branch from root nor, for that matter, that tree from you or me." (C. P. 33) 'A River' is a poem which describes the destruction or deluge of the river Vaikai. The poem conveys the suggestion that the harmful attitude of mankind towards natural objects is the main cause of human degradation: Every summer a river drives to a trickle in the sand baring the sand-ribs, (C. P. 38) Now, the poor condition of the river in the summer season is due to lakes, dams and the harmful depredatory attitude of man against nature. The poet, perhaps, presents this picture because he harbours and the anxiety about how to conserve nature in the midst of the conservation of nature ravages and disasters. In the same breath the poet criticizes some poets of Madurai as they did not pay heed to the destruction of a pregnant woman and two cows, namely Gopi and Brinda. 'A Hindu to his Body' is a poem dealing with nature-oriented theme. The poet again makes natural objects his focal point: ... "to rise in the sap of trees let met go with you and feel the weight of honey-hives in my branching and the burlap weave of weaver-birds in my hair" (C. P., 40) In the poem 'The Hindoo': he does not hurt a fly or a spider either", the poet again refutes anthropocentric norm as an ardent supporter of non-violence. The poet does not want to kill any living organism and thereby proves himself a deep ecologist. In this regard He writes: "It's time told you why I'm so gentle, do not hurt a fly. Why, I cannot hurt a spider either, not ever a black window" (C. P., 62)

There is a series of poems where the poet expresses his consciousness towards the environment. 'Love poem for a wife" again is a poem in which the poet describes his wife through the examples of natural objects. Ramanujan writes here thus: "chosen of all faces, a pouting difficult child's changing in the chameleon emerald wilderness of Kerala" (C. P.83). Spirituality sometimes adds to the creation of proper environment; for example, 'Yagya' purifies air. The adoration of Peepal, Banyan, Neem, Vindhya Mountain,

Kamad Giri (mountain) offers a spiritual-cum-religious touch in the life of a Hindu.

'Prayers to Lord Murugan' is a poem which contains an admirable amalgamation of spirituality and environment. Lord Murugan is as quoted in Ramanujan's Collected Poems, "an Ancient Dravidian god of fertility, joy, youth, beauty, war and love. He is represented as a six-faced god with twelve hands". Murugan is Kartikeya who is the elder son of Lord Shiva. The poet adores him as a god of nature and writes thus: "Lord of green growing things, give us a hand in our fight with the fruit fly. Tell us, will the red flower ever come to the branches of the blueprint city?" (C. P., 114) The Poem 'Elements of Composition' manifests Ramanujan's ecological prudence to a large extent. First of all, he describes the four essential elements of human body- earth, air, fire and water and these are all natural objects. The poet writes as follows: "father's seed and mother's egg gathering earth, air, fire mostly water, in to a mulberry mass, moulding calcium" (C. P.121). The poet concludes the poem with a minute observation of a small insect called caterpillar which is also a part of nature. This clearly shows the poet's „deep ecological" sensibility.

In the poem 'Ecology' the poet manifests his serious preoccupation with nature. Here, the poet also expresses his ecological sensibility through the common metaphor of family. Ramanujan presents anti-anthropocentric outlook in this poem through his mother who does not allow to cut down "the three Red Champak trees". Prof. A.N. Dwivedi remarks on this poem in his book *The Poetic Art of A. K. Ramanujan*: "Ecology' deals with the change of season and atmosphere and therewith the flowing of the three Red Champak trees, giving the poet's mother "her first blinding migraine of the season" and rendering the poet furious. The poet actually wants to cut down those trees, but his mother does not permit him to do so. After all, the trees were the source of supplying sweet smelling flowers to her gods and her daughters and her daughters' daughters, but for cousins they also necessitated "a dower of migraines in season" (15). The 'season' referred to here is the rainy season. (110) Ramanujan, in this way, does not allow the trees to be cut down and reveals his strong ecological concern as he writes thus: ... but mother, flashing her temper like her mother's twisted silver, grand children's knickers wet as the cold pack on her head would not let us cut down a flowering tree. (C. P.124)

In the poem 'Connect' the poet wants to connect all his dispersed things such as family and relations. But the depiction of the mango grove is noteworthy here: "... and search the mango grove unfolding leaf and twig living for the zebra-striped caterpillar in the middle of it. Waiting for a change of season" (C P 112) In brief, the poetry of A.K. Ramanujan has an explicit relationship with the physical environment, with the abnegation of the idea of anthropocentricism. Even though the family plays a crucial role in his poetry, he manifests his environmental awareness and pays considerable heed to the conservation of natural objects. Hence, his poetry can be interpreted in the light of eco-criticism.

In the end it can be summarised that an ecocricial consciousness demands to have an impersonal relationship with nature and environment for the better co-existence. An array of poetry written in India during different periods, from varied viewpoints and tones have the same message to convey that it is the need of an hour to form the harmonious relationship between man and nature.Nissim Ezekiel and A. K. Ramanujan very clearly express their consciousness towards the fast-putrefying environment in most of their poems and other works. Both the poets assert through their poems that all living and non-living beings are connected with each other in the ecological system and they need to be cared and protected for the sustenance of a better future.

Works Cited:

Abrams, M.H. and Geoffery Galt Harpham. *A Handbook of Literary Terms*. New Delhi: Cengage Learning India Private Limited, Third Indian Reprint, 2009.

Dharwadkar, Vinay. "Some Contexts of Modern Indian Poetry" in Aditya Behl and David Nicholls, (eds.) The Penguin New Writing in India. New Delhi: Penguin India, 1994: 221-236.

Dwivedi, A. N. *The Poetic Art of A.K. Ramanujan*. Delhi: B.R. Publishing Corporation, 1995.

Ezekiel, Nizzim. *Collected Poems: 1952-1988*. New Delhi: OUP, 1989.Print. (Referred in the text as CP with Page numbers).

Frederick, Suresh. "Suicidal Motive: An ecocritical Reading of Four Poems." *Essays in Ecocriticism*. (ed.)Nirmaladasan, Salvamony Alex. New Delhi: Sarup and Sons, 2007.

Glotfelty, Cheryll and Harold Framm, (eds.)*The Ecocriticism Reader: Landmarks in Literary Ecology*. Athens and London: University of Georgia Press, 1996.

Garrard, Greg. *Ecocriticism*. Oxfordshire: Routledge, 2007 (First Indian Reprint).

Ramanujan, A. K. *Collected Poems*. New Delhi: Oxford University Press, Twelfth impression, 2012.

Srivastav, Hemlata. *Signature of Literature on Society: Society, Culture and Literature* Agra: Associated Publishing House, 2013.

Chapter 4

Dilemma with Nature and Quest for Identity: Eco-critical Study of Margaret Atwood's Journals of Susanna Moodie

Sanju Choudhary

Abstract

Geography and landscape have always posed questions of identity. The wilderness settings are sites for the negotiation of identity and power relationships. The pioneers, settlers, tourists who form the core of Canadian culture are extensively used as protagonists in her poetry. *The Journals of Susanna Moodie,* is a postcolonial reading of a colonial text. Thisis possibly Margaret Atwood's finest collection of poetry; it unquestionably is her most tightly organized book of poems. Atwood's writing explores a wide range of concerns and "expand the brackets" of traditional literary genres, establishing her status as a major author in Canada and worldwide.

Keywords: Postcolonial, Identity, Culture, Wilderness, Power

Margaret Atwood is a prominent figuree and a prolific novelist, poet, short story writer, essayist, critic and editor. She is perhaps the most remarkable and prominent figure in the contemporary Canadian literature. Atwood's writing explores a wide range of concerns and "expand the brackets" of traditional literary genres, establishing her status as a major author in Canada and worldwide. W.J. Keith describes her as "the most brilliant, controversial, versatile, abrasive and enigmatic figure in Canadian literature" (Keith,1998:93) Shenon Hengen, a Canadian critic remarks that "She is an integral figure in the Canadian awakening of 1960's and 1970's, Atwood hopes to encode in her writing the potentially renewing powers of change" (Hengen, Shannon, 1993:45).

Geography and landscape have always posed questions of identity. The wilderness settings are sites for the negotiation of identity and power relationships. The pioneers, settlers, tourists who form the core of Canadian culture are extensively used as protagonists in her poetry. Margaret Atwood writes that "Canada is an unknown territory for the people who live in it". She says, "I am not talking about Canada as state of mind, as the space you inhabit not just with your body but with your head. It is that kind of space in which we find ourselves lost". (Frye, Northrop, 1995:78) 'Exploration' is a recurring motif in Canadian literature. The question of identity is deeply connected with Canadian nature and environment. The question "who am I" or "who we are"? has never been a stable question for Canadians. Canadian writers have always tried to understand nature, the wilderness as an alternate mode of perceiving the dark side of one's mind often they are hypnotized by it and would like to return to it in search of peace and tranquility.

The Journals of Susanna Moodie, is a postcolonial reading of a colonial text.This ispossibly Margaret Atwood's finest collection of poetry; it unquestionably is her most tightly organized book of poems.The book derives its shape and cohesiveness, of course, from the persona of Moodie herself as the writer traces the change -the growth and development - in Moodie's response to the land. She moves from her initial alienation to her attitude at the end where, as Atwood explains in the *Afterword,* that "Susanna Moodie hasfinally turned herself inside out, and has become the spirit of the land she once hated." (Margaret, Atwood, 1970:1)

The poems are tiedtogether not only by the persona, but also by a number of key images: trees, fire, light and darkness.It is especially in terms of the reversal of Moodie's attitude towards light and darkness that Atwood charts her growth and transforms her from a typical early Victorian lady to a person with a distinctly modern sensibility. The use of this imagery begins, in fact, with the collage that precedes the first journal. The opening collage reveals this to be Mrs.Moodie's state in the new land - she is artificially stuck into the wilderness, and lacks any true connection with the land. The sharp border of light surrounding Moodie reveals the cause of her separation from the land. Her initial commitment is to all those things associated with light: civilization, reason, order.But when she enters here she comes to accept the darker side of herself, and of nature.In the *Journals of Susanne Moodie*, as in much of Atwood's poetrythe exploration of a new land is also a psychological exploration of the self.

Journal I, covering Mrs. Moodie's years in the bush (1832-1840) takes us through the beginnings of her transformation. 'Disembarking at Quebec'the opening poem, portrays hertotal alienation from the land. She regards herself as "a word / in a foreign language."(JSM 23) But the poem also establishes, through the questioning tone of Moodie's voice, the possibility that her disharmony with the land is of her own making. She writes "or is it my own lack/ of conviction which makes/ these vistas of desolation, /omens of winter." Her alienation may be caused by her foreign habits of mind.

Atwood's Moodie starts taking tentative steps towards coming to terms with the new land, and towards greater self-understanding. In *Further Arrivals* the land is seen as "a large darkness" but she realizes: "It was our own / ignorance we entered." She does manage to make her initial gesture towards reaching out to, understanding, the darkness, but her dominant response to the land, and to her unknown inner self, is one of fear: "My brain gropes nervous/ tentacles in the night, sends out/ fears and demands lamps." (JSM46) The use of "tentacles", the animal's organs for sensing its way, suggests that her transformation has begun. This poem clearly shows her lack of conviction that creates, "sends out", fears. She still "demands lamps", the artificial light of society, to see her way, but knows that eventually she will need "wolf's eyes to see / the truth". She will have to come to terms with the darkness, see with the eyes of the wilderness, and that means the ability to see, as the narrator in *Surfacing* comes to realize, beyond the realm of logic, reason, and civilized order. (Atwood, Margaret 1972:67)

By the conclusion of the poem 'The Planters'Mrs. Moodie is well on her way to this kind of perception. The image of "planting" is the key image throughout the poem, and as Moodie watches her husband and the other man attempting to plant the garden, attempting to tame and humanize the wilderness, she realizes that if they:

> open their eyes even for a moment
> to these trees, to this particular sun
> they would be surrounded, stormed, broken
> in upon by branches, roots, tendrils, the dark
> side of light
> as I am.(JSM89)

These stanzas bring together the central images of trees, and darkness and light. She feels assaulted by the bush and regards it as threatening but another view seems implicit in her remarks. The image of "the dark" comes somewhat as a surprise at the end of the line above, for "branches, roots, tendrils" are, after all, simply the living forms of the natural world. Although at this point Moodie perceives the natural, the wild, as "dark", she is on the verge of a different and more complex perception. The line break produces another surprise; it conveys her realization that it is "the dark / side of light".Oxymoron indicates that Moodie's original, Victorian categories, which make a sharp separation of darkness and light, are beginning to break down.

Moodie's experiences and her increased feelings of alienation cause her to become more introspective and she begins to question who she is - and who her husband is. The poem 'The Wereman' shows her new awareness of her separation fromher husband: "my husband walks in the frosted field / an X, a concept / defined against a blank, / he swerves, enters the forest / and is blotted out."(JSM67)The phrase "Blotted out" suggests that she still sees the forest as something that simply threatens, obliterates one's identity.

In the following stanza, however, the opposite possibility is suggested: "Upheld by my sight / what does he change into / what other shape / blends with the under- / growth." Here he "blends" with the "undergrowth" and his identity is seemingly transformed positively by his achieving a new harmony with the land. The general theme of this poem that of lovers fixing an image of each other in their mindsis a common image in Atwood's work, but it takes on a new dimension here as she explores the impact of the land on identity.

In the poem 'Paths and Thingscape' Mrs. Moodie makes her own attempt to "blend in", to find meaning in her new world, but she is not yet fullyready. The opening sections of the poem suggest a growth in positive perception: "Those who went ahead / of us in the forest / bent the early trees / so that they grew to signals: / the trail was not / among the trees but / the trees." It is not entirely clear whether "those who went ahead" refers to earlier pioneers, or to the Indians; more probably it is the latter, but in any case the important fact is that the trails are not something man-made imposed on nature, but are made in harmony with nature.Certainly there is a suggestion that Mrs. Moodie is beginning to come to terms with the land, and beginning to recognize that the trees are her guide in her journey to self-understanding and self-realization.

The following two stanzas carry further the idea of

finding meaning, and order, in nature:

> and there are some who have dreams
> of birds flying in the shapes
> of letters, the sky's
> codes;
> and dream also
> the significance of numbers.(JSM90)

The first part, of course, refers to a form of augury. Both are seen as different kinds of "signals"; different ways of unlocking the order in nature, of discovering a natural pattern that exists apart from the meanings that man imposes.But at this point in Mrs. Moodie's experience the possibility of there being a meaning in nature is raised only to be discounted. The next lines in the poem show a shift in her attitude:

> In the morning I advance
> through the doorway: the sun
> on the bark, the inter-twisted branches,
> herea blue movement in the leaves,
> dispersed calls/ no trails; rocks
> and grey tufts of moss(JSM112)

Moodie fails to see any meaning in the things around her, but there is a suggestion that the sun, branches, blue movement could be seen in a unified way. Atwood deliberately juxtaposes "calls / trails". The "calls" are there, but Moodie can't understand them as she's still looking for the wrong kind of order. She perceives only the meaningless cycle of nature, but the poem points to the possibility that even in the fall of the, petals there may be some undiscerned pattern.

The poem concludes with Moodie longing for union with the world around her, longing for a vision of the world moving harmoniously "each / thing ... into its place." Because of her assumptions, however, Moodie is not ready for such a vision, and the union can't come until she undergoes a further transformation. The poem 'The Two Fires' portrays the experience that makes that transformation possible. This poem is one of the most brilliant examples of how Atwood uses Susanna Moodie's *Roughing it in the Bush* for her own purposes. The poem makes possible Moodie's new relation to the land, and to herself.

She creates a symbolic difference between the two fires in, order to portray Moodie's growth. The summer fire traps her in the house and against the "shapeless raging" of the wilderness fire, she attempts to raise up a charm: "concentrate on / form, geometry, the human / architecture of the house, square / closed, doors, proved roof-beams, / the logic of windows." In the face of the fire she turns to her belief, faith, in rationality implicitly in the whole cast of mind she brought with her from the old world. As Atwood's line-break - "the human / architecture" suggests, however, she mistakenly identifies the "human" with excessive rationality and abstraction, with "form, geometry". In the *Winter Fire* her situation is reversed and she writes:

> all those corners
> and straight lines flaming, the carefully-
> made structure
> prisoning us in a cage of blazing bars.(JSM135)

Here the structure, metaphorically of rational thought, is seen as a prison and cage that must be broken out of. The fire thus forces her outside into the wilderness she has so far resisted, and the dream of imposing the old order is "scorched", lost and given up.

As Atwood goes on to observe, she herself is on the side of the curve, and after the fires, so too is the Mrs. Moodie of her poems.By the conclusion of the poem *The Two Fires* Mrs. Moodie recognizes "each danger / becomes a haven". The danger has forced her to come to terms with the wilderness and the fires"have left charred marks / now around which 1 / try to grow." Purged by the fire of her false notions of order she is now, like the fire-weed of the previous poem which grows out of burnt soil, able to become part of the land.Her growth is presented partly through the use of tree imagery, and certainly in the following poem we see signs of her change.

In the poem *Looking Ina Mirror* Mrs. Moodie realizes that her civilized self has been destroyed by the land. She writes "religious / black rotted / off by earth". The loss, in fact, the discarding of the values of the old world is further implied in the lines: "the China plate shattered / on the forest road, the shawl / from India decayed." Her metamorphosis has begun as she perceives her "skin thickened/ with bark and the white hair of roots." and. her "fingers/ brittle as twigs"' She is not, it is true, yetaccepting the change:"the sun here had stained / me its barbarous colour". The values of the old world speak in the verb "stained" and in the adjective "barbarous", but she is on the verge of perception; her eyes are "almost / blind / buds" about to open, to flower. And by the end of the poem she has attained the recognition that she has never fully known herself:"you find only / the shape you already are/ but what/ if you have forgotten that/ or discover you / have never known."(JSM 56)

This recognition is, however, as far as she gets at this point, and her transformation is not completed before she leaves the bush. While the final poem of *Journal I* opens positively - "I, who had been erased / by fire, was crept in / upon by green" she is aware that her change is partial. She has not lost her fear of the land and of the animals: "I was frightened / by their eyes (green or/ amber) glowing out from inside me." Nor has she come to terms with the darkness: "I was not completed; at night/ I could not see without lanterns."(JSM 89)

*Journal II*purportedly covers the years 1840-1871, Moodie's years in Belleville; in fact, most of the poems return to her experience in the bush. While the arrangement of Journal I is perfectly clear, the poems follow Moodie's change, increasingly positive, response to the land.Moodie's attitude to the land becomes, consistently more positive; rather, the later poems show that she is in a continuing struggle to accommodate her new insights about the land. The journal begins with Moodie achieving a new relation to the land, but in the poems of the middle section, her old fears are revived.

In the opening poem *Death of a Young Son by Drowning* Atwood turns Moodie's own note, in *Life in the Clearings,* about the death of her son in the Moira river, into a key incident in Moodie's coming to accept her new land. At the beginning of the poem Moodie refers to "the land I floated only not touch to claim".But the death of her son finally establishes her link with the land. When he drowns he is "hung in the river like a heart"; he becomes the centre of her new feelings towards nature. At his death, she realizes:

My foot hit rock. The dreamed sails
collapsed, ragged
I planted him in this country like a flag.(JSM 189)

"Like a flag", of course, used in the discovery and claiming of a new land. The epigrammatic ending, so characteristic of Atwood's poetry, summarizes the change in Moodie's attitude. The dream of returning to England is ended, and her son's death gives her new roots.

Atwood opens the second journal with this poem is obviously of considerable importance, and thepoem*The Immigrants*portrays a further growth in Moodie' sunderstanding. She now realizes not only that the dream of return to England has collapsed, but also that the immigrants falsify, idealize, their memories of the old country. "the old countries rod, become/perfect, thumbnail castles preserved/ like gallstones in a glass bottle." The actual details of life in the old country, the real pain and suffering—implied by"gallstones" - are forgotten. All that remains in memory is the idyllic pastoral world shown "in a light paperweight-clear." But Moodie now realizes that if they go back, their idealized versions of the old country will be shattered by the reality: "their ears/are filled with the sound of breaking glass," this signifies shattering of her dreams of returning to her space left behind.

Moodie further understands that the old order cannot be re-created in the new land. Having come to the recognition that there is no going back, Moodie's mind, in the last two stanzas of the poem, turns to the land, that she must now find her identity.These opening two poems follow quite naturally from the first journal, showing Mrs.Moodie's response progressing in a straightforward line. But in the later series of poems we see that, at a deeper level, Moodie is still torn in her feelings about the land. In the *Afterword* Atwood provides a note on the construction of this journal: "At the beginning of this section Mrs. Moodie finally accepts the reality of the country she is in, and at its end she accepts the inescapable doubleness of her vision" (JSM 63). The poems show Moodie's recognizing the reality of her new country, but it is not at all clear that she accepts it. In many ways her years in the bush have left her with feelings of revulsion and terror towards her new land, and she is still struggling to come to terms with it. This may be what Atwood means by the"inescapable doubleness of her vision"that is, consciously committed to the new land, but she is also horrified by it.

The first dream poem, *The Bush Garden,* reflects the ambivalence in Moodie's attitude. In her dream the vegetables in the garden are seen as pulsing with life: "the radishes thrusting down/their fleshy snouts, the beets / pulsing like slow amphibian hearts." This surrealistic image of vegetables turning into animals is grotesque, yet is also positive as the land is becoming alive. The succeeding image is entirely positive: "Around my feet/ the strawberries were surging, huge/ and shining."(34) This poem apparently represents the vital energy in the land that attracts Mrs. Moodie. But the concluding stanza of the poem reveals a very different attitude:"In the dream I said / I should have known / anything planted there / would come up blood." The reference to "blood" is a shocking ending to the poem, and it reveals the great distance that still exists between Moodie and Nature. Within this single poem then we see Moodie's divided response, "the inescapable doubleness of her own vision". And, while the first two poems of this journal portray a conscious change in her attitude, the dream poem shows that in her unconscious, to some extent, her fear and revulsion remain intact.

The next three poems also deal with the spilling of blood and with Mrs. Moodie's attempt to confront the violence in the new land. The violence of the past, of the 1837 war, remains in the present, recorded in a child's drawing. In *Charivari* Atwood brings a particularly violent experience from our past front and centre, and, under the guise of Moodie, makes a direct, didactic appeal to us to change: "Resist those cracked/ drumbeats. Stop this. Become human." But these three poems are less important in trying to understand Moodie's attitude to the new land and society than the third dream poem, *Night Bear Which Frightened Cattle.*(JSM 170)

This dream poem picks up from *The Bush Garden* and reveals the terror that the wilderness still evokes in Moodie. Susanna Moodie's rather comic description, at the end of the poem *The Fire* she projects cattle being frightened by the bear, is transformed by Atwood into a probing exploration of what the wilderness now means to Moodie. At the beginning of the poem Moodie remarks that at night the cows were frightened, "the surface of my mind keeps/ only as anecdote". This particular scene remains in Moodie's conscious mind only as a memory to be laughed at, but the poem examines what lies beneath her conscious memory, and, moreover, what lies beneath the whole romantic conception of nature she brought with her:

> though beneath stories
> where forgotten birds
> tremble through memory, ripples across
> water
> and a moon hovers in the lake
> orange and prehistoric.(JSM 198)

This is one of the most overtly "poetical"stanzas in the collection:the birds "tremble", the moon "hovers", and these images evoke a romanticized nature. But "beneath stories", beneath this false peaceful natural setting, and beneath her conscious mind, lurks a sense of nightmare and terror.In the dream - "I lean with my feet grown intangible / because I am not there" - she comes to accept the reality of the wilderness. Although she does not actually see the bear, she realizes

> but it is real, heavier
> than real
> I know
> even by daylight here
> in this visible kitchen
> it absorbs all terror.(JSM 99)

The stanza takes us back to the early poem *Further Arrivals* depends on who lives there"which concludes "Whether the wilderness is/ real or not". Nowand "this visibleback -the wilderness is real to her. Apparently this refers to Moodie in Belleville, thinking back that the wilderness is real to her.

The penultimate stanza of the poem is of particular interest because it shows Moodie, in the dream, caught, or poised, between the world of the bear and that of the lighted cabin. In the actual scene in *Roughing It in The Bush*Moodie is with her family in the lighted cabin at night. In the dream Atwood changes the situation; Moodie is separated from her family:

it moves toward the lighted cabin
below us on the slope
where my family gathers.(JSM 187)

There is a certain ambiguity in the stanza, but "us", in the second line appears to refer to Moodie and the bear. She has now grown apart from the world of "the lighted cabin" civilization - and has moved out into the wilderness.*The Deaths of the Other Children*takes us back to the experience of the opening poem of this section, *Deathof a Young Son By Drowning*.

The two poems, portraying Mrs.Moodie's new roots in the land, provide a frame for the poems which come in between. She recognizes that the buried body"joins itself / to the loosened mind, to the black- / berries and thistles". As it will be for Mrs. Moodie herself, the union with the land takes place only in death. The conclusion of the poem makes it clear that these deaths have strengthened her ties to the land:"They"here refers to the children and the briers. The children have in fact become part of nature, and the land reaches out toclaim Mrs.Moodie.

In the third Journal Moodie's transformation finally occurs. The opening poem simply shows her out of place in the civilized world; the next three poems reveal her preference for the land over society, and her new preference for "the dark side of light". The poem *Daguerreotype Taken in the Old Age*shows the complete change from the early Moodie associates herself with "the granular moon"- she is a figure of the night. The analogy of Moodie as the moon is sustained throughout the poem: "I revolve among the vegetables", "I orbit", and the apple trees are seen as "white spinning/stars around me". The concluding lines bring the poem, and Moodie's change, to a focus: "I am being/ eaten away by light". Metaphorically light is no longer positive to Moodie. In *Life in the Clearings* Susanna Moodie remarked: "Light! Give me more light!' were the dying of Goethe; and this should be the constant prayer of all rational souls to the Father of light."(5) Atwood has none of Moodie's commitment to rationality and to Christianity- to light. Rather, Atwood wants the irrational, the dark side of nature and the self.

She believed that there should be a full recognition and acceptance of the darkness is the point of Mrs. Moodie's wish in the poem *Wish: Metamorphosis to Heraldic Emblem.* In her old age Moodie is already seeing her transformation: "On my skin the wrinkles branch / out, overlapping like hair or feathers." As the line break at"branch"indicates, Moodie is beingmetamorphosized into all aspects of nature, a tree as well as an animal (a bear, no doubt), and a bird. And she imagines the kind of emblematic forerunner she would like to become:

> I will prowl and slink
> in crystal darkness
> among the stalactite roots, with new
> formed plumage
> uncorrodedgold and
> Fiery green, my fingers
> curving and scaled, my
> opal
> no
> eyes glowing(JSM 256)

She will "prowl and slink" in opposition to the civilizationcommitted to light-that has excluded the land and darkness.For Moodie, the darkness is now "crystal darkness"; it is understood, and no longer feared. The bird that she imagines herself to be is "uncorroded" by society and its colour, "fiery green", symbolizes the energy and passion she now admires. At the end of the first journal she was frightened by "eyes (green or /amber) glowing out from inside me". The fear is gone and she is almost computed; she now desires that the land speak through her.As Mrs. Moodie turns to the land she becomes increasingly distanced from the society around her. By the end of the poem *Visit to Toronto, With Companions,* the separation is final.

The poem"Lunatic Asylum" in *Life In The Clearing*; from then on the poem is entirely, and distinctively, her own. Moody herself is now apparently "mad"; there is certainly a suggestion of controlled madness in her seemingly inappropriate gesture: "I sat down and smoothed my gloves." But this is "madness" as close to a breakthrough as to a breakdown, and is analogous to the madness of the narrator in *Surfacing* when she returns to a primitive state and identifies herself with the land:

> I lean against a tree,
> I am a tree leaning...
> I am not an animal or a tree,
> I am the thing in which the trees
> and animals move
> and grow,
> I am a place.(JSM 189)

Moodie never gets this far, but in the fourth stanza of the poem, as she steps into "a different kind of room" she encounters, or rather, imagines she encounters, the land, the wilderness now excluded by the city. Moodie is still not fully in harmony with the land: "The landscape was saying something / but I couldn't hear." But *Disembarking at Quebec*she felt *The rocks ignore,* here" One of the rocks / sighed and rolled over." There is some response, at least. Moodie rejects the appeal to return to the city for she prefers to attend to her visions:

> I shook my head. There were no clouds,
> the flowers
> deep red and feathered, shot from among
> the dry stones,
> the air
> was about to tell me
> all kinds of answers.(JSM 212)

In the earlier poem *Paths and Things cape*Moodie saw only the cycle of nature in the fireweeds; here the same flowers seem to shoot forth with significance. But the air is only"about" to tell her answer Moodie's change is not total and it is only in death that she can become one with the land.

Moodie's final word, just as she dies is "toro NTO"; Atwood may be playing on the Indian meaning of the word - "meeting place". In any case, in the poem *Alternate Thoughts From Underground*, as Mrs. Moodie, after dying, speaks out against the new order, "the inheritors, the raisers / of glib superstructures", she is identified with the land. She sets herself with Nature and totally against modern civilization; her heart prays: "O topple this glass pride, tireless / rivetted Babylon, prays / through subsoil / to my wooden fossil God." The key adjective "tireless" captures the reason for her revulsion from modern society, and also indicates the complete reversal from her original attitude. That she now prays to a"wooden fossil God". Nature that has no place in present society — prepares us for the transformation in the poem "Resurrection". The theme of the concluding part of "Alternate Thoughts" is strikingly similar to that of Al Purdy's *Lament for the Dorsets*. The giant reptiles, like the Dorset giants are "done under" by something they don't understand, in the same way Mrs. Moodie is done under by modern civilization, for which she feels "scorn but also pity"; scorn because of the shallowness of the present, pity because she knows it too will pass away.

The final transformation of Mrs. Moodie's attitudes occurs in the poem *Resurrection.*The first part of the poem shows traces of aChristian attitude towards resurrection, but there is also a perception of a resurrection of a different kind:

> I hear now
> the rustle of the snow
> the angels listening above me
> thistles bright with sleet
> gathering. (JSM 167)

Atwood makes superb use of her line-spacing to present two different perceptions; on the one hand Mrs. Moodie hears the angels, on the other hand she is aware of Nature. As Mrs. Moodie waits for the time to reach her "up to the pillared/ sun, the final city", she still seems to have a Christian idea of resurrection in mind, but in the concluding lines her attitude shifts:

but the land shifts with frost
and those who have become the stone
voices of the land
shift also and say
god is not
the voice in the whirlwind
god is the whirlwind
at the last
judgment we will all be trees. (JSM 213)

She rejects the notion of god as the Logos, or Word existing outside of, apart from nature; moreover, what she accepts is not what we ordinarily think of as pantheism: to say "god is the whirlwind" implies an acceptance of all the chaotic energy of nature. The concluding line, of course, brings all the tree imagery of the book to a focus.

In the final poem, *A Bus Along St. Clair: December,* the pattern of reversal is completed, and the tightly-structured *The Journals of Susanna Moodie*is brought to a fitting conclusion.Now it is not nature which is seen as threatening, but the city- "an unexplored / wilderness of wires." And Mrs. Moodie now is committed to "destroying, the walls, the ceiling", the boundaries and order she once supported. She has at last, as Atwood remarks, "become the spirit of the land she once hated.''

Works cited:

Atwood, Margaret, *The Journals of Susanna Moodie*. Toronto: OUP, Press, 1970.

Keith, W.J. "Significant Moments with Margaret Atwood" *Queens Quarterly,* 1998.

Atwood, Margaret. *Selected Poems I (*1966-1976) Toronto: O UP, 1976.

Hengen, Shanon. *Margaret Atwood's Power: Mirror, Reflections and Images inSelect Fiction and Poetry.* Canada: Second Story Press, 1993.

Sherril E. Grace, *"Moodie and Atwood: Notes on a Literary Reincarnation,"* in John Moss, ed., *Beginnings: A Critical Anthology, Vol.2* of *The Canadian Novel,* Toronto: E.C.W., 1980.

Atwood, Margaret. "Afterword," *The Journals of Susanna Moodie,* Toronto OUP, 1970.

Atwood, Margaret. *Survival: A Thematic Guide to Canadian Literature*Toronto: Anansi, 1972.

Weir, Lorraine, "Atwood in a Landscape," in Sherill Grace and Lorraine Weir, eds., Margaret Atwood: Language, Text and System Vancouver: U of British Columbia P, 1983.

Bilan R. P., *"Margaret Atwood's The Journals of Susanna Moodie,"* Canadian Poetry 2, 1978.

Chapter 5

Women and Nature: A Discussion of Female Characters in Anita Nair's novels in connection with Ecosystem

Neelofar Kohri

Abstract

The environment or eco-system has always been an inspiration for literature. Now a days, English literature and eco-criticism have become synonyms for each other. Increasing environmental disasters has become a topic of discussion for every debate. The sensitive writers cannot leave this issue unexplored. Literature now engages with the environment from a creative approach. In this scenario environmental degradation and gender studies have often been linked. Women writers of fiction frequently link their female characters to the natural world and ecosystem. The writers' pursuit of social justice for their female protagonists is closely associated with the concept of harmony in the natural world. Anita Nair is well-known for portraying the suffering that female characters endure due to discrimination on the basis of their gender. She also addresses the issues of patriarchy in connection with the ecological concerns.

Keywords: nature, loneliness, patriarchy, women, eco-feminism, novels etc.

"A definition of language is always implicitly or explicitly a definition of human beings in the world." (Williams 21)

-Raymond Williams

As William says, the combination of ecocriticism with feminism has resulted in ecofeminism. Both women and nature are responsibility of the human world. A political and intellectual movement that blends ecology and feminism is called ecofeminism. It looks at the relationships that exist between women and nature and makes the case that capitalism and patriarchy are to blame for both environmental damage and women's oppression. Eco-feminists apply feminist theory to ecological concerns, ecofeminism highlights the ways in which patriarchal society subjugates both gender-marginalized individuals and the natural world. In an interview with Barbara Gates Susan Griffin says,:

"I know I am made from this earth, as my mother's hands were made from this earth, as her dreams came from this earth and all that I know, I know in this earth, the body of the bird, this pen, this paper, these hands, this tongue speaking, all that I know speaks to me through this earth and I long to tell you, you who are earth too, and listen as we speak to each other of what we know: the light is in us" (e-source).

As a philosophy and movement, ecofeminism argues that the same male mindsets and behaviour that are associated with the patriarchy also link the marginalization of women to the subjugation of nature. Regaine Folter explains ecofeminism in simple words, she says

"Women are more likely to experience poverty and have less socioeconomic power than men, which makes it more difficult for them to recover from weather disasters that are becoming more and more frequent. Ecofeminism is a movement that aims to address this problem. It recognizes that life in society as well as nature should be maintained by means of collaboration instead of domination- and that the domination of women and nature stem from the same roots."(e-source)

The term ecofeminism is credited to French author Francoise d'Eaubonne in the year 1974. D'Eaubonne calls ecofeminism a branch of feminism that examines the connections between women and nature. D'Eaubonne contends that because of restrictions on abortion and the fact that certain people cannot obtain contraception, the "phallocracy" is to be held accountable for widespread pollution, capitalism, industrialism, and overpopulation. According to D'Eaubonne, each of these elements contributes to the planet's devastation, endangering all living things. Later ecofeminism included not only women but all the marginalized such as the downtrodden, and the queer. But conventionally, ecofeminism speaks of the women and nature.

To quote Alicia H. Puleo.

"An easy way to explain ecofeminism is to define it as a meeting between feminism and ecology. Today, ecofeminism is on the rise, mainly among young women, and is gradually leaving behind a long period when it was little known or poorly understood. It was believed that all forms of ecofeminist thought identified women with nature and that they were a kind of biologism." (Puleo 28)

In ecofeminist literature, women and the natural world are portrayed as co-victims of progress, with historical exploitation and dominance occurring hand in hand. Given that women are perceived as being closer to nature than men, it is assumed that any harm done to the natural world also affects women.

Mack Canty writes:

"From ecology, it learns to value the interdependence and diversity of all life forms; from feminism, it gains the insights of social analysis of women's oppression that intersects with other oppressions. Eco-feminism, in its use of ecology as a model for human behavior, suggests that we act out of a recognition of our interdependency with others, all others: human and nonhuman."(Canty 154-179)

Not a single piece of ecofeminist literature makes an effort to prove this connection using compelling data or persuasive reasoning. But there are connections between ecology and eco-feminism as well. The foundation of ecofeminism is found in literature. The linguistic and literary elements of theories and ideologies in literature have benefited from the contributions of ecocriticism and feminist literary criticism. Even though ecofeminist literary critique is not new, it is still developing, particularly when it comes to post-colonial literature. To Quote Ariel Salleh,:

"The word 'ecofeminism' might be new, but the pulse behind it has always driven women's efforts to save their livelihood and make their communities safe. From the Chipko forest dwellers of North India some 300 years ago to the mothers of coal mining Appalachia right now, the struggle to create life-affirming societies goes on. It intensifies today as corporate globalization expands and contracts, leaving no stone unturned, no body unused." (Foreword in Mies in Shiva, 7)

In Indian literature, ecofeminism manifests as a vibrant discourse that deftly interweaves issues of gender, ecology, and environmental activism amid the intricate social and cultural fabric of India. This discourse celebrates the beauty, spirituality, and interconnectedness of nature with human life while shedding light on the complex relationship between women's roles as environmental cultivators and victims of deterioration through a variety of literary forms, including stories, verses, essays, and more.

India is a country that values the natural world. Thus, the veneration of the sun, moon, planets, rivers, and so forth. The patriarchal society in India has also devalued women and the natural world in order to satisfy their own egotistical demands. From the bold and honest lyrical poetry of Kamala Das to the redolent stories of Mahasweta Devi; from the emotional world of Anita Desai to the chaos in Arundhai Roy; from the acute themes of Vandana Shiva's essays to the perennial themes of Gita Mehta, Indian women writers are attempting their hand at a variety of artistic mediums.. They address the concerns of marginalized individuals and promote environmental justice and sustainability through their thought-provoking writings. Women who have championed environmental causes include C.K. Janu, Medha Patkar, Mahashweta Devi, and Arundhati Roy. Some authors, such as Anita Desai, relate female characters to nature. Other well-known pieces were Kiran Desai's Hullabaloo and Arundhati Roy's The God of Small Things.

Vandana Shiva rightly quotes in her book *Staying Alive*:

"Women in India are an intricate part of nature both in imagination and in practice. At one level, nature is symbolised as the embodiment of the feminine principle, and at another, she is nurtured by the feminine to produce life and provide sustenance... prakriti is worshipped as Aditi, the primordial vastness, the inexplicable, the source of abundance, she is worshipped as Adi Shakti, the primordial power. All forms of nature and life in nature are the forms, the children in mother nature, who is nature itself born of the creative play of her thought." (Shiva 219)

The well-known Indian novelist Anita Nair is well-known for her works that examine social, cultural, and gender-related themes. With an eco-feministic perspective, the themes, characters, and storylines of Anita Nair's whole body of work will be examined here. By analysing Nair's writing, one can discover how, as a female writer, she ties feminist viewpoints to ecological concerns, emphasizing the relationship between gender and ecological integrity. Anita Nair frequently uses environmental issues as her main topics in her works. Her works, like *Ladies Coupe, The Better Man and Mistress*, address the issues of environmental deterioration and the necessity of preservation. She emphasizes the significance of environmental activism as a form of resistance by highlighting the effects of patriarchal power structures on women and the environment through her characters.

In her interview with Krishna and Jha, Nair says:

"[W]hether it is environmental protection or anything, women are the primary agents of change. Whatever rules are made, ultimately, women are the practitioners of change as they are engaged with the daily aspects of life in a daily basis.....[W]omen, whether they belong to rural or urban areas, they can initiate change." (Krishna and Jha 148)

Women in Nair, be it Akhila, or Radha, they are free spirits who want to take life in their own hands and want to monitor it on their own. One can recognize feminist patterns and draw a link between them by examining the ecological framework of nature. Anita Nair's 2005 novel, *Mistress* is situated in the famous literary and artistic district surrounding the Nila River, Kerala's own Ganges. There have been many immortal writers and Kathakali performers who have passed away and some who are still living. *Mistress* showcases the idea of a free woman as extending beyond her social or economic boundaries and instead having to do with her mental and emotional state of mind and general well-being. Radha's unfettered spirit is represented by the river "Nila," and Saadiya's inner longing for freedom is represented by the vast, open sea. The river "Nila," which is nearly completely dry, represents the dirty minds of those who live nearby. Their lust and greed have tainted the God-given spirits in their care, and their dirty habits have tainted the river's purity. Once more, their authority over this river demonstrates the tyranny that restrains Radha's longing and spirit of independence. In the same way that the river "Nila" suffers, Radha is constrained by borders and chains. Saadiya, on the other hand, desires to be unrestricted and free like the sea. She desired to ride the waves of life, much like the waves in the sea. She was against her father's plan to keep her confined to the house; she wanted to go and gain independence. She endured much suffering in order to gain this freedom, and in the end, she gives herself over to the lure of water and dives in to find her way out.

Further investigation into the river "Nila" will reveal that people with contaminated mindsets, such as "Shyam," exist. Despite his declarations of genuine affection for Radha, all he desires is complete control over her character. However, Chris, her lover, also exploits her body in the same way as others do with the water of the "Nila" river. As a result, this river also acts as an example of human life.

Saadiya is also dominated by the male ideology like Radha. Because of both the important male characters in her life, her father and her husband, she feels herself trapped in the cage of patriarchy. Living in an orthodox Muslim family, Saadiya wants to change her life and wants to explore the outer world, which is not allowed for women.

"Life: Life in so many colors and shapes. Life that breathed and walked. Life that chewed

and spat. Life that screamed and shouted. Life that mumbled and tumbled, hissed and crawled. Life that waited. Life that never be hers." (Nair 102)

Finally when she elopes with Sethu and gets married, she gives birth to a son, Koman. The concept of giving birth, regeneration is also symbolized by eco feminism; mother earth, that gives birth to new life. Carolyn Merchant observes:

"What draws together the various components of the eco-feminist movement is the concept of reproduction in its widest interpretation that includes biological reproduction and social reproduction of life, with the common aim of restoring the natural environment and improving life in the planet." (Merchant 58)

In Nair's *Ladies Coupe,* the six stories, each narrated by a woman from a different social background aboard a train, explore themes of power, gender, and relationships with the natural world. The socioeconomic strata represented by

Akhila, Prabhavathi, Sheela, Shanthi, and Marikolunthu demonstrate how gender oppression interacts with other oppressive institutions to sustain inequality. They display a range of cultural customs. The stories of the female protagonists in *Ladies Coupe* converge, highlighting the necessity of an inclusive feminism and environmental activist movement as well as the variety of difficulties they confront.The women speak up for their rights and autonomy by questioning social norms and claiming their agency. Nair also looks at how harmful behaviors affect nearby populations and ecosystems.

Akhila or Akhilandeshwari, the spinster, and Prabhavati, the devoted mother and wife, are just a few examples of the different facets of women's personality. Akhila's starched, rigid sarees represent her lack of empathy with the outside world, which has no understanding of her needs. Her own trip to Kanyakumari is a response to the call of nature. She wants to spend a few special minutes in nature's company and escape the selfish world because only nature can fulfil her demands for pleasure and the outside world will never be able to comprehend what she wants.

Nair herself says in an interview:

"To me, feminism in the Indian context is about recognizing the importance of the female self and to be able to nurture it. Very often, we Indian women tend to negate ourselves as something that is expected of us. In fact, there may be no pressure at all from extraneous sources for us to do so. Perhaps it is conditioning or perhaps it is lack of self-esteem, we do not consider ourselves important enough and so we tend to put our needs and desires on the back burner. This is what needs to be addressed. And this to me is what feminism ought to tackle". (Interview by Sneha Subramanian Kanta) (e-source)

Prabhavati's strong desire to learn how to swim and float serves as a metaphor for how nature returns all kindness.

Marikolanthu is a lower-class member who is not respected in society. Her rape is comparable to how anti-environmental actions are destroying Mother Earth. It is against nature for Sujata and Marikolanthu to have a sexual connection that may be described as a lesbian romance. Sujata and her husband oppress Marikolanthu, a lower-class woman, simultaneously. Like Mother Earth, she is always taken advantage of as a woman. Thus, Nair gives a comprehensive presentation of the predicament of femininity.

The picturesque beauty that Nair captures in her writing is a testament to her appreciation of the natural world. Her appreciation of the natural world is also evident in the novel *The Better Man*. In the words of Mukundan, she depicts pepper, mango trees, and paddy fields in her book.

"The fields were everywhere. Endless shades of green the stretched into the horizon on one side and the foot of the Pulmooth Mountain on the other. Speckled only with the bright blouses of thewomen as they stood ankle-deep in water-logged mud and pulled out the young paddy plants. When a breeze blew, the tops of the paddy rippled and turned the sheets of sedate jade into gleaming splashes of emerald. He knew that soon the sun would disappear behind thick grey clouds that would frown down unrelentingly. Then it would be time to seek the dry confines of the house. Until then he would stay here and look at the view he had banished from his memories for many years now." (Nair 50)

In addition to describing this stunning scenery, Nair discusses women's rights. Here are some lines that demonstrate her ecofeminist ideas. She writes:

"Like the firefly trying to match the brilliance of the stars, I had let the limits of my knowledge rule me. Man cannot change the movement of the planets with the sweep of his hands. Every man is guided by a force that is individual and unfathomable. Man can heal, but a little. Man can aid self-discovery, but only a little. No man is the master of another man's destiny. For man is no God. And fireflies are not stars." (Nair 168)

The three novels that were just examined are all set in Kerala's breathtaking landscape. Her works depict many locations, such as the beauty of Kanyakymari, Pulmooth Mountain and the Nila River, with a feeling of familiarity for the readers. These natural settings appear to represent the protagonists' internal turmoil. The pain they carry in their heart is also a part of nature. Rosemary Reuther writes in 1975 in her book:

"Women must see that there can be no liberation for them and no solution to the Ecological crisiswithin a society whose fundamental model of relationships continues. To be one of domination.They must unite the demands of the Women's movement With those of the ecologicalmovement to envision a radical reshaping of the basics Socioeconomic relations and theunderlying values of this society". Reuther 204)

Abuse of power can have an adverse effect on nature, just as it does on women who are oppressed. The environment and people could coexist harmoniously in a complementary, non-exploitative relationship. Therefore, just as it is every individual's duty to protect the environment and natural resources, it is also the responsibility of the male-dominated society to protect women's rights. The world could then only become more balanced and a better place to live. The treatment of women in Nair's novels is merely a fictionalized depiction of real-life events; some of the protagonists commit suicide to get the freedom they desire, some give in to their circumstances, and yet others flee from the inconsiderate society with their ambitions and dreams. Nair writes with the expectation that society will fundamentally change. And writing is a necessity for the same. Hence, she raises these sensitive issues in her novels.

Work Cited:

- Alicia H. Puleo. "What is Ecofeminism?" https://www.iemed.org/wp-content/uploads/2021/05/ What-is-Ecofeminism_.pdf. Pg 28
- Ariel Salleh in *Ecofeminism*. Maria Mies and Vandana Shiva, 1993, 2014 Foreword (2014)
- Canty Mack, C. (2004). "Third-Wave Feminism and the Need to Reweave the Nature/Culture Duality." NWSA journal, pg.154-179.
- Françoise d'Eaubonne. *Feminism or Death*, Verso. 1974.
- Krishna, Niyathi R and S Jha. "Interview with Anita Nair". The Atlantic Critical Review. Vol: 12, No: 4 (Oct-Dec 2013). Print Pg 148
- Merchant, C. (2008). *Eco-feminism*. Madrid Spain: La camera blu. Pg 58
- Nair, Anita. *Mistress*. New Delhi: Penguin Books.(2005).
- Nair, Anita. *The Better Man*. New Delhi: Penguin, 1999
- Nair, Anita. *Ladies Coupe*. New Delhi: Penguin, 2001
- Shiva Vandana & Maria Mies. *Ecofeminism. With a Foreword by Ariel Salleh*. Zed Books. 2014. Pg 7
- Shiva Vandana. *Staying Alive*. Zed Books. 1988.pg. 219
- Williams, R. 1977. *Marxism and Literature*, Oxford. Pg 21.
- "What is ecofeminism?" Regiane Folter, Women's Media Center, (09 December 2019) https://womensmediacenter.com/fbomb/what-is-ecofeminism
- Made From This Earth: A Conversation Toward Healing, With Susan Griffin. By Barbara Gates. https://inquiringmind.com/article/0401_01_gates-griffin-interview/ Ecofeminism:Historic and International Evolution Pg 204. https://systemicalternatives.org/2016/01/18/ecofeminism-historic-and-international-evolution/#:~:text=In%20one% 20of%20the%20first,to%20be%20one%20of%20dominat ion.

Chapter 6

Religion and Environment in James Camaron's Movie Avatar

Tamishra Swain

Abstract

Climate change in the whole world make everyone bother. The environmental exploitation is going on endlessly everywhere. However, it is high time to make people aware of its dangerous impact in future and we must understand what kind of future we restore to the future generations. These environmental changes and its impact have been the buzz words in every discourse. The present book chapter analyzes James Camaron's 'Avatar', a dystopian movie through the lens of Eco spirituality propagated by Bron Tayor.

Keywords: Ecospirituality, Eco criticism, Ecofeminism, Environmentalism

Introduction

Ecospirituality or dark green religion is all about the spiritual connection between humanand nature which links religion and environmental activism. The earth is the creator andnurturer of all the living and non-living species, and it provides enough for the sustenance of every creature, however human beings exploited nature and environment out of greed andselfish desires. From this perspective, current human practices toward nature are a sacrilege.Hence, the modern ecological crisis has created a need for environmenttally based religionand spirituality. Ecospiri-tuality is a critic of consumeristic and materialistic human society. Itsees this massive humanization of earth-and humans; sanguine attitude towards it–as self-idolatry. Humans ultimate concern is to domesticate and manipulate ecosystems. James Camaron's Si-fi film 'Avatar' is one of the examples of the depiction of fantasy landand the problem of colonizing the land of Pandora and to plunder the land ecologically. Ithighlights the nuances of the evils of the society through its depiction of contemporary issuesand counters the age-old practices by providing a counter narrative. This paper attempts toanalyze the movie "Avatar" through the lens of Dark Green Religion a term popularized byBron Taylor. Henceforth, the term ecospirituality and Dark green religion will be used interchangeably.

This paper begins with the idea of Eco-criticism then it discusses Ecospiritualism /Dark Green Religion the term popularized by Bron Taylor in his book *Dark Greene Religion: Nature Spirituality and the Planetary Future* published in 2010. Then the book chapter analyzes a couple of scenes from the movie 'Avatar' that reflects or supports the idea of Dark Green Religion where Nature is treated as sacred which is commonly associated with the indigenous people. All the Natural elements including man, animal, plant and non-human elements shared a kinship and all have that part of sacred elements in them that make everyone equal. Hence, Eco spiritualism rejects the hegemonic idea of Anthropocentrism means man as superior to all other elements of Nature.

With the rising temperature of the earth the discussion on environmental degradation crops up. There are various events happened that make everyone think about the preservation of nature. However, to create an awareness among the common people there are certain discourses disseminated in the public domain. Literature is one of the discourses that create an awareness among readers. Nonetheless, it is also important to note that how nature is represented in literature. The definition of ecocriticism was provided in the book *The Ecocriticism Reader* (1996) that it is the study of the relationship between "Literature and the Environment" (Qtd in P.K Nair 242). Majorly eco criticism seeks to study the anthropocentric and exploitative attitudes towards nature. Cherry Glotfelty defines Ecocriticism as

Ecocriticism is the study of the relationship between literature and the physical environment. Just as feminist criticism examines language and literature from a gender conscious perspective, and Marxist criticism brings an awareness of modes of production and economic class to its reading of texts, ecocriticism takes an earth-centered approach to literary studies (xix).

When we talk about ecocriticism it seeks to explore nature writing texts, environmental awareness in canonical texts etc. To understand the exploitation of nature one needs to look at the place of "nature' in western thought. Thomas Hobbes in 17th century believed that the 'state of nature' was a primitive one and similarly John Locke believed that the land /nature should be treated as private property. During 18th century the civilization witnessed the growth of two movements, colonialism and capitalism. In the name of growth and development two contrasting things happened. One materialistic growth and second subjugation of those who are at the periphery, here periphery means women, nature who do not have the voice to resist the injustice done to them. Since then, one can see the degradation of nature as nature is used as a materialistic object, an object which can serve humans, hence exploitation of nature begins.

Darwin links human and non-human life forms which altered the Western thought towards nature. According to Darwin those who adapted to nature can survive. He called for a greater understanding of the human dependance on nature. Similarly, Enlightenment thinkers believe that human progress was based upon a careful exploitation of Nature. This idea has been rejected by many western thinkers like J.S Mill, who argued in his essay "Nature" against the exploitative ideas. Following J.S Mills there are other theorists who reject the exploitative ideas of Nature.

Eco spirituality/ Dark Greene Religion is a term coined

by Bron Taylor. He links religion to many forms of environmentalism. Rachel Wheeler said, " Eco-spirituality describes how one relates to the sacred within the context of our natural global and even cosmic eco-system (or homes) of which we all from a part." (10) Eco spirituality/ Dark Green Religion related to two terms they are 'ecology' and 'religion'. Religion has a Latin root *Leig* meaning 'to bind' or 'tie fast' or 'religare', means 'to reconnect' – it can be concluded that religion connects people to that which they most value, depends on and considers sacred. When religion is associated with nature it means "religious perceptions and practices that are characterized by a reverence for nature and that consider its destruction a desecrating act. Adherents often describe feelings of belonging and connection to the earth- of being bound to and dependent upon the earth's living system" (Taylor 5). This idea of 'nature religion' has been discussed in many of the texts like E.B Taylor's Primitive Culture (1871), Max Muller's Natural Religion (1888), James G. Frazer's The Worship of Nature (1926) Mircea Eliade's Patterns in Comparative Religion (1958) etc.

Religion and nature relationships have been majorly discussed by Baruch Spinoza and Jean Jacques Rousseau. "Spinoza makes sense, for if every being and object is a manifestation of God or God's activity, then everything has value, which presents a fundamental challenge to the prevailing anthropocentrism"(Taylor 8). Rousseau'e religious thought is more influential than Spinoza's pantheistic philosophy in promoting nature religion. "Rousseau rejects the idea of Christian orthodoxy in favour of 'natural religion' in which God's existence could be perceived in the order of nature. For Rousseau, natural religion and an epistemological turn to nature could lead the way to a life free from the alienation and materialism of western civilization" (Taylor 9).

Hettinger in his paper entitled "Ecospirituality: First

Thoughts" opined that, "Religion is an incredibly powerful force in human life and our spiritual attitudes toward the earth, its teeming life forms and human presence, has had and will have powerful effects on the human-nature relation" (83). As Lynn White puts it, "What people do about their ecology depends on what they think about themselves in relation to things around them. Human ecology is deeply conditioned by beliefs about our nature and destiny-that is, by religion". (Qtd in Hettinger 83). Hence, treatment of nature is majorly affected by the mindset of human beings. Bron Taylor talks of two terms one 'green religion' and the other is 'dark green religion'. Green religion means friendly behaviour with nature is a religious obligation and dark green religion is nature is sacred has intrinsic value and is therefore must be worshipped. Dark green religion is related to religious environmentalism which means religions that are becoming more environmentally friendly. Lynn White Jr. in 1967 critiqued Christianity by saying that it rejects ancient paganism and creates dualism of man and nature but also insisted that it is God's will that man exploit nature for his proper ends. "Paganism and animism are more nature friendly than chrisitanity as Christianity was the most anthropocentric religion the world has seen and as a result helped precipitate the environmental crisis" (White 11). White is also of the opinion that science and technology will facilitate more exploitation of nature hence humans need to find a new religion or rethink the old one. He gave emphasis upon 'Gaia' or 'Paganism' which believes in the concept of "Earth First".

In the contemporary age after globalization there is increased immigration and the strict boundary of nation has been blurred. Not only the boundary but also the religious belief, custom, culture etc became hybridized. Multireligious culture has become the norm in the west. With more number of different people, the idea of fixed religion has been challenged and new religion/s have been created that supports the subjective idea of religion, God and spirituality. So, the new religions are fluid and transnational according to Christopher Patritdge "There is in the West, for example, a move away from traditional forms of belief, which have developed within religious institutions, toward forms of belief that focus on the self, on nature, or simply on "life" (17).

Paul Heelas and Linda Woodhead's book "The Spiritual Revolution" inspired by Charles Taylor's concept of the great modern subjective then religion since 18th century talks about how in West there has been a slow turn away from external institutional authority to towards quest from freedom and self-fulfillment. Heelas and Woodhead talked about spiritual revolution in West since 1960's Subjective turn of religion " it has to do with states of consciousness, states of mind, memories emotion, passion bodily experience inner conscience and sentiments including moral sentiments like compassion" (3).There is a turn towards paganism and Wicca (1060s) which shows the support for the subjective life. Similarly, Colin Campbell argued about the Easternizaton of Western Culture constitute a paradigm shift in which ideas once perceived as marginal have come to represent the norm. Campbell further adds that the 18th century paradigm metaphor of the Great Chain of Being has been replaced by Gaia/ Earth.

Talking about New Religions, Lorne Dawson has distilled some of the key features of new religions as "dualisms are rejected and a common holistic belief in the interconnectedness of spirit and matter the mind and the body the individual and the community and the sacred and the profane"(132). The New religions challenge the existence of rigid religion that believes in a particular fixed structure, belief system rather it accepts plural ideologies. Gradually a trend in Hollywood movies has been developed where they encourage this idea of new religions. Another point of New religions is the easternization and this has been portrayed in the film like Hollywood like The Lion King, Lord of the Flies, Bambi, Star wars etc combined green religion and indigenous spirituality

The movie 'Avatar' directed by James Cameron portrayed how humanity is faced with a global energy crisis. Man has managed to exhaust Earth's natural resources, and looking for a new universe known as Pandora. Human scientists have managed to create avatars, half-human, half-Na'vi hybrid clones that can freely move around and operate in Pandora's poisonous atmosphere. A paraplegic marine named Jack Sully is given the responsibility to visit Pandora and observe their activities.In that land, Jack Sully was attacked by an animal and saved by female Na'vi name Neytiri. Neytiri's mother and spiritual leader, Mo'at, orders her to induct Jake into their clan. Jake soon becomes supportive of the Na'vi's plight as he gains a better understanding of their ways, and he proves himself to be a worthy Na'vi warrior. He is eventually integrated into the tribe and Neytiri chooses him as a mate. However, Pandora's soon came to know about Jack Sully's betrayal. Wishing to win back favor with the Na'vi, Jake sets into motion, Jake, supported by the new tribal chieftain Tsu'tey, gathers and unites the remaining tribes to fight the Resource Development Adminstration. The RDA's superior techno-logy and weaponry overwhelm the Na'vi, but the animals of Pandora join in the fight, and change the course of the battle. Neytiri takes this to mean that Eywa has heard Jake's prayer and has responded by sending assistance.

The Film 'Avatar' is a term borrowed from Hinduism. The Greene religion believes that nature is sacred, human have no dominion over it and that it is not a resource for humans. The movie Avatar tries to disseminate the similar idea. In the movie Avatar two contrasting elements are portrayed Jake Sully's wheelchair on the street emphasizes extreme overpopulation; TV extinction of Bengal tiger- is being cloned back to existence shows how the strong prey on the weak. The beginning of the movie talks of overpopulation, extinction and survival talk. Greene religion can be understood as based on a felt kinship with the rest of life, derived from a Darwinian understanding that all forms of life have evolved from a common ancestor and hence related interconnectedness and the idea of interdependence. Dark Green religion according to Bron Taylor is ' it not only oriented towards nature, it preferences nature" fundamentally talks of harmonious relationship with nature.

The Na'vi population lives in the lap of nature instead of thinking themselves above nature they consider themselves as part of nature. They have a strong connection with their environment, and they pray the natural elements, as they pray trees, animals etc they normally don't harm them. They lead a harmonious life with everything that is part of nature. Most importantly, Neytiri is an extremely powerful woman, and she is constantly shown as being connected to nature. There are scenes where Neytiri was shown to have a good bonding with all the animals of that land, in one of the occasions where she has to kill an animal to save Jack, she shows her repentance and anger towards the killing. There is another place (a huge tree) where all the Navi's offer prayer and they call this tree as 'soul tree' and it is a belief that their prayers are answered there. When Neytiri considered Jake as the people of Omaticaya, he is permitted to make his bow from the wood of Hometree. Harold Linde argues that, James Cameron's 'Avatar' is without a doubt the most epic piece of environmental advocacy ever captured on celluloid. Similarly, Parth Bhattacharjee says, "Cameron demonstrates that Avatar can be taken as one text which deals with the context of nature writing text with its strong environmental messages"(99).

Another example of Navi's strong bonding with nature is "Tsahaylu" or the neural bonding that help them to feel the orders from Eywa; they can interact with Ewya, send prayers through tree. Eywa is the mother goddess. The Navi's create connection between animals through neural bonding. Later, Jake also made the bond with his horse, by using the same "Tsahaylu".

The Navi people worship nature and show their gratitude towards it. They protect the 'Soul tree' as sacred. Unfortunately, when the people of earth attacked Pandora, they destroyed the 'soul tree' and Navi people suffered a lot of casualty. Initially Jake shows his loyalty towards the RDA however, later he supports the Navi. Jake connects himself with a dragon-like creature through his neural bond and finds refugee at the sacred tree of souls. Jake unites the clan to battle the RDA which was headed by Quaritch. During the battle when Navi started losing the battle unexpectedly all the animal gathered to protect the land. This they believed as the answer of Eywa to Jake's prayer. When the battle between Navi's and RDA's from earth began, initially it was difficult for Navi's to win the battle, but eventually the whole Pandora's supported the Navi's (which include all kinds of animals). The ultimate winning of Pandora's over science and technology shows the benefits of harmonious relationship between man and nature.

The movie "Avatar" tries to disseminate the idea of dark green religion that can save the earth from further exploitation. By bringing the earth to the center one can revere the earth and resist humans from further devastation. It is the only way of protecting nature, environment and human beings. The movie 'Avatar' is all about the shifting focus of "Antrhopocentric" to "Earth centric" ideology. The idea of "Earth First" not only protects nature but also all the elements of nature including human beings.

Works cited:
Bhattacharjee, Partha. "Humans, Humanoids and Animals in Eywa: An Eco-critical Reading of James Cameron's Avatar."https://bcjms.bhattercollege.ac.in/V3/14_Ecocriticis m_James_Cameron_Avatar.pdf (date of access 17 June 2024)
Dawson, Lorne L. "Anti-Modernism, Modernism, and Postmodernism: Struggling with the Cultural Significance of New Religious Movements." *Sociology of Religion* 59.2 (1998): 131–56. Print.
Erb, Cynthia. "A spiritual blockbuster: Avatar, environment-talism, and the new religions." *Journal of Film and Video* 66.3 (2014): 3-17.
Garrard, Greg. *Ecocriticism*. Routledge, 2004.
Glotfelty,C. and Fromm, H.(eds) *The Ecocriticism Reader: Landmarks in Literary Ecology*, London: University of Georgia Press,1996.
Heelas, Paul, and Linda Woodhead. *The Spiritual Revolution: Why Religion Is Giving Way to Spirituality.* Malden: Blackwell, 2005.
Hettinger, Ned. "Ecospirituality: First Thoughts." *Dialogue and Alliance* 9 (1995): 81-98.
Linde, Harold. 2010. "Is Avatar Radical Environmental Propaganda?" Mother Nature Network, 4 January. http://www.mnn.com/technology/ research-innovations/ blogs/is-avatar-radical-environmental-propaganda.
Lynn White, "The HistoricalRoots ofOur Ecologic Crisis," *Science 155*, #3767 (10 March 1967), p. 1205.
Partridge, Christopher, ed. *New Religions, a Guide: New Religious Movements, Sects, and Alternative Spiritualities.* New York: Oxford UP, 2004.
Taylor, Bron. *Dark green religion: Nature spirituality and the planetary future*. Univ of California Press, 2009.
Wheeler, Rachel. *Ecospirituality: An Introduction.* Augsburg Fortress Publishers, 2022.

Chapter 7

Eco-Consciousness as Reflected in Female Life Narratives : Insights into Nayantara Sahgal's Autobiographies

Sanjana Sharma

Abstract

A woman's autobiography, vibrant with the hues of human emotions, serves as portal through which readers gain a profound understanding of the then prevalent political, societal and economical concerns. Women writers have always touched upon the myriad issues pertaining to environment and have tried to generate eco-consciousness among readers. Worshipping nature and harbouring love for nature and natural resources have their roots in ancient Indian culture since Vedic era and Indian women have successfully carried on this cult of worshipping and protecting nature since time perennial. Women, being nurturer like nature, have greater understanding, and sensitiveness towards the issues that are threatening to the earth and its environment. Nayantara Sahgal's two autobiographies elaborately delineate her diverse perspective towards nature. The paper tries to explore how Sahgal's life's journey is interwoven with the Indian Himalayan region and how does she accentuate eco-consciousness through her life narratives.

Keywords: Autobiography, wildlife, eco-consciousness, urbanization, temperature, light, noise, monsoon.

Nayantara Sahgal is a novelist and columnist of great repute. She has written two autobiographies, *Prison and Chocolate Cake* (1954) and *From Fear set Free* (1962). *Prison and Chocolate Cake* is full of reminiscences from the family record, with emphasis on the political life of the family at Anand Bhawan in Allahabad. Sahgal's another autobiography *From Fear Set Free* is a sequel to the first one. It unravels Gandhian influence on the writer.Through her autobiographies she has tried to emphasize the significance of nature in our life.In both of her books, she resolutely voices for every citizen's right to inhabit a clean, safe and wildlife-rich environment.

Sahgal's life narratives advocate that we belong not only to human community but to a community of all nature as well. In "Personal and Social Transformation: A Complementary Process towards Ecological Consciousness" Yuka Takahashi too has pertinently stated that we are at a critical moment in history where we are not only facing ecological and other social crises of an unprecedented scale, but we are also challenging the destructive forces that give rise to these crises and are attempting to create new possibilities. All around the world, there are individuals, groups of individuals, and organizations that are participating in the process of creating ecologically sustainable and just societies (169). Through generating eco consciousness and environmental awareness among the readers regarding the environmental limits and the consequences of human actions damaging the planet's basic life support system, Sahgal shows her serious apprehension for reduction of the natural resources. Sahgal's father Ranjit Pandit's great love was Khali, an estate situated high in the Kumaon hills near Almora. Sahgal has given a great importance to it in both of her autobiographies. According to her it was his retreat from the noisy clamor of politics. Appreciating her father's spirit she claims that in spite of frequent draughts and lack of modern comforts, he succeeded in making Khali a beautiful home and a place where Sahgal could spend her summer vacations. Sahgal has drawn an amazing picture of the time spent at Khali with her pen:

Khali brings to mind early suppers eaten on the porch, from which we watched the sunset casting a rosy glow over the snow peaks of the Himalayas; fragrant pine-cone firs crackling every evening in the living-room, picnic lunches taken to the many beauty spots in the forest around the house; pure, sweet, icy sparkling water drunk from mountain streams; the walled orchard of cherries, apricots and peaches where we played; the lonely mountain paths where more than once we saw a graceful tawny panther prowling at sundown; and above all like a constant refrain, the look, the smell, the soft regular swish of the slender pines with their spicy-sweet dry odor (Sahgal *Prison* 36).

In the article "Being Eco-Conscious: Your Ecological Mindset and Its Impact on the Environment" Brad Stevens observes that eco-consciousness is a state of mind where you have an innate understanding of your role as a human being on earth. This means being fully aware of your effects on the environment and everything connected to it, big or small. It's about knowing the importance of preserving and saving nature at its core. This doesn't just include animals, trees, and insects. It also includes the bigger things: mountains, bodies of water, the air, and the sky, and all that makes Earth alive and everything walking on its soil. It's you and me, and down to the tiniest cell the naked eye can't see. Stevens states that being eco-conscious starts with you and your mindset. Once we're truly aware of what impacts nature and life on earth, we begin to understand the importance of the choices we make in our daily lives. We need to protect and save what's ours as long as we have it, including animals, trees, and every part of the earth. While travelling towards Darjeeling after her marriage, Sahgal is reminded of time and care lavished by her father on Khali. Her father had transformed the wildness he had found into a fruit and poultry farm, "With an abiding love for the land and all its produce he had never been able to resist its invitation, and the earth had amply repaid him, blossoming to his touch, banishing the fatigue and frustration of all life lived away

from his true talent. He had been happiest in the Himalayas"
(Sahgal *Fear* 123).

Groundbreaking article "Cities and Nature: The Issues"
maintains that exposure to nature can render significant
physical and mental health benefits whilst inspiring care for
the natural world. Sahgal's works reflect her ardent
conviction in the healing powers of nature. After her father's
untimely death during Indian freedom struggle, whenever
Sahgal thought about him, it was in Khali that she pictured
him. It was only Khali which was a suitable frame for his
many-sided personality. There he could live and breathe
freely and joyfully. From there he wrote her rambling letters
commenting on the state of the nation in bantering fashion
and gave her a detailed picture of the estate:

The letter then went on to give us detailed and
scintillating account of affairs at Khali: of the fields covered
with golden, ripening wheat, of the thriving poultry farm, of
the flourishing grapevines brought from Quetta and Kashmir,
and the trees loaded with apple, cherries, and figs, of the
masses of wild raspberries, strawberries, and mulberries, of
the primary school he had started for the little folks children,
and the tannery he had set up. He would proudly tell us of
his country breakfast of coffee, Khali honey, Khali bread,
Khali butter, and Khali Leghorn eggs (Sahgal *Prison* 37).

Interestingly, in foregoing lines Sahgal mention of
locally grown food and appears to be advocating for 'vocal
for local' decades ago.Itis a concept that urges Indians
nowadays to back native products, stimulating economic
advancement and self-sufficiency. Article"What is Vocal for
Local? How is the Government aiding Local Artisans?" too
explains the concept that 'just as in the era of the Swadeshi
movement, this forward-thinking approach is dedicated to
the upliftment of our local producers and artisans'. Again
and again, at all juncture of her life, Sahgal remembers her
father and his loved estate Khali. Here she helped her father

in up keep of the various gardens with her two sisters and mother. After marrying Gautam, she went to Almora to see the house at Khali, *'Ritusamhar'*, as Ranjit Pandit had named it. She walked in the long wild grass and sat on a tree stump. Around her, the treacherous pins were reminders of something that had slipped away. Her father had once told her that life always went on in one form or another, but for Sahgal, something had ended, "The seasons would change at Ritusamhar, summer mellow at autumn. The apricots in the orchard would ripen pine cones drop to the ground to be gathered and crackle in fragrant fires. The pageant of beauty would go on, but not for me. The hills would never have the same magic for me either, or so I thought" (Sahgal *Fear* 124).Recollecting the memories of her early childhood, Sahgal states that before shifting to Anand Bhawan, the Pandits lived in a house with dark green shutters, a garden full of spreading trees, and a lawn bordered with roses. Both her parents took great care of the gardens of their different homes in whichever city they lived. Such efforts of her parents inculcated love and care for nature in Sahgal's heart and mind.

Nayantara Sahgal highlights the issue of unplanned urbanization and believes that it has brought about dramatic environmental changes pertaining to temperature, light, noise, traffic etc. in our cities. When Sahgal moved to Bombay i.e. Mumbai with her husband after marriage, she faced the disadvantages of urbanization here. About Bombay she remarks that this city has a social life of elegance and a citizenry unsurpassed in India for its enlightened civic consciousness. It has everything but a sufficient number of playgrounds and parks. Her four-year-old daughter asked her about parks and the outside. Sahgal writes that with so many buildings hemming them in 'the outside' was hard to find. Like all city children Moni and Ranjit, two sallow wraiths, spent most of their time indoor. She searched for them a nursery school hoping it might solve the problem of playspace. She found one where a mixed group of Indian, European and American children were taught. During her first monsoon in this city, Sahgal recalled with nostalgia the welcome rains of north India:

Here it was three months of sunlessness and mildew, of gusty ocean winds showering salt spray over furniture, spreading rot and rust. It was a steady, heavy monotony flooding the streets, where gleeful urchins earned coins pushing cars stalled in the slush. ....And when the sky seemed to have vomited its last of the deluge, and the city looked forward to a breathing spell; it rained again (Sahgal *Fear* 155-156).

During monsoon, between showers, Bombay steamed hot and wet, black tarred roads gleaming, puddles never drying before another deluge flooded them again. The Sahgals woke to dripping mornings and watched the damp soak through their walls. Sahgal has enchantingly pictured the mighty monsoon of Bombay:

The sea churned uneasily, expectantly. The sky, like old discolored silk, ripped and tore, emptying its contents into the Arabian Sea. In instant response the slate-blue turned a coffee colour, its narrow trimming of lace-like forth disappearing under a wall of rain. Wind-goaded, the rain swept across the Breach Candy Garden, lashing the trees. The coconut palms at the water's edge whirled their fronds in a frenzied dance (Sahgal *Fear* 175).

Article "Impacts of Urbanization on Environment" observes that due to uncontrolled urbanization all over the world, environmental degradation has been occurring very rapidly and causing many problems like land insecurity, worsening water quality, excessive air pollution, noise and the problems of waste disposal. For Sahgals, escape from the heat and crampedness of Bombay came with their going to Kashmir for a holiday in the summers of 1958. There they lived in an island cottage, surrounded by an arc of mountains and under the clear water of Dal Lake, they could see a forest of long shining red lotus stems and a thousand silver minnows flashing in and out among them. Beauty in Kashmir was everywhere and everlasting:

It rose with the sun over terraced rice-fields. It wavered in the reflection of a lone shikara poised like a bird on the tranquil evening waters of the lake. It ran riot in fields of wild red and yellow poppies and grass embroidered with daisies. The formal gardens designed by the Moghuls with their groves of chenar trees imported from Iran enshrined it, as did the workmanship of the Kashmiri craftsman in everything he fashioned with the skill and inherited knowledge of generations. Above all there was the beauty of the peasant girls whose faces were lit as though by lamps from within, shepherded boys who in their loose robes and round skull caps looked like illustrations from the bible (Sahgal *Fear* 184).

The Sahgals felt oppressed at the thought of leaving the wealth of natural beauty around them and returning of their confines in Bombay. It was time to have a home instead of merely having a place to live. To Sahgal's husband Gautam, home always meant Punjab. He decided to get it built in Chandigarh and according to Sahgal, they were fortunate to have Monsieur Jeaneret as their architect who was one of the distinguished planners of the city. The Sahgals shifted to Chandigarh leaving behind the polluted and mundane city of Mumbai to breathe fresh in the midst of Mother Nature.

Sahgal's autobiographies reveal that by making peace with ourselves and each other, we gain the capacity to make peace with mother-earth, that earth is our larger body, the sacred whole that we dwell within. Her major concern has been her worry for the inconsiderate actions of human beings towards nature. Developing ecological consciousness successfully exposes the realization that must take place in order to rejoin the community of life. Sahgal emphasizes that the world was not made for human beings, but these are the human beings who have been made for the world.

Works Cited:

Sahgal, Nayantara. *Prison and Chocolate Cake*. New York: Alfred Knopf, 1958. Print.

---.*From Fear Set Free*. Delhi: Hind Pocket Books, 1962. Print.

Stevens, Brad. "Being Eco-Conscious: Your Ecological Mindset and Its Impact on the Environment". Web. 18.4.2024 "<https://www.tamborasi.com/being-eco-conscious/>"

Takahashi, Yuka."Personal and Social Transformation: A Complementary Process towards Ecological Consciousness" p.p.169-182 *Learning Toward an Ecological Consciousness Selected Transformative Practices*. Ed.Edmund V.O'Sullivan and Marilyn M. Taylor. Palgrave Macmillan: New York (2004) Web. 21.2.24 "<https://link.springer.com/chapter/10.1007/978-1-349-73178-7_11>"

Uttara S., Nishi Bhuvandas, Vanita Aggarwal. "Impacts of Urbanization on Environment"*JREAS*Vol. 2, Issue 2 (February 2012) ISSN: 2249-3905. Web. 18.4.2024 "<https://www.researchgate.net/publication/265216682_Impacts_of_urbanisation_on_environment>"

"What is Vocal for Local? How is the Government aiding Local Artisans?" Web. 15.2.24 "<https://www.narendramodi.in/what-is-vocal-for-local-how-is-the-government-aiding-local-artisans-579458>"

"Cities and Nature: The Issues" Web.23.3.2024"<https://iucnurbanalliance.org/cities-and-biodiversity-the-issues/>"

Chapter 8

Reading Panchatantra as Narratives of Ecological Awareness

Karthika V.P.

Abstract

Folktales, which are ancient narratives passed down to generations function as a powerful tool in fostering a holistic awareness of the various dimensions of life among people. These ancient narratives are major vehicles for transmitting values, knowledge, and practices that are fundamental in the creation of communal identity and awareness.The *Panchatantra* which is a compendium of ancient fables is one such enduring piece of Indian folklore that has fervently impacted the conceptual framework of the community. This paper aims to understand and underscore the influence of *Panchatantra* Tales in inculcating ecological consciousness among people. This research work is an exploration of the ecological wisdom conveyed by these ancient narratives in the light of ecocriticism to reinstate its indelible position in the contemporary ecological discourse.

Keywords: Ecological awareness, folklore, man-nature relationship, compendium,

In recent years the escalating global ecological crisis has triggered a re-examination of the human-nature relationship and has prompted academicians to turn their attention towards ecological perspectives across various academic disciplines. William Rueckart, an American academician has termed this interdisciplinary inquiry which explores the intersections among literature, culture, and environment as 'ecocriticism' in his book *Literature and Ecology.* Ecocriticism is a theoretical perspective that examines how literary texts, cultural artifacts, and human narratives perceive the natural world and delineates the moral implications of human actions on the environment. Ecocriticism as a critical concept garnered attention with the publication of two seminal works *The Ecocriticism Reader* (1996) by Cheryll Glotfelty and Harold Fromm and *The Environmental Imagination* (1995) by Lawrence Buell.

Cheryll Glotfelty in her 1996 book, *The Ecocriticism Reader: Landmarks in Literary Ecology* defines ecocriticism as "the study of the relationship between literature and the physical environment (xviii). She further articulates, "in most literary theories "the world" is synonymous with society – the social sphere. Ecocriticism expands the notion of the world to include the entire ecosphere." (xix). The fulcrum of ecocritical inquiry is the concept of ecological consciousness, which reflects an understanding of the interrelation of all living beings and the acknowledgement of humanity's place within the broader context of the ecological community. In the present context, when the world is grappling with numerous environmental challenges (from climate change to biodiversity loss), it is highly pivotal to have a heightened sense of responsibility toward preserving the health and sustainability of our ecosystem. Therefore it is very pertinent to inculcate environmental awareness as well as a sensible attitude towards behaviors and practices that contribute to its preservation and sustainability, among People, especially the younger generation. An eco-centric reading of books, especially folktales/fables, helps in comprehending the intricate relationship between living beings and the natural world.

This research paper examines the ecological conscious-sness entwined in the Panchatantra tales and explores the environmental themes woven within the narratives. Though numerous studies have been done on multiple aspects of *the Panchatantra,* there exists an unexplored research gap regarding the eco-philosophical themes present in these tales. This study aims to address this gap by examining the ecological aspects of selected tales from t*he Panchatantra.*

Folktales, deeply rooted in natural settings, employ animals, plants, and landscapes to reflect an intimate understanding of the natural world and the interconnectedness of all living things. These narratives emphasize environmental stewardship, underscoring the importance of respecting and protecting nature by illustrating the consequences of ecological imbalance and the benefits of sustainable living. Furthermore, folktales embed traditional ecological knowledge, encompassing insights into seasonal cycles, agricultural practices, and resource management, essential for sustainable living and conservation. They also highlight the cultural significance of landscapes, which are often biodiversity hotspots, thus fostering community engagement in conservation efforts. Through the use of symbolism and metaphors, folktales make complex ecological principles relatable, representing broader environmental concepts in a manner that enhances comprehension and promotes ecological awareness. *The Panchatantra* has been a cornerstone of Indian folktales.

The Panchatantra, a compendium of stories, each imbued with moral teachings, originally written in Sanskrit is one of the most widely translated non-religious books from India. The title is derived from the Sanskrit terms "pancha" meaning five and "tantra" signifying principle, and denotes its thematic essence of "Five Principles." Despite the elusive nature of its authorship, the widely accepted speculations attribute authorship to the ancient sage Vishnu Sharma,an ancient sage and scholar supposed to have lived around 200 BC. At present, innumerable adaptations, translations, and abridged versions of *Panchatantra* are available. The primary source for this paper is *Vishnu Sharma Panchatantra: Translated from Sanskrit by Rohini Chaudhary* published in 2017.

The *Panchatantra* consists of five books, each dedicated

to one of the five principles, or "tantras." The"Prologue" to the book sets the stage by narrating the plight of the ignorant sons of the king of Mahilaropya, who, lacking in education and wisdom, are deemed unfit to inherit the throne. The king sought guidance from his ministers regarding the education of his sons but all of them except one considered it to be an arduous task. The one minister who gave an affirmative response was Sumati, according to whom:

true knowledge does not come from learning the rules of grammar, the points of law ,or even by mastering one or all of the many branches of learning. True knowledge must be distilled and extracted from life itself. The princes do not need years and years of lessons. Instead, they need a new method of learning and a new teacher who can open their minds and guide them towards worldly wisdom. (2)

Sumati suggested the name of the scholar Vishnu Sharma to teach wisdom to the "blockhead" sons of the king. Vishnu Sharma employed fables as a pedagogical tool to impart essential knowledge and values to the princes,which have been compiled as the *Panchatantra*. The stories he narrates to educate the sons of the king have been organised into five parts which are *'Mitra-bheda'*: 'The Falling Out of Friends', *'Mitra-labha'* or *'Mitra-samprapti'*: 'the Gaining of Friends', *'Kokolukiya'*: 'Of Crows and Owls', *'Labdhapraṇāśam'*: 'Loss of Gains', *'Aparkitakraka'*: 'Unconsidered Actions'. ("*Panchatantra*")

The stories are predominantly set in rural and natural landscapes rather than urban environments. The first book, *Mitrabheda*, exemplifies this by beginning with *'the Story of Sanjivaka the Bull and Pingalaka the Lion'*. It recounts the tale of a merchant from the city who ventures into the wilderness with his bulls, Nandaka and Sanjivaka. During the course of journey, Sanjivaka gets injured and the merchant abandons him. However, Sanjivaka eventually recovers and thrives on the fresh green grass of the forest.

One day, he meets a lion, who gets frightened when he hears bellowing. But later, they become friends as the advisor of the king introduces the bull as an angel sent by the god. Later on, the same advisor instigates the lion against the bull which culminates in the death of the bull.

The narrative vividly describes the lush forest, abundant with diverse flora and fauna such as acacias, sals, dhaks, elephants, tigers, bears, deer, and wild oxen. The depiction of the forest, with its pristine waters and caves, immerses the reader in a picturesque natural setting, offering a stark contrast to the bustling city life. This portrayal not only transports readers to a tranquil environment but also serves as an educational tool, providing insights into Indian forest ecosystems and fostering an appreciation for the richness of nature.

One may also observe undertones of environmental themes through the story of Sanjivika, abandoned by his owner after sustaining an injury.Sanjivaka's fall into the mud is an example of the unpredictability and dangers of the natural world. The narrative highlights the significance of the environment in facilitating the survival of animals. Sanjivika's gradual recovery, aided by the natural nourishments, underscores the self-sustaining capacity of natural ecosystems. The story vividly reinstates the protective nature of Nature. It describes:

He wandered through the forest until he reached the banks of the River Yamuna. Here grew, fresh green grass, sweet and juicy, such as Sanjivaka had never eaten before in his life. Day by day, Sanjivaka regained his strength, till he became as healthy, strong, and beautiful as the White bull of Lord Shiva himself. (3)

This transformation from a wounded bull to a strong and healthy bull emphasizes the restorative power of nature. Conversely, Sanjivika's eventual demise at the hands of Pingalaka, orchestrated by the jackals Karataka and

Damanaka, illustrates the workings of the food chain. As natural predators, lions prey upon animals like bulls, while scavengers like jackals exploit the remains of deceased creatures. Through this portrayal, the narrative subtly imparts an understanding of the inherent order and dynamics of the natural world. It unveils the duality of nature, which is capable of both endangering and sustaining life.

Similarly, 'The Story of the Cobra and the Crow', illustrates interconnectedness among species, the natural world as well as the survival strategies in the human world. The story depicts the predicament of a pair of crows living in the branches of a huge banyan tree, who were constantly facing the threat of a cobra eating their chicks. Despite the pleading of the female crow to leave their nest and fly away to a place that did not pose a threat from the cobra, the male crow decided to live there and sought the counsel of his friend Jackal. The Jackal advised them to steal the queen's necklace and drop it near the hole. The attendants in pursuit of the necklace saw the cobra and killed it. The recurrent attack of the cobra exemplifies the predatory aspect of nature and the crow's struggle to survive reflects the real-world struggle of the species to overcome the environmental threats. The intervention of the jackal shows the pertinence of harmony and cooperation in overcoming ecological challenges.

Another story highlighting the delicate balance of ecosystems is 'The Story of the Wild Geese and the Bird Catcher', It narrates the story of a flock of wild geese who abided in a huge Banyan Tree. An old goose cautioned them against the growth of a wild creeper around the tree as it can help bird catchers. The warning was ignored by other geese and the creeper grew and as predicted by the old goose, it helped a bird catcher to trap the flock. However, the resilient old goose advised others to feign death until the bird catcher released them and they escaped together. The Banyan tree can be identified as a microcosm of the ecosystem, and the creeper can be identified as a threat that has the potential to disturb the entire ecosystem. Initially, the creeper seemed to be harmless and was not given importance by the inhabitants. However, it grew to dominate the tree and affect the geese's habitat. This reflects how ignoring small changes in the ecosystem can result in potential disasters. The bird catcher represents the human encroachments on the natural habitat, leading to the destruction of wild life.

The narrative *'The Turtle and the Geese'*, portrays the symbiotic relationship between geese and a tortoise as they navigate a challenging environmental situation. Faced with the drying of their habitat due to a severe drought, the animals collaborate to find a new source of water. The geese, capable of flight, devise a plan to transport the tortoise by carrying it on a stick held in its mouth. However, the tortoise's inability to remain silent, as instructed, leads to ridicule from humans encountered along the journey. This episode highlights the vulnerability of nonhuman beings in the face of human mockery and underscores the inherent power dynamics between humans and animals. Despite the animals' cooperation and ingenuity, their efforts are met with ridicule and derision from humans, reflecting a broader theme of human dominance and exploitation of the natural world. Furthermore, the narrative sheds light on the ethical dimensions of human-animal interactions, emphasizing the importance of empathy and respect towards nonhuman beings. By depicting humans as antagonistic forces that undermine the animals' endeavors, the narrative prompts readers to reflect on their attitudes and behaviors towards the environment and its inhabitants. Ultimately, *'The Turtle and the Geese'*, serves as a poignant commentary on human arrogance and the need for greater compassion towards all living beings.

In the story *'The Story of the Unfortunate Weaver'*, one

may observe the existence of nature as an omnipotent backdrop orchestrating events that challenge human ambitions. The story revolves around a talented weaver Somilaka who struggles with poverty despite his skills. Determined to mitigate his poverty he ventures to another city in search of good fortune. He successfully earns money, however, loses it twice due to some mysterious occurrences in a forest. However, through divine intervention, he learns the true meaning of happiness. The narrative implicitly conveys the interconnectedness of destiny and the natural world. The forest, with its imposing banyan tree and mysterious voices, throws light into the mysteries of the natural world as well as nature's inimitable role in guiding human destiny. The interaction with Guptadhana and Upabhuktadana, instilled in him the realization to be contented with the judicious use of the available resources.

'The Story of the Three Fishes', is another narrative of adaptability. It recounts the story of three fishes who are known for their foresight, quick thinking, and reliance on luck respectively. One day they overheard some fishermen's plan to catch all the fish, the next day. Recognizing the imminent threat, the first two fish decide to leave the pond; however, the third one dismisses the warning, choosing to stay back due to a fatalistic belief in destiny. The fishermen returned and caught all the fish that remained. The story demonstrates the importance of recognizing the danger and taking proactive measures to tackle it. The fish's decision to leave the pond exemplifies adaptive behavior in response to a threat. It also shows the consequences of underestimating the severity of a threat. It also indicates that adaptation and migration are effective survival strategies for wildlife facing habitat degradation.

Stories such as *'The Blue Jackal',* provide insights into the pack behavior of jackals, illustrating how the jackal's instinctual response to the call of its kin leads to its eventual capture. This narrative underscores the inherent social dynamics within animal communities and their survival strategies. Similarly, there are stories focusing on the interplay between crows and owls, offering detailed observations on the nocturnal nature and predatory habits of owls. These depictions serve to educate readers about the ecological roles and behaviors of these animals.

The fable *'The Monkey and the Crocodile'*, highlights the consequences of habitat displacement for animals. The narrative illustrates how the monkey, an arboreal creature, loses its survival instincts when taken into the aquatic environment by the crocodile, an amphibian. The crocodile's ignorance of terrestrial life is starkly evident when it naively believes the monkey's ruse about leaving its heart on a tree. This story serves as a poignant reminder of the dangers and misunderstandings that arise when animals are removed from their natural habitats, further emphasizing the need for ecological sensitivity and awareness. It also depicts how the crocodile's betrayal of the monkey's trust disrupts the natural harmony, serving as a metaphor for the consequences of ecological imbalance.

Many *Panchatantra* tales emphasize the importance of respecting nature and its creatures. *'The Brahmin and the Crab'*, illustrates how a Brahmin saves a crab, which later rescues him from a deadly snake. This story underscores the reciprocal relationship between humans and animals, advocating for kindness and respect towards all living beings. Similarly, in the story *'The Elephants and the Mice'*, a group of elephants inadvertently destroys the homes of a colony of mice. After the rat king negotiates with the elephant chief, the elephants agree to take a different path, sparing the mice's homes. Later, when the elephants are trapped by hunters, the rats repay the favor by gnawing through the nets, showcasing interspecies cooperation and mutual aid.

The bond between humans and serpents is intricately explored in the tale *'The Serpent Who Painted in Gold'*, illustrating a symbiotic relationship wherein humans benefit from snakes' natural role in controlling rodent and insect populations, thereby protecting food supplies and crops. This narrative emphasizes the ecological importance of serpents, often misunderstood and maligned in human society.

In the story, a Brahmana recognizes this value and extends an act of kindness by offering a cup of milk to a serpent. This gesture of goodwill is reciprocated by the serpent with a gold coin, symbolizing a harmonious coexistence based on mutual respect and benefit. However, this delicate balance is disrupted when the Brahmana, needing to travel to a nearby city, instructs his son to continue the ritual. Driven by greed, the boy plots to murder the serpent and steal its wealth, an act that underscores human avarice and its destructive impact on the natural world.

This tale critically examines human attitudes towards animals, highlighting how acts of kindness can foster beneficial relationships, while greed and betrayal lead to discord and loss. The serpent's intended offering of gold coins can be seen as a metaphor for the untapped potential and rewards of respecting and preserving nature. The boy's treachery, on the other hand, reflects a broader pattern of exploitation and environmental degradation perpetrated by humans.

The character of the wise old crow in *'The Crow and the Pitcher'*, demonstrates resourcefulness and intelligence in utilizing natural resources. The crow's innovative method of dropping pebbles into a pitcher to raise the water level exemplifies the principle of sustainable use of resources. This tale teaches the importance of using intellect to solve environmental challenges without depleting resources.

In brief, narratives in *the Panchatantra* reflect a deep understanding of ecological principles, emphasizing the interconnectedness of all living beings and the ethical dimensions of human interactions with nature. It vividly illustrates the interconnectedness of all life forms, a core principle of ecological consciousness. Some narratives show that survival and well-being are often contingent on cooperation and respect between different life forms. By depicting these relationships, the tales foster an awareness of the delicate balance within ecosystems and the importance of each species in maintaining this balance.

The Panchatantra consistently underscores the ethos of environmental stewardship, advocating for the ethical and considerate treatment of nature and its denizens. Through tales like *'The Elephants and the Mice'*, the text illuminates the critical role of empathy and understanding in navigating interspecies conflicts. The elephants' deliberate choice to alter their course to avoid harming the mice, alongside the mice's proactive efforts to free the trapped elephants, underscores humanity's ethical responsibilities towards the environment and its inhabitants.

Furthermore, *the Panchatantra* contains lots of old wisdom about nature that's important for grasping and protecting natural environments. Stories teach us about how animals behave and survive. This ancient knowledge is super useful for living sustainably and looking after the environment, giving us practical lessons we can still learn from today. Its enduring appeal lies in its ability to foster ecological awareness through engaging and instructive narratives. By portraying animals and natural settings in a relatable manner, the tales educate readers about the importance of ecological balance and the ethical dimensions of human actions. They serve as a reminder of the wisdom inherent in traditional narratives and their potential to inspire a deeper understanding and appreciation of the natural world.

In the context of the escalating global ecological crisis, the ecological consciousness embedded in the *Panchatantra* is more relevant than ever. These tales offer valuable lessons on sustainable living, environmental stewardship, and the ethical treatment of nature. They advocate for a harmonious coexistence with the natural world, a principle that is critical in addressing contemporary environmental challenges.

The Panchatantra, through its rich narratives and moral teachings, is a cornerstone of ecological education. It underscores the importance of understanding and respecting the natural world, fostering a sense of responsibility toward environmental conservation. By bridging traditional ecological knowledge with modern environmental ethics, the *Panchatantra* serves as a powerful tool in promoting ecological awareness and sustainable living. As we navigate the complexities of the ecological crisis, these timeless tales remind us of the interconnectedness of all life forms and the ethical imperatives of caring for our planet.

Works Cited:
Environmental Consciousness in Indian Fables: How and What the Pañcatantra Can Teach Our Children, www.researchgate.net/publication/335273047_Environment al_Consciousness_in_Indian_Fables_How_and_What_the_P ancatantra_can_Teach_Our_Children. Accessed 10 July 2024.
Chowdhury, Rohini, et al. *Panchatantra Vishnusharma. Translated from Sanskrit by Rohini Chowdhury*. Penguin Books India, 2017.
Glotfelty, Cheryll, and Harold Fromm. *The Ecocriticism Reader Landmarks in Literary Ecology Ed. by Cheryll Glotfelty and Harold Fromm*. Univ. of Georgia Press, 2009.
Kumaravelu, Shanmugapriya, and G Christopher. "Eco-Philosophy of Indian Classical Fables:" *Ecocycles*,

www.ecocycles.net/ojs/index.php/ecocycles/article/view/286
. Accessed 4 July 2024.

"Panchatantra." *Wikipedia*, Wikimedia Foundation, 18 Jan. 2024, en.wikipedia.org/wiki/Panchatantra. Accessed 9 July 2024.

Chapter 9

Mapping Ecocritical Concern in W.H. Auden's "In Memory of W. B. Yeats"

Ambika Gahlot

Abstract

The aim of this paper is to bring to the forefront the ecological understanding between nature and man as beautifully sewn in the fabric of the poem "In Memory of W.B Yeats." This modernist masterpiece was composed in 1939, shortly after the death of the Irish poet W.B. Yeats. It was published in Auden's collection "Another Time" in 1940. Traditionally the poem is an elegy which laments the demise of W.B Yeats. But the poem has sharp and profound ecocritical undertones. The poem may be approached through an ecocritical lens by examining the multidimensions it serves in the way it reflects upon humanity's relationship with the natural world and how life and death are interconnected in this natural world. While Auden's elegy primarily mourns the death of the poet W.B. Yeats, it also contains broader ecological themes that resonate with the concerns of ecocriticism.

Keywords: Ecocriticism, Elegy, Nature, Environment, Ecology.

Eco is short of *ecology*, which is concerned with the relationships between living organisms in their natural environment as well as their relationships with that environment. By analogy, ecocriticism is concerned with the relationships between literature and environment or how man's relationships with his physical environment are reflected in literature.(Toši) Ecocriticism tends to delve into the works with an analogical framework that speculates the text not merely as artefacts of human expressions, but also reflections of humanity's relationship with the natural world.

The paper limns on a journey taking into account W.H. Auden's elegy on the death of W.B. Yeats, guided by an ecocritical perspective, to uncover the ecological threads woven into its fabric.

W.H. Auden's "In Memory of W.B. Yeats" is an obituary, a poignant tribute to one of the greatest poets of the 20th century. Yet, the magnificenceof the elegy does not overshadow its ecological concerns rather embellish it with multiplicity of meaning. Beyond the poem's overt themes of mourning and remembrance liea rich tapestry of ecological imagery which provides a new essence and depth to the overall interplay of its structure of being an elegy. Through the lens of ecocriticism, we delve into the interplay between nature and culture, life and death, as manifested in Auden's elegy.

This paper digs into the terrain of human mortality and environmental degradation, intertwining the passing of Yeats with broader ecological concerns as navigated by W.H. Auden. By examining the poem through an ecocritical lens, we seek to unearth the deeper meanings and implications that lie beneath its surface.

Auden's elegy does justice to the techniques and nuances of the art of composing poetry, paying particular attention to the ways in which it engages with ecological themes and imagery. Through close reading and contextual analysis, the text of the poem illuminates the ecocritical dimensions shedding light on its significance within the broader discourse of environmental literature.

This exploration of Auden's elegy is an attempt to unearth the elegy not only as a testament to Yeats' legacy but also as a reflection of humanity's intricate relationship with the natural world. Through the ecocritical lens, we endeavour to unveil the ecological resonances that reverberate through Auden's verses, enriching our under-standing of both the poem and the environmental ethos it embodies.

The poem starts with a beautiful depiction of nature symbolising winter with death. The description grapples us with use of adjectives in the opening stanza when the poet jots-

"He disappeared in the dead of winter: The brooks were frozen, the airports almost deserted, And snow disfigured the public statues; The mercury sank in the mouth of the dying day. What instruments *we have agree* The day of his death was a dark cold day."

(Poets, "In Memory of W. B. Yeats by W. H. Auden - Poems | Academy of American Poets").

The opening stanza of the poem relates the interconnectedness of nature with the death of a human being. Eco criticism also views nature as a separate entity and not as an element of the Anthropocene world. The very opening of the poem underlines the setting and determines the tone of the work. How nature has a cyclic connotation. The use of adjectives plays a crucial role in the process of meaning making adding depth to the figurative description of the text. The use of the adjectives such as 'dead of winter', 'deserted', 'dying', and 'dark' underline the relationship of nature with the death of the poet. How nature elevates the setting with a symbolism that speaks for itself. 'Dead of winter' is not only the season of winter in which the poet dies but it is also presenting winter as a separate entity which is dominant and everywhere. Auden here deploys the season as all powerful which makes the brooks frozen, airports deserted, and disfiguring the statues thereby rendering the day as 'dying.'

Thus, the day of the death of the poet W.B Yeats has one omnipresent characteristic that it was a dark cold day. The symbolism of nature is supreme even in death which is praiseworthy in the text. How nature envelops the activities of man and yet is ignored by humans. The setting of the poem depicts a desolate, barren landscape devoid of any humans and natural blissthat in a way reflects upon the degradation of the natural world. This elegy is an elegy for the Irish poet but also a lament of the depleting modernist natural world.

The poem's setting is characterized by dryness, decay, and amputation, symbolizing the environmental devastation wrought by human exploitation and neglect. The poem is a traditional elegy which talks about the death of an Irish poet, W.B. Yeats but in the demise of the poet Auden here is echoing the degeneration of an entire culture, the tradition which boasts of grandeur and the very nature and beauty of the country Ireland. The opening of the poem is closer in its appeal to *T.S Eliot's* masterpiece *"The Wasteland"* when he writes-

> "April is the cruellest month, breeding
> Lilacs out of the dead land, mixing
> Memory and desire, stirring
> Dull roots with spring rain. *"*

(The Waste Land by T. S. Eliot | Poetry Foundation)

These lines contradict the traditional association of April with rebirth and rejuvenation with the harsh reality of a world where nature struggles to recover from human-induced destruction. The modernist landscape of the time is evident in the text. The similarity in the very opening of both the poems and the subsequent symbolism touches upon the ecocritical themes. The image of "dead land" suggests a landscape that has been marred by human activities thus rendered lifeless, while the mention of "dull roots" hints at the inability of the natural world to regenerate and flourish.

The next stanza of the poem illuminates the very essence of the elegy and the lifelessness of nature. The poet writes –

"Far from his illness The wolves ran on through the evergreen forests, The peasant river was untempted by the fashionable quays; By mourning tongues The death of the poet was kept from his poems. "

(Poets, "In Memory of W. B. Yeats by W. H. Auden - Poems | Academy of American Poets")

The poet here talks about the illness which has knocked the poet down but how nature administers its daily routine religiously. These lines are reminiscent of the ignorance of nature towards the trivial topics such as death of a human being.

Throughout the poem, Auden utilizes natural imagery and references to the elements to evoke a sense of the cycle of life and death. For example, in the opening lines, Auden writes:

A traditional elegy laments the death of a person; this elegy is special for it shadows the potential death of a planet, which has enveloped the anthropocentric world. The poem is a dialogue between the discourse of death of a person and the death of nature. How death foretells the concept of birth and our consciousness about nature is shaped and envisioned in the poem. The poem channelizes the potentiality of the poet Yeats by using the course of nature debunking the roots of Shallow Ecology which states that how man is the centre of the world and in a way, it debunks the primacy of humans in the meaning making process. Auden here uses metaphors of nature to establish the supremacy of the all-pervading nature. Thus, man is not used to glorify nature; rather this role is reversed where each stanza has a background of nature speaking for itself. This spectrality has a deeper understanding than the mere interplay of words talking about the death of the poet.

"Now he is scattered among a hundred cities And wholly given over to unfamiliar affections, To find his happiness in another kind of wood..."

(Poets, "In Memory of W. B. Yeats by W. H. Auden - Poems | Academy of American Poets")

The penultimate section of the first part of the poem emanates the transcendentalist appraisal of the poet W.B. Yeats. The dead poet is not to be found in body and flesh and is now all pervading and omnipresent. Here the spectrality of the presence of Yeats is overplayed with nature. *A hundred cities, unfamiliar affections, and another kind of wood* refer to the deep connection of the dead poet with nature. These words form a bridge between the death and nature. Yeats after death is elevated to be a part of *another kind of wood.*

"Earth, receive an honoured guest: William Yeats is laid to rest. Let the Irish vessel lieEmptied of its poetry."

(Poets, "In Memory of W. B. Yeats by W. H. Auden - Poems | Academy of American Poets")

Here, the earth is personified as a recipient of Yeats's body, emphasizing the interconnectedness between humanity and the natural world. The image of the "Irish vessel" being "emptied of its poetry" suggests the transience of human life and the return to the earth from which all life emerges.Additionally, how the poet is capturing the permanence of nature over the temporality of human life. The line "Let the Irish vessel lie Emptied of its poetry" can be interpreted as a metaphorical return of Yeats to the earth, symbolizing his integration with the natural cycle of life and death. The use of the word "vessel" implies that Yeats' body is a container for his poetic spirit, which is now released and returned to the Earth. The stanza is also symbolic of the Earth being a career of the humans and their spirits being shaped and transformed by it. Yeats' Irishness is enhanced by the natural landscape of Ireland, its traditionsand culture, reflectingon the juxtaposition of human culture and the natural environment. Furthermore, the phrase "Emptied of its poetry" can also be interpreted in a broader sense to reflect the idea that poetry, as a form of artistic expression, draws inspiration from the natural world. By returning Yeats' poetry to the Earth, Auden may be suggesting that poetic creativity is inherently linked to the cycles and rhythms of nature.The tone of the poem here veers between the artistic calibre of the poet and the musings provided to it by nature. These exquisite lines from Auden's mind evoke themes of interconnectedness between the human and the natural world, emphasizing the Earth's role as both a physical and symbolic repository for human existence and creative expression. How Earth is a vessel having regenerative power and potential to train and direct the flow of human mind and be the metaphorical and literal recipient of it. The stanza has philosophical connectedness with the stanza of Emerson's Hamatreya, when the poet writes-

"Where are these men? Asleep beneath their grounds:
And strangers, fond as they, their furrows plough.
Earth laughs in flowers, to see her boastful boys
Earth-proud, proud of the earth which is not theirs;
Who steer the plough, but cannot steer their feet
Clear of the grave."

(Poets, "Hamatreya by Ralph Waldo Emerson - Poems
|Academy of American Poets")

Emerson here fosters a deeper understanding of nature where there is a balance between life and death. Both the stanzas have a profound sense of mortality,humility, and the integration of human existence with the Earth's cycles, reflecting from theecocritical point of view. There is a similarity abiding these two. The Earth is not a mere recipient of humans but rather act as a transformative power. Another important aspect of the treatment of nature lies in the unfolding of the treatment given to Earth.Emerson's stanza critiques human pride and arrogancedominating the anthropocentric view on Earth, claiming its supremacy and demanding ownership of it. On the contrary Auden's poem suggests a humble acceptance of Yeats' integration withEarththereby becoming one with it. Here nature is not secondary, but its primacy is acknowledged.In both cases, there is recognition of the limits of human control and the need for humility in the face of the Earth's vastness and power.They highlight the transient nature of human existence, the importance of humility and stewardship, and the interconnectedness between human culture and the Earth's ecosystems.

Furthermore, Auden's elegy explores themes of continuity and regeneration in nature. He acknowledges the passing of Yeats while also recognizing the enduring presence of his legacy and influence. This reflection on the cycle of life and death can be interpreted as a broader meditation on the resilience of the natural world and its capacity for renewal.

Additionally, Auden's elegy raises questions about humanity's place within the larger ecological community. By mourning the loss of a great poet and reflecting on the significance of his contributions in literature, Auden delineates the importance of artistic expression in fostering a deeper understanding of the natural world and our place within it.The text is a perfect example of a traditional elegy combining ecocritical themes within atraditional lyric framework.

Works Cited:
Poets, Academy of American. "Hamatreya by Ralph Waldo Emerson - Poems | Academy of American Poets." Poets.Org, https://poets.org/poem/hamatreya.
"In Memory of W. B. Yeats by W. H. Auden - Poems | Academy of American Poets." Poets.Org, https://poets.org/poem/memory-w-b-yeats.
The Waste Land by T. S. Eliot | Poetry Foundation. https://www.poetryfoundation.org/poems/47311/the-waste-land.
Toši, Jelica. Ecocriticism–Interdisciplinary Study of

Literature and Environment.

Rueckert, William. "Literature and Ecology: An Experiment in Ecocriticism." Glotfelty and Fromm, 1996, pp. 105-123.

Strehle, Susan. Fiction in the Quantum Universe. University of North Carolina Press, 1992.

Knoepflmacher, U. C., and G. B. Tennyson. Nature and the Victorian Imagination. University of California Press, 1977.

Williams, Merryn. Thomas Hardy and Rural England. Macmillan, 1972.

Chapter 10

The Vedic Pantheon and Deep Ecology: A Study of the Indian Ecocentric Approach to Environmental Crisis

Shruti Dubey

Abstract

Nature worship and deification of natural entities has been one of the most significant features of almost all the ritualistic practices inherent in Hinduism ever since its inception. Of all the ceremonies surrounding human life and the major events as those of birth, death, cremation, marriage, etc. nature and the entities associated with it have enjoyed a revered position and have been irreplaceable by any other phenomenon. As the Vedas are believed to be the foremost in establishing the cult of nature worship and the major religious principles and rituals associated with it, an enquiry into the ecocentric tendencies of the same may lead any curious observer into the representation therein of natural entities as deities and figures of power and authority having a major role to play in shaping the lives of humans. Especially in the context of the ensuing climate crisis, the need for such an approach gains more prominence as the only viable solution today as against the anthropocentric approach that places human at the centre of the crisis and its resolution. The paper attempts to study the Vedic figures and their representation from an ecocentric standpoint and to analyse how the supplication of natural elements as deities can be read as an attempt on the part of the forerunners of civilisation to incorporate the ethos of caring for nature and ensuring sustainability in all human endeavours.

Keywords: Deep Ecology, Ecocentrism, Vedic Pantheon, Environment, Nature worship.

Myth has it that Rishi Aurava once got so angry with the kings ruling on the earth that he decided to eradicate them. The kings were on the path of *adharma* and had abandoned every form of *dharma*. He was so angry that his wrath took the form of fire but as he was pacified by other rishis that man should be given a chance to change, he transformed this fire into a fire-breathing mare-Vadavagni. It is believed that this stays at the bottom of the large water bodies and is instrumental in the water of the seas and oceans getting evaporated so that the natural cycle of the rains is maintained and water may not overflow on the earth. But if man keeps pestering nature, this would spurt out of the ocean as a volcano destroying the earth and all that exists therein. It is also believed that this shall be the vehicle of Kalki at the end of Kalyug.

This myth, one of the most significant eschatological myths in the Indian mythology, clearly indicates the predicament of human atrocities and their fatal consequences at once drawing a dynamic inherent relationship between human and all that is non-human on the planet. This also stands as a testimony to the fact that the belief system as was practiced by the people of the yore revered mother-nature as a tolerant and patient being who can however turn vengeful when mistreated. Such delineation forms the part and parcel of the mythological structure of our culture. In the context of present day pollution the need for such narratives gain even more importance because it draws the attention on humans part to conserve, revere and sustain all that is non-human but crucial for his own existence and it is in this pursuit of the fullness and wellness of life that the vedic approach offers us a way through its ideology of nature worship.

One of the most pressing concerns in today's times is the degradation of environment and its fatal consequences that have now started manifesting themselves in a wide variety of phenomena as those of extreme temperature variations, excessive rains, landslides, floods, droughts, etc. Environmental crisis today constitutes climate change and global warming; air pollution, deforestation and biodiversity loss, melting glaciers and ice sheets and these have become instrumental in causing devastation not limited to a particular geographical region but all around the globe. "Disasters linked to climate and weather extremes have always been part of our Earth's system. But they are becoming more frequent and intense as the world warms. No continent is left untouched, with heatwaves, droughts, typhoons, and hurricanes causing mass destruction around the world."("The Climate Crisis Race We Can Win")

Studies have pointed out that the current lifestyle as is being pursued by most of the humans today requires extreme exploitation of Earth's resources and that if this is to continue we would need almost half an Earth more to survive. Almost three fourths of the land surface and roughly sixty six per cent of ocean area on Earth has been badly affected by human activities. This has resulted in extinction of many animal and plant species on the planet and could negatively affect the biodiversity in the near future too. As humans the greatest share of this bleak reality lies with us and therefore we owe the responsibility to undo and alter the current ways of our lives in accordance with the principles of nature that may help in reversing the damage caused to the environment.

One of the ways academia can address this issue is through exploring literary texts and culture in relation to the aspects of nature degradation and impending climate crisis. Ecocriticism as a literary theory deals with this aspect. Used for the first time by William Rueckert in 1978, the term denotes an approach where literature is analysed and studied through the lens of ecological concerns and is defined as, "the application of ecology and ecological concept to the study of literature" (Glotfelty & Frommxviii)

According to Greg Garrard an ecocritical approach, "...wants to track environmental ideas and representations...to evaluate texts and ideas in terms of their coherence and usefulness as responses to environmental crisis"(4).

Closely related to the concepts of ecocriticism is the approach of deep ecology that focuses on egocentrism rather than anthropocentrism as the key to arriving at some sustainable solution to the aforementioned crisis. Deep ecology proposes and envisages egocentrism or the centrality of all living entities rather than just the human agency as the panacea for the crisis faced today as it blames anthropocentric tendencies for the same. It proposes the replacement of the latter with ecocentric approach as it believes that all the non-human entities also provide value addition to the life of humans on the planet. According to Garrard, "Eco philosophers often criticise the arrogance of anthropocentrism, sometimes using the Ancient Greek term 'hubris' for this fatal flaw of overweening self-righteousness and wilful misuse of power. The history of the world in the last 200 years, and especially the history of the developed world in the last 50 years, supplies ample evidence of such hubris..." (179).

The basic idea therefore as suggested by deep ecology is that if the human societies, communities and civilizations have to thrive, they will have to do so in communion with nature and all the entities surrounding them. For this it is required that a radical shift be made from the anthropocentric ethic to the ecocentric one which rejects human as the centre and places the non-human world at an equal pedestal that too needs to be cared for and given an equal opportunity to thrive.Therefore an ecocentric approach is the need of the hour and the ancient Indian ideology can serve as a guiding principle in this regard. Revisiting our cultural roots and delving deep into the timeless wisdom of the ancient seers can provide us with the much required solutions to the current crisis.

The Hindu religion since its inception has been such that nature and its entities have acquired a prominent place in every aspect of culture and civilization and the Vedas are an example of the same wherein we find incorporation not only of the animal forms but also of vegetative entities and abstractions.

...the Indus Civilization also seemed to attach a religious significance to certain animals such as, the tiger, buffalo, crocodile, elephants and even multiheadedmonsters and hybrid creatures as well as trees and auspicious symbols such as the swastika. (Bary, et al. 3)

The term *Veda* originates from the root word *vid* meaning knowledge and consists of a vast and varied literature that encompassed centuries and enquired about the "unchanging Principlethe *sanatana* or the eternal timeless being"(Radhakrishnan 29). Known to have come into existence around 1500 BC, these scriptures are believed to be *apaurusheya* i.e. not composed by any mortal but revealed to the seers who then passed them onto the upcoming generations majorly through verbal medium and consist of *Samhitas, Brahmanas, Aranyakas*and the *Upanishads* or the hymns, liturgical books, forest texts and the knowledge portion respectively. *Upanishads* being a significant part of the *Vedas* consist of the truthful utterances which are not mere subjective disclosures but are the objective time transcending truths that form the very core of existence. According to Radhakrishnan:

As a part of the veds, the Upanisads belong to sruti or revealed literature. They are immemorial, sanatana, timeless. Their truths are said to be breathed out by God or visioned by seers. They are the utterances of the sages who speak out of the fullness of their illumined experience. They are not reached by ordinary perception, inference or reflection but *seen* by the seers...the sages are men of direct vision in the words of Yaska, sakshat-krta-dharmanah, and the records of their experiences are the facts to be considered by any philosophy of religion.(22)

All the four Vedas, namely the Atharvaved, Rigved, Yajurved and Samved emphasize the need for environmental consciousnessas they speak of the interrelation between the well-being of humans and the non-human entities that surround and sustain life and have enormous influence on each and every aspect of the same. According to Radhakrishnan, "…in the Rig Veda we find the first adventures of the human mind made by those who sought to discover the meaning of existence and man's place in life, the first word spoken by the Aryan man"(44). Believed to be the foremost in composition among the four Vedas, Rigveda consists of ten books and more than a thousand hymns.The natural entities like *varuna, agni, dyausmithra,ushas, vayu, savitr, surya* among others have been deified in the Vedic literature. These figures from nature that are crucial in providing sustenance to the human life were so revered in the Vedic era that they had occupied the status of the deities whose invocation and supplication formeda crucial part of the ritualistic practices of the Hindu household. The major rituals around birth, death, marriage, cremation, etc. focused on the supplication of one or more of the aforementioned deities.

The Rig Veda, which comprises 1017 hymns divided into ten books, represents the earliest phase in the evolution of religious consciousness where we have not so much the commandments of priests as the outpourings of the poetic minds who were struck by the immensity of the universe and the inexhaustible mystery of life. The reactions of simple yet unsophisticated minds to the wonder of existence are portrayed in these joyous hymns which attribute divinity to the striking aspects of nature. (Radhakrishnan30)

In ritualistic practices like those of *yagya* during

ceremoniesthe lord *Agni* holds a special place. *Agni* is considered as next in prominence to *Indra* in the *Rig Veda*. There is a distinction between three forms of *Agni*, namely that of the sun, the lightening and that of the sacrifice. Functioning as a messenger, a sort of a mediator between heaven and earth, it fulfils the duty of conveying to the deities the oblations of their worshippers. It is the messenger who invites the Gods to descend to the place of the *yagya*or the ritual sacrifice.*Vayu*is invoked in the *Rig Veda* after *Agni*in conjunction with *Mithra* as one who presides over day and night and is aspowerful as to destroy the demons and negative forces and as one who can carry the fumes of the sacrifices to far off thereby purifying the atmosphere around. He is also supplicated together with *Indra* who is considered the most powerful God as per the Vedic hierarchy and is believed to use a thunderbolt for a weapon against the negative forces that bring about droughts and deforestation; he resides in the clouds and also looks after the rainfall and so any issues regarding the water cycle of the nature comes under his domain thereby making him responsible for the ensuing fertility and sustenance of life. *Varuna* is considered to be the deity related to water bodies and with a golden bird named *hiranyapaksh* as his messenger. *Usas* or the crimson coloured divine being of dawn is a female deity who drives darkness away and awakens the humans for the new day. She is the wife of sun, sister of *Nisha* or nightand the daughter of *Dyaus* or the sky.

Surya or the sun god is considered as the source of all life, knowledge and the fatherly centre around whom all the forms of life revolve. *Prithvi* or the Earth is revered as a mother who bears the burden of the gigantic mountain ranges, holds on the flood of rivers and sustains the land and the people therein. The phenomenon of Earth revolving around the Sun is depicted in the *Vedas* as a calf adoringly following his mother. Such representation can be read as one of the instances of what Greg Garrard terms as, "culture as a rhetoric… production, reproduction and transformation of large scale metaphors" (7).

Apart from these, the Vedic tradition also accords great significance to the animal world. *Indra* it is believed has the mighty white coloured elephant*Airavat* as his vehicle. Cow in the Vedic texts is supplicated in the tradition of *Kamdhenu*.Not only the animals but also the birds as *shukadev* and *Garuda*also find elevated to Godly levels. The *Ashwins* or the *ashwinikumars* are believed to be the deities in the form of horse who are known to have cures to all the maladies.

In this way, some of the deities mentioned in the *Rig Veda* along with the manner of their supplication depict the high regard that the forerunners of the civilization placed on Mother Nature and its entities who were very much instrumental in influencing human. The deified figures, all of them being natural entities that are instrumental in creating and sustaining life, are invoked and supplicated so as to induce a sense of reverence, empathy and concern for the non-human entities and in this way to ensure that man stays aware of his position in the great phenomenon called life. Garrard speaks of the same ethos of megalopsyche- a term he borrows from the Greek philosophers, "The Ancient Greeks proposed a virtue that combined the proper pride of a clever, resourceful animal with reasonable acceptance of the human place in a world we can neither wholly predict nor control. They called it ['megalopsuche'], which translates roughly as 'greatness of soul', and I would suggest this as a worthy aspiration" (179).

Not only the deification of the natural forces but also the very fact that the trait of being "revealed" as attributed to Vedas points at the deliberate avoidance of anthropocentric tendencies on the part of the seers and the precursors of the vedic ideology. Radhakrishanan summarizes the thought as,

"Though the knowledge is an experience of the seer, it is an experience of an independent reality which impinges on his consciousness. There is the impact of the real on the spirit of the experiencer. It is therefore said to be a direct disclosure from the 'wholly other', a revelation of the Divine symbolically, the Upanishads describe revelation as the breath of God blowing on us (23). The very attribution of the Vedic wisdom as revealed and the natural entities mentioned therein as deities are sufficient to delineate the ecocentric approach of the precursors of the Indian culture.

VasudhevaKutumbakam, the ideal that finds manifesttation in the Vedic literature proposes a kind of co-existence not only between humans of varied backgrounds but also of all the species transcending the human and between non-human divide. It is a sort of an acknowledgement of the mutual well-being of both. As the paper attempts to show, this has been the crux not only of the classic Indian religious ethos but also of the other significant cultures as those of the ancient Greek philosophers who have all unanimously agreed that if human has to survive in peace and thrive, there is no other way than the ecocentric ethos as is summarized in the Vedic prayer *"Sarvebhavantusukhinah, sarvesantuniramyha"* -the all-encompassing ideal that ought to be followed in letter and spirit.

Glossary
1. Adharma- Religious/Ethical Unrighteousness;
2. Dharma- Ethical Righteousness;
3. Vadavagni- The underwater fire/ A fire-breathing being believed to be seated at the bottom of large water bodies;
4. Kalki- Believed to be the last avatar of Vishnu who will arrive to destroy and end the cycle of ages;
5. Kalyug- the last age in the cycle of existence;
6. Veda- Religious texts;
7. Apaurusheya- Not composed by humans;
8. Sruti- Heard/Revealed;

9. Swastika- holy sign used at ritualistic practices;
10. Sanatana- forever/ associated with Hindu ideology;
11. Yagya- Fire sacrifice, an important part of rituals;
12. Hiranyapaksh-Golden hued bird;
13. Airavat-White Elephant and the vehicle of Indra;
14. Kamdhenu- the wish fulfilling cow found in heaven;
15. Shuka- Parrot deity;
16. Garuda- Eagle;
17. VasudhevaKutumbakam-the entire Earth as one family;
18. Sarvebhavantusukhinah, sarvesantuniramyha- May bliss and perfect health be there for one and all.

Works Cited:
Bary, Theodore de, et.al, *Sources of Indian Tradition.* Columbia U P, 1963.
Basham, A.L., *A Cultural History of India.* Oxford U P, 1975.
Basham, A.L., *The Origins and Development of Classical Hinduism.* MotilalBanarsidas, 1990.
Garrard, Greg. *Ecocriticism: The New Critical Idiom.* Routledge, 2004.
Glotfelty, Cheryll and Harold Fromm, editors. *The Ecocriticism Reader: Landmarks in Literary Ecology.* University of Georgia, 1996.
Michael, Aloysius, *Radhakrishnan on Hindu Moral Life and Action.* Concept Publishing Company, 1979.
Radhakrishnan, S. *The Principal Upnisads.* George Allen & Unwin Ltd. 1953.
Rigved Vol.I. Trans. by Dr. Tulsi Ram, Vijaykumar Govindram Hasanand, 2013.
Sharma, O.P., *Indian Culture: Ancient Glory and Present Gloom,* Intellectual Publishing House, 1993.
United Nations. *The Climate Crisis – A Race We Can Win.*

www.un.org/en/un75/climate-crisis-race-we-can-win.
Accessed 06 July 2024.
Wallis, H. W. *The cosmology of the Rigveda: An Essay.*
Williams and Norgate, 1887.

Chapter 11

Environmental Justice Movement

Rishika Verma

Abstract

In this Research paper, I will discuss about the concept of Environmental Justice and its definition. Environmental Justice is defined by Miller (2003) as the fair treatment and meaningful involvement of all people regardless of race, color, sex, national origin, or income with respect to the development, implementation and enforcement of environmental laws, regulations, and policies. Fair treatment means that no population, due to policy or economic disempowerment, is forced to bear a disproportionate share of the negative human health or environment, impacts of population or environmental consequences resulting from industrial, municipal, and commercial operations or the execution of federal, state, local and tribal programs and policies. As this definition indicates, there are both distributive and participative (or procedural) justice issues involving the environment. I will discuss here the 17 principles of Environmental Justice and how Environmental justice movement started and why environmental justice movement is important.

Keywords: Environmental Justice, Its Principles, Movement, Protection, tragedy.

The word **"Environmental Justice"** was first used in the movement born in the United States in struggle against waste dumping in North Carolina in 1982. Activist-authors such as Robert Bullard (1992), Civil Rights activists with no academic affiliation and members of Christian churches saw themselves as militants of environmental justice. By October 1991, an assembly of "leaders of peoples of color" in Washington DC proclaimed the 17 principles of Environmental Justice which went beyond a focus only in the United States. The meeting was in Washington DC but the terms "environment" and "justice" were used in ways that challenged US capitalist domination; certainly not a Western celebration of coloniality and racism, on the contrary. The document included affirmation of the sacredness of mother Earth and the right to be free from ecological destruction; peoples' right to self-determination; rights of participation and enforcement of principles of informed consent; rejection of military occupation, repression and exploitation of land, people, and culture and other life forms.

The concept of environmental justice as a mobilizing force emerged in the US in the last forty years, in opposition to practices that were classified as environmental racism. This is defined as 'any policy, practice or directive that differentially affects or disadvantages (whether intentionally or unintentionally) individuals, groups or communities based on race or color' as defined by (Bullard RD, 1996). Environmental justice is the principle that "all people and communities are entitled to equal protection of environmental and public health laws and regulations." In the words of Bunyan Bryant, "Environmental Justice is served when people can realize their highest potential."

Environmental Justice is defined by Miller (2003) as the fair treatment and meaningful involvement of all people regardless of race, color, sex, national origin, or income with respect to the development, implementation and enforcement of environmental laws, regulations, and policies. Fair treatment means that no population, due to policy or economic disempowerment, is forced to bear a disproportionate share of the negative human health or environment, impact of population or environmental consequences resulting from industrial, municipal, and commercial operations or the execution of federal, state, local and tribal programs and policies. As this definition indicates, there are both distributive and participative (or procedural) justice issues involving the environment.

Distributive justice concerns the allocation of burdens and benefits in societies. One important environmental burden is exposure to environmental hazards. Research has shown that low-income and high-minority communities are disproportionately exposed to environmental hazards, particularly chemical exposure and air and water pollution, stemming from living and/or working near transportation depots, industrial facilities, and waste processing facilities. In the United States, race is significant to exposure above and beyond income, sometimes leading to the use of the term environmental racism. The United States is not anomalous in this respect; low-income and marginalized communities all over the world are disproportionally exposed to ecological hazards from, for example, mining, agriculture, and global climate change.

Unequal exposure to environmental hazards might not itself be unjust, if there were good justification for the inequality. For instance, justice might allow unequal exposure even to the economically worst off, if those who shoulder the burden also get associated benefits, or if exposure is the result of a sufficiently fair social and political process. However, this is rarely the case. Any plausible theory of justice must accept that race and wealth are not appropriate bases for differential treatment or political standing. To deny this would be to accept racism and classism and to reject the equal moral worth of people.

Participative justice means the involvement of those affected by decisions in making the decisions. Critics have pointed out that many people adversely affected by policies, institutions, and choices about environmental matters have no say in their formation. This is a violation of participative justice.

Environmental Justice can be distinguished from environmental inequality (or environmental injustice), which refers to a situation in which a specific social group is disproportionately affected by environmental hazards. A specific form of environmental inequality is the phenomenon of environmental racism. Chavis (Bullard RD. 19992/2000) first defined the term environmental racism in the following manner: "Environmental racism is racial discrimination in environmental policy making, the enforcement of regulations and laws, the deliberate targeting of communities of color for toxic waste facilities, the official sanctioning of the life-threatening presence of poisons and pollutants in our communities, and the history of excluding people of color from leadership of the ecology movements". Thus, environ-mental racism "refers to any policy, practice, or directive that differentially affects to disadvantage (whether intended or unintended) individuals, groups, or communities based on race or color" (Bullard RD, 1996).

Studies on environmental justice began in the early 1970's; a substantial body of literature was developed that documents the existence of environmental inequalities in the United States. These early findings were later amplified by a series of studies focusing on the location of hazardous waste sites, beginning with a study conducted by the U.S. General Accounting Office in 1983. This study documented that African American communities in the southern United States were playing host to a disproportionately high number of waste sites.

In 1990, Bryant and Mohai organized the Conference on Race and the Incidence of Environmental Hazards at the University of Michigan. The Michigan conference brought together researchers from around the nation who were studying racial and socioeconomic disparities in the distribution of environmental contaminants to discuss their findings and implications. Since 1990, scholars have produced an extensive and sophisticated literature on dimensions of differential environmental risks based on race and socioeconomic class position. Bryant and Mohai were the first to perform a systematic meta-analysis of empirical studies shedding light on race and class disparities in the distribution of environmental hazards. All these studies found environmental disparities based on either race or income or both.

In a more recent review of the literature regarding differential exposures to environmental pollution, Evens and Kantrowiz (2002) found that significant relationships exist between the ethnic and class characteristics of a community and levels of exposure to environmental risk. Across a wide variety of environmental components, including proximity to hazardous waste sites, exposures to air and water pollution, high levels of ambient noise, residential crowding, quality of housing, quality of local schools and the work environment, communities composed of people of lower SES and people of color were consistently exposed to higher levels of environmental risk.

The key points considered in the environmental justice are that it opposes the destructive operations of multi-national corporations. It demands the cessation of the production of all toxins, hazardous wastes, and radioactive materials, and that all past and current producers should be held strictly accountable to the people for detoxification and containment at the point of production, Environmental justice renewable resources in the interest of a sustainable planet for humans and other living things.

Environmental justice calls for universal protection from nuclear testing, extraction, production, and disposal of toxic hazardous wastes and poisons that threaten the fundamental right to clean air, land, water and food. It affirms the fundamental right to political, economic, cultural and environmental self-determination of all people. It also advocates protecting the right of victims so that one gets full compensation and reparations for damages as well as quality health care. Environmental justice affirms the right of all workers to a safe and healthy work environment, without being forced to choose between an unsafe livelihood and unemployment. It also affirms the right of those who work at home to be free from environmental hazards.

Environmental justice demands that public policy be based on mutual respect and justice for all people, free from any form of discrimination or bias. It requires that we, as individuals, make personal and consumer choices to consume minimum earth's resources to challenge and re-priorities our lifestyles to insure the health of the natural world for present and future generations. Environmental justice affirms the sacredness of earth, ecological unity and the interdependence of all species, and the right to be free from ecological destruction.

The Bhopal gas tragedy is a well-known phenomenon that happened at mid night on 3rd December 1984 in Bhopal. It was a manmade tragedy that caused suffering to the poor living around the industry and about 3000 person including children died due to leakage of gas called MIC (Methane Isocyanides). Did the victims of Bhopal get justice in court of law and at international level? Not to the level that damage was done as law was only looking into scientific factors, not the social and economic ones which were more critical as the population that suffered the most was poor, vulnerable and minority in characteristics. Although people were compensated monetarily, the loss theysuffered in health, family and livelihood could not be compensated. Therefore, it is imperative to know what is environmental justice and how to help people to safe guard themselves from environmental damages which have non-tangible factors associated with it.

The environmental justice movement was born from

communities of color and Black communities in particular-organizing in opposition to environmental policies that systematically expose them to disproportionate levels of toxins and pollution. This racist distribution of environmental burdens is accompanied by the unjust distribution of environmental benefits as well. In addition to fighting for distributional justice, the environmental justice movement has grown to encompass procedural justice as well by working to redistribute power over ownership and environmental decision-making processes.

The Principles of Environmental Justice: The people of color, gathered together at this multinational People of Environmental Leadership Summit, to begin to build a national and international movement of all people of color to fight the destruction and taking of our lands and communities, do hereby re-establish our spiritual interdependence to the sacredness of our Mother Earth; to respect and celebrate each of our cultures, languages and beliefs about the natural world and our roles in healing ourselves; to environmentally safe livelihoods; and, to secure our political, economic and cultural liberation that has been denied for over 500 years of colonization and oppression, resulting in the poisoning of our communities and land and the genocide of our peoples. At the First National People of Color Environmental Leadership Summit in 1991, delegates drafted and adopted 17 principles of Environmental Justice. These are:

1. Environmental Justice affirms the sacredness of Mother Earth, ecological unity and the interdependence of all species, and the right to be free from ecological destruction.

2. Environmental Justice demands that public policy be based on mutual respect and justice for all peoples, free from any form of discrimination or bias.

3. Environmental Justice mandates the right to ethical, balanced and responsible uses of land and renewable

resources in the interest of a sustainable planet for humans and other living things.

4. Environmental Justice calls for universal protection from nuclear testing, extraction, production and disposal of toxic/hazardous wastes and poisons and nuclear testing that threaten the fundamental right to clean air, land, water, and food.

5. Environmental Justice affirms the fundamental right to political, economic, cultural and environmental self-determination of all peoples.

6. Environmental Justice demands the cessation of the production of all toxins, hazardous wastes, and radioactive materials, and that all past and current producers be held strictly accountable to the people for detoxification and the containment at the point of production.

7. Environmental Justice demands the right to participate as equal partners at every level of decision-making, including needs assessment, planning implementation, enforcement and evaluation.

8. Environmental Justice affirms the right of all workers to a safe and healthy work environment without being forced to choose between an unsafe livelihood and unemployment. It also affirms the right to those who work at home to be free from environmental hazards.

9. Environmental Justice protects the right of victims of environmental injustice to receive full compensation and reparations for damages as well as quality health care.

10. Environmental Justice considers governmental acts of environmental injustice a violation of international law, the Universal Declaration On Human Rights, and the United Nations Convention on Genocide.

11. Environmental Justice must recognize a special legal and natural relationship of Native Peoples to the U.S. government through treatises, agreements, compacts, and covenants affirming sovereignty and self-determination.

12. Environmental Justice affirms the need for urban and rural ecological policies to clean up and rebuild our cities and rural areas in balance with nature, honoring the cultural integrity of all our communities, and provided fair access for all to the full range of resources.

13. Environmental Justice calls for the strict enforcement of principles of informed consent, and a halt to the testing of experimental reproductive and medical procedures and vaccinations on people of color.

14. Environmental Justice opposes the destructive operations of multi-national corporations.

15. Environmental Justice opposes military occupation, repression and exploitation of lands, peoples and cultures, and other life forms.

16. Environmental Justice calls for the education of present and future generations which emphasizes social and environmental issues, based on our experience and an appreciation of our diverse cultural perspectives.

17. Requires that we, as individuals, make personal and consumer choices to consume as little of Mother Earth's resources and to produce as little waste as possible and make the conscious decision to challenge and reprioritize our lifestyles to ensure the health of the natural world for present and future generations.

Environmental Justice Movement in India

The environmental justice movement in India has a long history. The Chipko Andolan of 1973 is seen as the first environmental justice movement of the country, although concerns for environmental protection can be traced back to protests against the commercialization of forests in the early twentieth century under the British rule (Guha 2000; Sahu 2007). Such early grassroots resistances with ecological undertones like the Bengal peasant revolt of 1859-63 against Indigo plantations are considered to have resemblances to the recent day protests against industrial tree plantations movement also rang with concerns for the ecosystem and its people. After independence, there was a heavy boost to large infrastructure for nation building such as multi-purpose dam projects and steel plants. Although this impetus on rapid industrialization could not bring the desired economic growth, it unwittingly ushered in a wave of environmental justice movements in the country, such as the Narmada Bachao Andolan or the Appiko movement or the Silent Valley protest. The protests over the Bhopal accident of 1984 have lasted until today. Since 1991, after the liberalization of the Indian economy, 283 cases of ecological conflicts have been reported in the Environmental Justice Atlas as of 24 December, 2018. These cases account for more than one-tenth of all the environmental justice movements documented worldwide in the Environmental Justice Atlas. Although this article draws from the Environmental Justice Atlas, we are aware of other outstanding repositories of documented environmental conflicts and movements in India such as the Green Files, India Environmental Portal and Land Conflicts Watch.

In the last 45 years, the hows and whys of environmental justice struggles in India have been reshaped in many ways. Yet, the basic premise of non-violent direct action, which follows from the Gandhian principle of Satyagraha, remains. It takes unique forms depending on the context, be it the Koyla Satyagraha (Environmental Justice Atlas 2016) against coal mining in tribal areas of central India or Zameen Samadhi Satyagraha (Environmental Justice Atlas 2017) against land acquisition in Rajasthan. These mostly peaceful manifestations are sometimes met with direct violence, as evidenced by the number of cases with high intensity of conflicts.

The goal of environmental justice is to ensure that all people, regardless of race, national origin or income, are protected from disproportionate impacts of environmental hazards. To be classified as an environmental justice community, residents must be a minority and or low-income group; excluded from the environmental policy setting and/or decision-making process; subject to a dispropor-tionate impact from one or more environmental hazards; and experience a disparate implementation of environmental regulations, requirements, practices and activities in their communities. (U.S. Environmental Protection Agency, Office of Environmental Justice, 2000). Determining "Environmental justice communities" becomes a matter for scientific analysis. In some EPA regions, for instance, administrators have developed protocol for using Geographic Information Systems (GIS) to demarcate such communities (e.g., U.S. Environmental Protection Agency, Region IV, 2000).

Still, in accordance with the directives of Executive Order 12898, interpretations of environmental justice within government agencies promote diverse conceptions of environmental issues. All federal environmental justice programs includeprovisions for both distributive justices, referring to the distribution on environmental quality among different communities and procedural justice, referring to the access of citizens to decision-making processes that affect their environment. While the EPA's environmental justice policies focus primarily on areas facing hazardous waste and pollution concerns, the program of the U.S. Department of Housing and Urban Developmentaddresses such problems as lead-based paint in inner-city public housing projects and the lack of basic infrastructural needs in many Native American reservation, migrant farm worker compass and colonies along the United States Mexico border. In the Federal Highway administration and Federal Transit Administration, environmental justice also means ensuring that minority and low-income population benefit proportionately from trans-porttation projects. In addition, in the policy of the FHWA and FTA, adverse impacts of concern extend beyond conventional health and environmental effects to such issues as aesthetic values, traffic congestion and community isolation or displacement. In spite of this variety of environmental justice issues recognized by government agencies, empirical investigations have typically failed to look beyond sites and chemical release documented in EPA databases.

Some slogans and banners of the global movement for environmental justice: There is another approach to research the global environmental justice counter-movement, and this is to look at its cultural expressions in the form of banners, murals, slogans, documentaries. While the ultimate causes of collective protest are the growth and changes in the social metabolism (flows of energy and materials), such protests exhibit cultural and symbolic elements that we gather in the EJAtlas. What is invisible and silenced in the official press and in academic writings becomes more visible and audible in the banners and slogans spontaneous or organized demonstrations within the limits of what state and company violence will tolerate and the participants fear allows.

Consider for instance the current conflict against the Pan American Silver mine in Chubut, Argentina. The "Navidad" mining project is one of the largest silver deposits in the world. While local inhabitants reject the project, the national government and mining companies are pressing for changes to the law that preventsits exploitation. The banner states that the place where the mine is located should not be a "sacrifice zone", a term that is used by the USA environmental justice movement.

Conclusion

Environmental Justice has travelled a long distance from the time it gained importance. It has gained significance starting with issues of solving problems of residents around the industrial areas to human right and indigenous communities' right. The legal development of discipline has also travelled a long distance and we have number of international treatises, international court of justice and international NGO to deal with environmental justice. The subject has gained importance in academic domain also.

An environmental justice perspective takes into account a contextual analysis of historical injustices and exclusion faced by indigenous and tribal communities and recognizes traditional conceptions of nature and justice still exist in indigenous and tribal communities. These are reflected on a daily basis in local, traditional norms and informal and hybrid systems of justice and governance which determine rights and decide on contested claims related to land and natural resource use within the community. Expanding social and environmental justice and rights for indigenous and tribal people recognizes that rather than being victims of the past, communities are agents of change in their own right with their own vision for the future of development and the natural resources, which they host.

Works Cited:
Adams. W. (1997) "Rationalization and conservation: Ecology and the management of nature in the United Kingdom," Translations of the Institute of British Geographers NS 22: 277-291.
Anderson, James, N. 1973. Ecological Anthropology and Anthropological Ecology. In Handbook of social and Cultural Anthropology. John J. Honigmann, ed. pp. 477-497. Cicago: Rand McNally & Co. Anderson James 1973.
Capek SM. 1993. The environmental justice frame: a conceptual discussion application. Soc. Probl. 40: 5-24.
Akula, V.K. 1995. "Grassroots Environmental Resistance in

India". In Ecological Resistance Movements: Grassroots Environmental Resistance in India edited by B.R. Taylor, 127-145, New York: Sunny press.

Bisht, A. and J.F. Gerber. 2017. "Ecological distribution conflicts (EDCs) over mineral extractives in India: An overview". Extractive Industries and Societies,548-563.

EJAtlas. 2016. "Coal mining conflict in Hazaribagh with NTPC in Jharkhand, India." In Atlas of Environmental Justice, http://ejatlas.org/conflict/illegel-land-acquision-for-coal-minig-and-violent-protest-in-hazaribagh-jharkhand.

EJAtlas. 2017a. "Zameen Samadhi Satyagraha agiant land acuquisition in Needanar village, Jaipur, Rajasthan, India" in Atlas of environmental justice. http://ejatlas.org/ conflict/ zameen-samadhi-satyagraha-by-villagers-agianst-land-acquision-for-infrastructure-of-needar-village-jiapur-rajasthan.

Millar, A and C. Sisco. (2002). Ten Actions of Climate Justice Policies, available at http://www.ejrc.cau. edu/summit2/SummiIIClimate Justice%20.pdf.

Bodley, J. 1982. Victims of Progress. Mayfield, Menlo Park.

Bryant B, Mohai P, eds. 1992. Race and Incidence of Environmental Hazards: A time for Discourse, Boulder, Co;Westview.

Sharma, M. 2018. Caste and Nature: Dalits and Indian Environmental Politics. New Delhi: Oxford University Press.

United nations Environment Programme (2019).

Environmental Rule of Law: First Global Report.

United Nations Environment Program, "What are environmental rights?" Accessed in December 2021.

Mary Robinson Foundation on Climate Justice, "Rrinciples of Climate Justice". Accessed in December 2021.ss

Chapter 12

Colonization and Green Culture History : The Glass Palace's Eco-Tale

Shruti Soni

Abstract

The Glass Palace entails the story of the colonization period of Burma in which the green culture is victimized by the hands of the colonizers. Historical events play a paramount role in the intricate plot of the novel. The places that the writer holds in the story are- India, Malaya, and Burma. Ecocritical concerns like- deforestation, pollution, depletion of natural resources, exploitation of animals, and domination of humans by humans are showcased beautifully and crudely exhibited in this research paper.

Keywords: Colonization, Ecocidal Damages, Green Culture, Social Ecology

The Glass Palace and Green Culture

The ecocritical study endeavours to fade away the dichotomy rooted in one's perception. The construction and destruction of nature knowingly or unknowingly is interconnected with man. One needs to accept this universal truth and Ecocriticism is the way, which allows the human world to walk on and confronts this indubitable reality. Glotfelty (1996) opines, "An ecologically focused criticism is a worthy enterprise primarily because it directs our attention to matters about which we need to be thinking. Consciousness raising is its most important task. For how can we solve environmental problems unless we start thinking about them?" (xxiv).

The Glass Palace expounds the crux of green culture's doom. The novel discloses the colonization era and interlaces the wreckage of green culture. The conglomerated characters assist in the enclosures of deteriorated conditions of the green surroundings in varieties. The characters like-- Rajkumar Raha, a young kalaa Indian boy; Saya John and his son Mathew from Malaya; King Thebaw and Queen Supayalat, their daughters and their little young girl attendants; Dolly, one of the princess' attendants and wife of Rajkumar; Uma, the collector's wife; Neel and Dinu, sons of Rajkumar and Dolly; Alison and Timmy, children of Mathew and Elsa; Bela, Manju, and Arjun, Uma's nieces and nephew; Jaya, daughter of Neel and Manju; Ilongo, illegitimate son of Rajkumar and other characters exhibit the plight and power of women, search of identity, colonialism, wars, and the ecocidal damages in Mandalay.

The story is set in 1885 and starts with one of the major characters of the novel, RajkumarRaha. He along with his mother moves to Mandalay from the port of Arakan- a port where Bengal and Burma meet with the help of sampan- a boat. During the journey, his mother dies on the sampan as she is suffering from the fatal disease, Akyab. Rajkumar's father, brothers and sisters also died of Akyab. The deadly disease compels Rajkumar and his mother to escape from the place but unfortunately, his mother fails to survive and leaves him all alone in this world.

In Mandalay, Rajkumar is known as a "kalaa from across the sea- an Indian" (3). He is eleven when he steps into Mandalay and finds a trivial job as a waiter at Ma Cho's food stall. Ma Cho, "she was half Indian and she ran a small food stall; small and harried looking, with spirals of wiry hair hanging over her forehead like a fringed awning" (4-5). At Ma Cho's stall, Rajkumar meets Saya John, a contractor of teak, on whom Ma Cho has a huge crush but couldn't make it into a sustaining relationship. Saya John has a son of almost Rajkumar's age, named Mathew, "he was seven, a handsome, bright eyed child, with an air of precocious self-possession"(11). Rajkumar and Mathew's intimacy turns into

136

an unbreakable friendship. Rajkumar shares his heart-wrenching story with Mathew about how he loses everyone in his family. In this way, both of them share an intimate and emotional bond. One day, both are discussing Mandalay as a place and the things that go around it. During the conversation, Mathew tells Rajkumar that the British would try to overpower Mandalay for the teak farms as they want to convert them into timber yards for commercial purposes. "The English are preparing to send a fleet up the Irrawaddy. There's going to be a war. Father says they want all the teak in Burma. The King won't let them have it so they're going to do away with him" (15). Rajkumar flabbergasts with the fact that "log of wood" (15) could be a reason for a war. The reason is indigestible for Rajkumar but it happens and the British colonizes Mandalay:

Two days later the whole city was gripped by rumors of war. A large detachment of troops came marching out of the fort and went off down river, towards the encampment of Myingan. There was an uproar in the bazaar; fishwives emptied their wares into the refuse heap and went hurrying home. A disheveledSayaJohn came running to Ma Cho's stall. He had a sheet of paper in his hands. 'A Royal Proclamation', he announced, 'issued under the King's signature'. (15)

The Royal Proclamation announces that the British would have a battle with Mandalay to destroy the King's reign but the King takes the pledge to protect his country and countrymen. This announcement gives a sense of security to the citizens but still, they have the apprehension to get colonized at the hands of the British.

The British enters Mandalay in 1885 and colonized it with the ten thousand soldiers of the British army which encompasses the two-third of Indian sepoys.

The British captures the Glass Palace and the day has come when the King Thebaw along with the Queen and their two daughters and their girl attendants are exiled from Mandalay to Ratnagiri in India and the actual beginning of the deterioration of the green culture in Mandalay.

Ghosh through the picture of the eighteenth century displays the picture of the present time—the age of environmental crisis.One can fairly observe this unanticipated attitude in Harold Fromm (1996) essay "From Transcendence to Obsolescence" where Fromm receives a letter and the writer mentions her human preferences over the ecological issues. She says:

Dear Sir:

Since all of the environmentalists who worry about pollution are also consumers of the products of these bleaching plants (the automobile for instance by which you reach your farm), what is the answer? Do we cut off our noses to spite our faces? Do we destroy our economy: eliminate many necessities of life' go back to living in tents for the sake of clean air? The answers are complex. (37)

This letter shakes and nonplussed Fromm what to reply to it. The writer comprehends the current environmental issues this biosphere is suffering from but her preferences are still materialistic ones. Fromm opines regarding this letter that then "what are the necessities of life in comparison with which clean air cannot be regarded as a necessity?" (37). The necessities of life that the writer is asking for are her wishes to live a full-fledged luxurious life where she can content her state of mind and physical prosperity. Fromm observes that "the necessity of clean air" that she is ignoring over "the necessities of life" is actually needed and the most required "for the sake of her own biological existence" (37). To clear the writer's thoughts and interpretations, Fromm takes some analogies to replace her statement like: "Do we eliminate necessities of life for the sake of clean air?" could equally well be represented as "Do we give up smoking for the sake of avoiding lung cancer?" Fromm compares "the necessities of life" with "smoking" and "for the sake of clean air" with "avoiding lung cancer"; and here the foundation of this research can be easily reflected. What does the human world compare with what? What the human world actually requires is ignored thoroughly. Fromm gives a well justified analogy that the human world is ready to give up "the clean air" for the sake of "necessities of life" which are ruining the body, mind and soul of human beings. One must not ignore this fact too that all are required a basic need of science and technology and our current life is incomplete without these basic necessities. The human community needs an air conditioner for the living; mobiles and other gadgets to be in touch with others; automobiles to travel in; internet to know the world around; basically, a life where the human community is helpless without technology. The revolution of science and technology should not demolish the presence of nature in human beings' life –this should be one of the norms that technology should work on. The scientists are searching for life on other planets as we are failing to save ours. These days it is not possible for anyone to go and build a tent or house in the countryside and live a happy life but it is possible to maintain the serenity of the natural surroundings. As Fromm replaces "avoiding lung cancer" with "remaining alive"(37) which modify the whole question again as in: "Do we give up smoking for the sake of remaining alive?"(38) and finally, if it can be quoted in the writer's statement then it will be "Do we give up the necessities of life for the sake of remaining alive"? (38). Further Fromm states that "the struggle between the "necessities of modern life" and the "environment" is the age-old struggle between the individual will and the universe . . ." (38).

Deforestation

In the third part of the novel, *The Money Tree,* Rajkumar ties the nuptial knot with his childhood love Dolly and returns to Rangoon. Saya gifts Dolly a gold bracelet and a spongy ball called rubber to Rajkumar as a token of love and blessings to the newly married couple. Rajkumar with astonishment asks Saya why he has gifted him this piece of rubber instead of any materialistic gift that he could use for his happy married life. Saya responds enthusiastically that he finds the rubber in his hometown Malacca or Malaya when Rajkumar is in India. Rubber as a business created chaos in Rangoon's market during that time.

Saya loves travelling and always pays visits to his friends and relatives. During his journey, he wishes to visit his wife's grave at Malacca so he stops and gets down into the city. To his surprise, the town is debasing, the place is choked up with dust and sand, the port looks ruinous, the sailors are moving either to Penang or Singapore for an uncontaminated life:

Malacca had been a town that was slowly dying, with its port silted up and its traders moving away, either northwards to Penang, or southwards to Singapore. But now suddenly, Malacca was a changed place; was a palpable quickening in the muddied veins of the sleepy old city . . . an area that had once been home to dozens of small spice gardens, where pepper plants grew on vines. But the vines were all gone now, and in their place there were long straight rows of graceful, slender-trunked saplings. (182)

The saplings are of rubber plants. A Chinese family of Mr Tan Chay Yan of Malacca converts their pepper gardens into rubber plantations for monetary gains. Earlier it was criticized by everyone because during the late 18th century it was a risk to the rubber business. But Mr Tan Chay Yan proves everyone wrong and flourishes the rubber plantation in Malacca within a short span of three years. After looking at his success, the British companies also follow his path to grow rubber and in a glimpse of time, they become rich. Various motor companies need rubber for the motor parts and "the profits beyond imagining"(182) regardless of its catastrophic and ruinous effect on the natural surroundings.

Saya purchases land near to the island of Penang and the port of Butterworth. But Rajkumar counters the thought of Saya as Mathew is completely unaware of rubber and its business so how is it possible for Mathew to run the business which he doesn't know about. Saya says, "Timber is a thing of the past, Rajkumar: you have to look to the future- and if there's any tree on which money could be said to grow then this it- rubber" (184).

Finally, Mathew comes back with his wife Elsa. Saya sells all his properties in Rangoon and settles down in Malacca with Mathew and Elsa. During that time, Dolly is pregnant and Saya promises that he will definitely come to the birth ceremony of their child. Dolly gives birth to their first child, a baby boy, named Sein Win in the Burmese and Neeladhri in the Indian language. After four years, Dolly again gives birth to a baby boy named TunPe and Dinanath and surprisingly they have received news from Saya that Elsa also gives birth to a baby girl named Alison. Saya invites Rajkumar and Dolly to Malacca for the ground-breaking ceremony of their new house. Rajkumar and Dolly are welcomed by Mathew and Elsa at GunungJerai. On the way to Mathew's house, Elsa flaunts their rubber plantation named as "Morningside Rubber Estate" (198) to Dolly and takes her to the area where the rubber trees are planting:

They headed through the rubber trees....The ground underfoot had a soft, cushioned feel, because of the carpet of dead leaves shed by the tress . . . It was like being in wilderness, but not yet. . . But this was like neither city nor farm nor forest: there was something eerie about its uniformity; about the fact that such sameness could be imposed upon a landscape of such natural exuberance... 'It's like stepping into a labyrinth,' she said to Elsa. (199)

The phrase "the carpet of dead leaves" profoundly discourses the callous activities which are performed by man. Unquestionably, man prefers materialism over spirituality. Modern technology gives a back foot to nature and conceals its identity in the name of progress. Man only feels nature's presence when it reverts by hitting him in the form of natural calamities until and unless human beings feel that nature is voiceless. William Rueckert (1996) says, "Green plants, for example, are among the most creative organisms. They are nature's poets"(111).

Literature presents the harsh social realities to the society itself to transform the humanistic mind-set and encourages the human world to work for a better position. Wordsworth is one of the romantic poets who idealise nature as the key component of human's life and his poems help to generate eco awareness and assess the moral responsibilities towards ecology. Wordsworth is of the opinion that our foremost responsibility as a human being is to love and admire nature and to protect it from any kind of harsh and severe intervention. In *Tintern Abbey* Wordsworth beautifies nature at every phase of life and also preaches the urgency to protect and preserve the natural surroundings. He admires nature as a divinity and influences the world to pay a tribute to the best gift bestows by the Almighty by protecting it from the materialistic hands. But, *The Glass Palace* shows us a counter scenario of what Wordsworth thought. The colonizers establish their timber business by clearing the teak forests and later on they move to the rubber plantation and the same is performed by the colonized people too and in this array of commercial growth, they forget Mother Nature who always stands as a guardian and nourishes them with the basic necessities.

Exploitation of Animals

Literature always demonstrates the inevitable and humble relationship of human and animal. *The Glass Palace* shares some incidents in the novel depicting the miserable treatment of the elephants. They are only used for human's profits irrespective of their health, their capabilities, and even their death. After the expulsion of King Thebaw and Queen Supayalat from Mandalay, the royal elephant of their reign died soon: "There was news from Mandalay that the royal elephant died . . . everyone had known that the elephant would not long survive the fall of the dynasty. But who could have thought that it would die so soon? It seemed like a portent. The house was sunk in gloom"(51).

The reason for the elephant's death remains fuzzy and blurrily. Before the colonization of Mandalay by the British, the King and the Queen possessed a very amicable relationship with their elephants. They treat them like their own family, take care of them like their children and this is the reason they are flourishing and enjoy good health during their reign but colonization makes their life hell and they are used to bearing the burden of their business. Kenneth Brown (2006) in his essay "Pastoral Concern in Relation to the Psychological Stress caused by the Death of an Animal Companion" says:

We share our existence with a great variety of other animals and throughout history these animals have played a significant role in our customs, legends, and religions in all parts of the world. These animals exist beside us, below us, above us and often with us. They are a feature of our natural world and a source of human curiosity, fascination and study. (411)

Animal advocates are of the opinion that the major problem lies with human beings' perception towards animals. Both the entities own equal rights on this earth. Sue Campbell (1966) in her essay "The Land and Language of Desire: Where Deep Ecology and Post-Structuralism Meet" also opines the same:

The most important challenge to traditional hierarchies in ecology is the concept of biocentrism – the conviction that humans are neither better nor worse than other creatures (animals, plants, bacteria, rocks, rivers) but simple equal to everything else in the natural world.(128)

When Saya and Rajkumar are in Rangoon for the timber business, Saya mentions the conditions of the *hsin-ouq*, the leader of the *oo-sis* group. They are the trainers of the elephants which are used to transport the log of teak woods from one place to another. Here comes another depiction where animals are used by the man for their commercial profits. Before colonization no one ever thought of utilising elephants for the human's profits. The elephants are always pampered but never used for the business purposes:

The team of elephants would go to work, guided by their handlers, their *oo-sis* and *pe-sis*, butting, prodding, levering with their trunks.

Yet until the Europeans came none of them had ever thought of using elephants for the purpose of logging . . . It was the Europeans who saw that tame elephants could be made to work for human profit . . . the entire way of life is their creation . . . this method of girdling trees, these ways of moving logs with elephants, this system of floating them downriver . . . . (69, 74-75)

Another deadly scene appears in the novel when Doh Say describes various fatal situations which are stalking the happy lives of the *oo-sis*. Anthrax is one of the deadliest elephant's diseases which attack the elephant and leave them in the most fatal and terrible condition. This disease is very common in the dense forest of Burma and it is very tough to prevent it. The disease is so fatal that the elephants can surmount to their death in a couple of hours. When the disease attacks the elephants a kind of volcanic energy erupts from them and become awfully insane that even attack at their private organs. Rajkumar encounters an elephant suffering from Anthrax along with Rajkumar and Doh Say. The encounter is very horrifying that they are stunned to look at the situation:

The infected elephant was quieter now than before, dazed by pain and weakened by its struggle with the disease. The swellings had grown to pineapple size and the elephant's hide had begun to crack and break apart . . . soon the pustules began to leak whitish ooze. Within a short while the animal's hide was wet with discharge. Rivulets of blood-streaked pus began to drip to the ground. The soil around the animal's feet turned into sludge, churned with blood and ooze. (95)

Jonathan Swift (1726), an Irish writer, emerges as an eco-writer in *Gulliver's Travels*[11]. Swift articulates about the terrible conditions of the animals especially horses during the eighteenth century likewise in *The Glass Palace* with elephants. The fourth part of the book *Gulliver's Travels* "A Voyage to the land of the Houyhnhnms" depicts the horrifying conditions of the horses during the eighteenth century. It was the time in the European countries where the animals were not treated properly, mostly they were neglected and ill-treated by humans and Swift was pained at this situation. Swift articulates that the horses are called Houyhnhnms. He describes:

The Houyhnhnms among us, whom we called 'horses', were the most generous and comely animals we had; that they excelled in strength and swiftness; and when they belonged to persons of quality, employed in travelling, racing or drawing chariots; they were treated with much kindness and care, till they fell into diseases, or become foundered in the feet; but then they were sold and used to all kind of drudgery until they died; after which, their skins were stripped and sold for what they were worth, and their bodies left to be devoured by dogs and birds of prey.(181)

Depletion of Natural Resources

The natural resource of Mandalay is the earth oil which seeps naturally at the coastal banks of Irrawaddy River at Yenangyaung. The texture is dark green with a little bit of sparkles in it which shines like a green filmed pool. This earth oil is globally acknowledged because of its medicinal value for the treatment of skin diseases. This attracts many merchants from different nations. *Twin-za*is the community who looks after this oil and uses it for market gains. Because of its booming demands, the *twin zas* dig the area so hard that the pools are converted into the oil wells which are surrounded by sand and the earth. Even Rajkumar notices foreigners at the oil wells, jumping from one oil well to another like a hungry dacoit whose main purpose is to rob the precious oil. He also notices the increased number of the foreigners over the oil wells in his every next visit:

Many of Yenangyaung's pools had been worked for so long that the level of oil had sunk beneath the surface, forcing their owners to dig down. In this way, some of the pools had gradually become wells, a hundred feet deep or even more- great oil- sodden pits, surrounded by excavated sand and earth. Some of these wells were so heavily worked that they looked like small volcanoes, with steep, conical slopes.

Whenever he returned, there were more and more of these men around the slopes, armed with instruments and surveyors' tripods. They were from France, England and America, and they were said to be offering the twin zas good money, buying up their pools and wells. Wooden obelisks began to rise on the hillocks, cage-like pyramids inside which huge mechanical beaks hammered ceaselessly on the earth. (123)

"Oil well" as "Small volcanoes" unmasks the repercussions of the edacious human mind in terms of the demolition of natural resources, which happens in Mandalay. Digging the Mother Earth to the core that oil well appears as a volcano advocates the human's mind which is engineered by the machines and leaves man at a position from where he can see himself as the only king of this biosphere.

Air and Noise Pollution

The bombardments, emission of the toxic gases in the environment, number of casualties, destruction of the waterfronts and mills etc. these are another achievement of the colonization in Burma. Here, Ghosh articulates the air and noise pollution in Burma caused by the colonization. After the British, the Japanese attacked Burma with their heavy force and "the planes were in flames" (383). The attackers have demolished the warehouses, oil tanks, mills, etc. The thriving sounds of bombarding and the hazardous clouds of smoke are the reflections of the heavy air and noise pollution:

Minutes later, with a blast that was like a moving wall of sound, the Japanese heavy artillery opened up. The first shells went skimming over the tops of the trees, sending down showers of leaves and small branches . . . the earth shook so violently as to send the water at the bottom of the trench shooting into their faces. Arjun saw a fifty-foot rubber tree rising gracefully from the earth and jumping several feet into the air before somersaulting towards them. They flattened themselves at the bottom of the trench just in time to get out of its way. The bombardment continued without a break for hours. (391)

The attack of the Japanese army over Malaya causes immense damage to the physical environment. Another scene appears when Rajkumar arrives at the bank to withdraw some money for his oo-sis as they are hired to brush off the Pazundaung timber yard in Rangoon. He is standing outside the bank in a queue. Suddenly, he sees the planes approaching from the east in a brash recurring sound and on the contrary the city's anti-aircraft guns open up with gloomy and throbbing noise. The eastern horizon is coated with the luminous silver sheet of the ashes of bombarding:

The first bombs fell several miles away, the explosions following in evenly spaced rhythmic succession. Suddenly

147

there was booming sound, several times louder than all the proceeding blasts. From somewhere in the eastern reaches of the city, a huge cloud of black smoke mushroomed up towards the sky, almost engulfing the bombers . . . they were targeting the city's long waterfront, aiming for its mills, ware houses, tanks and railway lines. People had been crouching along the walls of the telegraph office when the water source was hit. Many had died. Dismembered limbs could be seen in the pool that spinning around the main: there was a child's arm, a leg . . . . (461-62)

"Columns of smoke", "swirling clouds of smoke", "blanketed in flames", "clouds of smoke", "blackened with smoke", "booming sound", "loud rhythmic noise" —these phrases well-depict the air and noise pollution caused by the attacks, especially air pollution is the most prevailing during the attack.

The Domination of Human-by-Human - Ecological Issue

Murray Bookchin (2006) states that the oppression of the natural surroundings by the human world is the result of the oppression of human-by-human-powered by the authoritarian social world and termed it as "Social Ecology" where another human being does the domination of a human being. Thus, Social Ecology illustrates the fact that the ecological crises which turn out to be a lethal threat to the whole world, is actually the result of the "deep seated social problems" (Bookchin, *Social Ecology* 19). The oppression of the weak by the strong is always a social problem and this inherent instinct rules human nature and appears as a prime reason for the ecological destruction. Thus, it can be primarily said that the ecological problems and social problems have a common connection and probably have the same solution—the attitude of human beings in regard to power and authority. Colonization is a mirror to social ecology where the colonizers oppress the colonized societies to exhibit their power and supremacy and this supremacy dominates the human and the non-human worlds: "the hierarchical mentality and class relationships that so thoroughly permeate society are what has given rise to the very idea of dominating the natural world" (Bookchin, *Social Ecology* 20).

A scene appears in the novel where Saya and Rajkumar converse about the Europeans soldiers who are transported by the British to Mandalay as the workers to deforest the teak forests. But this proves the worst situation for the soldiers as they have not been paid proper attention by their masters and this makes their health miserable and deplorable. Saya says:

Think of the kind of life they lead here, these young Europeans. They have at best two or three years in the jungle before malaria or dengue fever weaken them to the point where they cannot afford to be far from doctors and hospitals . . . within a few years these men will be prematurely aged, old at twenty-one . . . it is only when they are freshly arrived seventeen or eighteen . . . during those days few years the company must derive such profit from them as it can . . . they send them from camp to camp . . . scarcely a break in between . . . sick and alone, thousands of miles from home . . . deep inside a forest. (74)

The power of colonizers over colonized is a picture perfect of what social ecology propagates that besides the biological facts of domination like "kin lineage, gender distinctions and age difference"(31), there are also some dominated powers outside who are "strangers"(32) and form a chain of exploitative oppressors according to their needs and requirements.

The Glass Palace recurs as the encasement of the disturbed ecological cycle and its disastrous result over the green culture. The novel emphasises the destruction of the green culture causing ecocritical concerns like deforestation, pollution, depletion of natural resources, exploitation of animals, and human predicaments. Social Ecology, another aspect of the environmental deterioration where humans are the enemy of another human and adds on to the ruling force over both the life forms—human and non-human. Thus, human beings need to investigate the righteous path for survival where both worlds can reside peacefully.

Works Cited:

Bookchin, Murray. *The Ecology of Freedom: The Emergence and Dissolution of Hierarchy.* Cheshire Books, 1982.

Brown, Kenneth. "Pastoral Concern in Relation to the Psychological Stress Caused by the Death of an Animal Companion." *Mental Health Religion &Culture*, vol.9, no. 5, 2006, pp. 411-422.

Campbell, Sue Ellen. "The Land and Language of Desire: Where Deep Ecology and Post-Structuralism Meet." *The Ecocriticism Reader: Landmarks in Literary Ecology*, edited by CheryllGlotfelty and Harold Fromm, Athens: The U of Georgia P, 1996, pp. 124-136.

Fromm, Harold. "From Transcendence to Obsolescence: A Route Map." *The Ecocriticism Reader: Landmarks in Literary Ecology*, edited by CheryllGlotfelty and Harold Fromm, Athens, Georgia: The U of Georgia P, 1996, pp. 30-39.

Ghosh, Amitav. *The Glass Palace.* Harper Collins. 2000.

Rueckert, William. "Literature and Ecology: An Experiment in Ecocriticism" *The Ecocriticism Reader: Landmarks in Literary Ecology*, edited by CheryllGlotfelty and Harold Fromm, Athens, Georgia: The U of Georgia P, 1996, pp. 105-123.

Swift, Jonathan. *Gulliver's Travels* (Wordsworth Classics). Wordsworth Editions, Hertsfordshire, UK, 1992.

Chapter 13

Imagining Sustainable Worlds : The Confluence of Eco ethics and Literature

Sunita Dhankhar
Pooja Khanna

Abstract

We find an inherent connection between nature and human society and this connection between literature and human society can best be examined through the lens of ecocriticism. Ecocriticism takes on the dominant anthrophonic narratives that have put the interests of humans above that of all living and non-living beings. This has been at the expense of the animal kingdom and the environmental health of the planet. It shifts the focus to the interconnect-tedness of all life forms and a need to balance the earth's ecosystem with a more democratic approach to the rights of all life form. A bio-centric approach is the need of the hour. Renowned environmental philosopher Holmes Rolston III in*Conserving Natural Value*states, "Nature is not something to be merely consumed by humans, but a community to which we belong and for which we are to care". A shift in focus from human centric approach to a more nuanced thinking that fosters a sustainable and more holistic approach to our relationship with the planet and all forms of life is the focus of this chapter.

Keywords: anthrophonic, ecocriticism, environmental health, sustainable development, eco ethics, ecological balance

This chapter aims to examine and study the various nuances of eco ethics and sustainable development through the lens of ecocriticism. Ecocriticism offers an interdisciplinary approach through which the environmental crisis being faced by the planet can be studied. The field of literature, environmental science, philosophy, and cultural studies are all examined to fix the moral and ethical responsibility that humans have towards the planet and all its inhabitants. It focuses on the need to change the approach of humans towards nature from being the conquerors and dominators to those of facilitators who harmonise human progress with ecological balance thusensuring that the Earth's resources are utilized in a manner that preserves the planet's health and diversity for future generations to be able to survive.

The issue at hand is complex; we will examine the vast and varied literature available to us. Rob Nixon in his book*Slow Violence and the Environmentalism of the Poor*focuses on the impact of wars and policies of the world institutions on the poor and marginalized people of the world. Lawrence Summers the president of the World Bank in his confidential memo advocates for shifting the "dirty industries to the Least Developed Countries". As per his logic, "countries in Africa are vastly under polluted; their air quality is probably vastly inefficiently low compared to Los Angeles". (Lawrence Summers, confidential World Bank Memo, December 12, 1991) Nixon examines how this attitude of the rich global north has led to what he refers to as 'slow violence.' He says:

We need to urgently rethink-politically, imaginatively, and theoretically-what I call "slow violence." By slow violence I mean a violence that occurs gradually and out of sight, a violence of delayed destruction that is dispersed across time and space, an attritional violence that is not typically viewed as violence at all. (2)

He states that if Summers had advocated an invasion of Africa the reaction would have been very different. Slow violence is difficult to recognise and elicits a very different reaction. According to him any calamity whose destructive impact is clearly visible will get a stronger reaction as compared to an event where the impact will be evident after a prolonged passage of time. According to him, this can be done by creating a narrative and visual imagery which can trigger an emotionalreaction.Another major concern of his is the impact of 'slow violence' on the lives of poor and disadvantaged sections of the society. The damage being done might be slow but its impact is long lasting and catastrophic.

If we look at the work of Ursula K. Heise in *Imagining Extinction: The Cultural Meanings of Endangered Specie-swe* find that she lays emphasis on the role storytellingin shaping our perceptions of biodiversity and its conservation. Culture also plays a pivotal role in how we perceive nature and its different resources. Different cultures lay emphasis on the preservation of different plants and animals. Different cultures worship different elements of nature and these belief systems get reflected in the stories, mythology, religious and cultural practices of that region. She shows how biodiversity conservation, extinction of species are issues not just of science but also the history, society and culture of the people. All this impacts how ecologically responsible certain communities and people are.

Storytelling plays an important role in shaping our perceptions of biodiversity and its conservation among different cultures and communities. Literature and culture can lead to a more empathetic, thoughtful, and sustainable engagement with the world around us. Through this we can come to a better understanding of how environmental challenges can be better addressed.

Ecocriticism has emerged as a distinctive field in the intersection ofthe study of environmental philosophy and literary criticism. Literature plays a dual role of both reflecting as well as shaping the attitude of the society in how the environment and nature are perceived by the people. Environmental philosopher Aldo Leopold has said,

We abuse land because we regard it as a commodity belonging to us. When we see land as a community to which we belong, we may begin to use it with love and respect....land is a community is the basic concept of ecology, but land is to be loved and respected is a basic concept of ethics. (XXII).

Today ecocriticism advocates the same philosophy. We need to view the planet as a community rather than as a pool of resources to be used and exploited by the humans. Ecocriticism has its roots in environmental ethics, a branch of philosophy that challenges the anthropocentric worldview. It advocates a more inclusive ethics based on the inherent value of all living beings. Literary and cultural expressions, narratives, and imagery can perpetuate or challenge harmful environmental ideologies.

Ecocriticism does not operate in isolation; it is influenced by ecofeminism, which links the exploitation of nature with the oppression of women, deep ecology, which advocates for the intrinsic value of all living beings regardless of their utility to humans among other environmental philosophies. A diverse perspective is thus provided to understand the relationship humans have with nature. Ecological science and literary critique are juxtaposed for a better understanding of the issues at hand. This engagement of science and humanities leads to a more holistic understanding of the environmental issues and the way they get portrayed in literature and culture. Rachel Carson a biologist and science writer through her book "Silent Spring" was able to bring about a radical change in the way pesticides were used in America. It is a testimony to how public Opinion can be galvanized by a well written book.

Lawrence Buell, in *The Environmental Imagination* states that:

Although the creative and critical arts may seem remote from the arena of scientific investigation and public policy, clearly they are exercising, however unconsciously, an influence upon the emerging culture of environmental concern....How we image a thing, true or false, affects our conduct towards it, the conduct of nations as well as persons.(3)

He emphasizes that language has immense power and impacts how we view the world and literary works go a long way in shaping the relationship man has with the natural world. His work highlights how ecocriticism bridges the gap between the affective dimensions of literature and the ethical imperatives of environmentalism, illustrating the field's commitment to fostering a deeper, more responsible engagement with the planet.

Ecocriticism's strength lies in its interdisciplinary approach, drawing on insights from philosophy, science, and the humanities to enrich our understanding of environmental issues. Through its cross sectional approach ecocriticism helps in arriving at a better understanding of human culture and natural environment leading to the emergence of a more ethical, sustainable, and interconnected worldview.

Ecocriticism has evolved as a complex field which reflects the complexity surrounding environmental issues. Now it encompasses fields beyond literary studies and engages with history, philosophy, media studies, and the social sciences. Although it was mainly concerned with the predominantly Anglo-American literature and landscapes, ecocriticism has broadened its scope to include diverse ecological traditions and perspectives from around the world thus acknowledging the interconnectedness of environmental issues which go beyond national and cultural boundaries. As a result the focus has shifted to examining and exploring the philosophies and literatures of other cultures and continents, native philosophies and cultural practices.

Ursula K. Heise in the book *A Sense of Place and Sense of Planet: The Environmental Imagination of the*

Global explainshow environmental issues and approaches are no longer localized but is interconnected in an increasingly globalized world linking different locales and regions. Heise writes that while,

some theorists criticize nationally based forms of identity and hold out cosmopolitan identifications as a plausible and politically preferable alternative, other scholars emphasize the importance of holding on to national and local modes of belonging as a way of resisting the imperialism of some forms of globalization (12).

Heise's central idea is of, "eco-cosmopolitanism" which according to her can be defined as an "environmental world citizenship," She mentions:

ecologically oriented thinking has yet to come to terms with one of the central insights of current theorists of globalization: namely, that the increasing connectedness of societies around the globe entails the emergence of new forms of culture that are no longer anchored in place...(13).

According to her considering the increasingly globalized world the better approach is to take up the environmental concerns and issues through this lens. Ecocriticism needs to adopt a more inclusive and international perspective.

Environmental Justice integrates social and environmental concerns, focusing on how environmental degradation excessively affects the members of marginalized and vulnerable communities. The environmental justice movement has shifted the focus on the need to address not only the ecological but also social, economic, and racial injustices being perpetuated through environmental degradation.

Evolution of ecocritical theory has been dynamic and been constantly adapting to the changing need of the hour dictated by environmental crises and cultural narratives. It has emerged as an interdisciplinary field that offers deep insights understanding about the complex relationships between human cultures and the planet.

Eco ethics has emerged as a challenge to theanthropocentric ethical frameworks that has prioritized human needs and desires, often at the expense of ecological systems and non-human entities. The era of the Anthropocene has had long lasting and harmful impact on the geology and ecosystems of the planet. Human activities have altered the Earth's ecosystem and there is an urgent need for a re-evaluation of how we interact with the natural world. Ethical concerns have to transcend the human world to include the planet in its entirety. The interaction between humans and the environment has to be more harmonious so that all can inhabit the earth in a sustainable manner. All living beings are interdependent and interconnected and nature is not merely a resource for human exploitation.

Aldo Leopold in his book *A Sand County Almanac* has argued for an expansion of ethics to include soils, waters, plants, and animals, or collectively: the land with his concept of the "land ethic". The idea of an ethical relationship with the land has had a major influence onsubsequent ecoethical thought process.Ecoethics challenges us to rethink our responsibilities and to envision a future in which human activity is in harmony with the natural world.

Henry David Thoreau in his book *Walden* reflects on living a simple life surrounded by nature and critiques the impact of industrial revolution on human life. Humans have gotten alienated from nature leading to life choices that have led to ecological degradation of the environment.His writings underline the intrinsic value of nature and the insights it offers to those who engage with it respectfully and attentively.

Barbra Kingsolver in her novel *Prodigal Summer* through three storylines celebrates the interconnectedness of life and the importance of ecological stewardship. She assimilates scientific understanding with empathetic story-telling, encouraging readers to recognize the complexity of ecosystems and the role of humans in them. She through the novel enumerates how human lives are deeply enmeshed with those of other species, each influencing the other's survival.

Margaret Atwood's through her *MaddAddam* Trilogy portrays a world ravaged by genetic engineering, corporate greed, and ecological collapse. The trilogy brings out an urgent need for adopting a more inclusive approach for the world to be able to overcome the current environmental and ethical shortcomings in the human and non-human interface. She through her work challenges her readers to find an alternative approach that will lead to a more ethical and sustainable relationship between humans and the environment.

Mary Oliver in her poem 'Wild Geese' says, "You do not have to be good... / You only have to let the soft animal of your body / love what it loves.... / Whoever you are, no matter how lonely, / the world offers itself to your imagination," She offers complex environmental and ethical insights through her work. She invites her readers to engage with nature at a deeper level to be able to get an honest understanding to enable a greater appreciation of the natural world.

Literature plays an important role in shaping the ecoethical thinking. It not only represents the reality of the damage done by a human centric approach but also challenges the anthropocentrism and advocates for a more harmonious and inclusive relationship with the environment. In order to bring about ecoethical awareness it is crucial that perception of humans toward nature is changed. This will go a long way in creating a more sustainable and just world.

According to William Cronon narrative plays a vital role in shaping our understanding of sustainability. "The challenge of sustainability is not simply one of finding the right technological solutions but of finding the right stories to tell about our place in the world." ("Uncommon Ground: Rethinking the Human Place in Nature", 1995) He moves beyond mere technological thinking of fixing the problem to addressing the core issue in a more holistic way of coexisting with nature, with it not away from it. The aim is to find a connection between human prosperity and environmental sustainability in an ecologically sustainable and ethical way.

Environmental issues have to be solved through a harmonious approach of integrating ecological, economic, and social realities. The focus in ecocritical discourse and sustainable development can no longer be just a policy objective but a cultural and ethical one. This can be envisioned through literature by imagining alternative futures and ethical landscapes.

Literature provides both dystopian views as well as positive narratives.Cormac McCarthy presents a stark, post-apocalyptic world ravaged by environmental catastrophe in his novel *The Road*. It is a cautionary tale about the dangers humanity faces if it fails to address ecological issues facing the planet. Octavia Butler through her novels *Parable of the Sower* and *Parable of the Talents* presents the themes of community resilience, environmental stewardship, and adaptive governance in the face of societal collapse. She through her writings establishes that sustainable development can be achieved through collective effort, empathy, and an ethical commitment to the planet and each other.

Kim Stanley Robinson's *Science in the Capital* trilogy highlights the possibility of reconciling technological advancement with ecological stewardship. His narratives suggest that science and technology, guided by ethical considerations and a commitment to sustainability, can play go on to play a critical role in addressing climate change and fostering a more equitable and sustainable world.

Richard Powers in his novel *The Overstory*presents a compelling narrative that spans generations and geographies.

He explores the intricate relationships between humans and the natural world by intertwining the lives of nine characters with the lives of trees. His scientific knowledge and ecological insight play a crucial role in shaping the narrative. He makes a powerful case for the conservation of forests and for recognizing trees as vital, sentient beings in their own right. Trees are depicted as characters thus challenging the anthropocentric viewpoint.

Barbara Kingsolver in the book *Flight Behavior* tackles the theme of climate change. This is achieved through the personal transformation that its main protagonist, Dellarobia Turnbow undergoes after discovering a colony of monarch butterflies that have veered off their migratory path. This has happened due to environmental changes. Kingsolver explores the complexities of addressing climate change especially in communities and societies where economic hardship and political ideologies are in the forefront thus pushing environmental concerns in the background. The novel highlights the interconnectedness of global environme-ntal issues and local livelihoods. The writer through its relatable characters and engaging narrative makes a strong case for a well thought out action and adaptive resilience in order to effectively face climate change.

We also have Mary Oliver who through her poetry both celebrates natural beauty while also lamenting its degradation. In her poems, "The Summer Day" and "Wild Geese," she draws readers attention to the inexplicable connection human life has with its environment. Through her work she urges the reader to first notice, appreciate, understand and ultimately protect the natural world. Both imagery and reflections are used to achieve this. She through her poetry encourages a shift in perspective. Instead of seeing nature in the backdrop of human activity there is a need to recognize it as a part of the interconnected web of life. We need to both respect and preserve it. Her poetry showcases the role that art, literature and poetry can play in generating an awareness about environmental issues by creating a sense of wonder towards the natural world. This will result in responsible behaviour in the reader and society.

Literature not only plays an important role in shaping the societal values and practices but also offers alternate visions. It has a critical role to play in challenging the established human centric narratives. New ethical and environmentally sustainable behavioural changes can be brought about in the society through Literature. Literary tools question the linear model of development, and challenge the fallacy that believes that uninterrupted economic growth which totally disregards the environmental costs and leads to the depletion of natural resources will result in human happiness and fulfilment.

The exploration of ecocriticism shows how literature intersects with eco ethics and sustainable development. A careful examination of various literary works, from novels and poems to speculative fiction has revealed that literature both reflects and moulds our understanding of the environment. Narratives not only challenge anthropocentric views but also advocate for a deeper ethical consideration in our interactions with the natural world, thus leading to alternative paths which will pave a way of life that is sustainable for the planet.

Ecocriticism offers critical insights into the interconnectedness of human and non-human worlds and helps in understanding the Anthropocene and makes us re-evaluate the traditional narratives of progress and development. It helps us in addressing the environmental challenges that are being faced by the world today. Literature helps us reflect on our actions by evoking empathy, which leads to positive action. It has emerged as a powerful tool that can help foster environmental consciousness and lead to ecoethical behaviour among humans.

There is a growing need to continue to engage in both intra disciplinary and interdisciplinary studies between the humanities and the sciences. This will help us in enriching our understanding of eco ethics and sustainable development. Literary studies, environmental ethics, and sustainability research taken together hold immense potential in helping us in finding a solution to the problems facing the planet today. As the poet Gary Snyder says: "Nature is not a place to visit. It is home." This statement encapsulates the essence of ecocriticism. It is through our value system, our beliefs, our thoughts, our stories, our writings and our actions that we can achieve a deeper, more respectful, and sustainable relationship with the Earth.

Works Cited:

Atwood, Margaret. *TheMaddAddam*. McClelland & Stewart, 2013.

Buell, Lawrence. *The Environmental Imagination*. Harvard University Press, 1995.

Butler, Octavia E. *Parable of the Sower*. New York: Four Walls Eight Windows, 1993.

----.*Parable of the Talents*. New York: Seven Stories Press, 1998.

Carson, Rachel. *Silent Spring*. Hughton Mifflin, 1962.

Cronon, William, ed. *Uncommon Ground: Rethinking the Human Place in Nature*.New York: W.W. Norton & Co, 1995

Heise, Ursula K. *Imagining Extinction: The Cultural Meanings ofEndangered Species*. The University of Chicago Press, 2016.

----. *Sense of Place and Sense of Planet: The Environmental Imagination of the Global*. New York: Oxford UP, 2008.

Homes, Rolston. *Conserving Natural Value*. Columbia

University Press, 1994.

Kingsolver, Barbara. *Flight Behavior*. New York: Harper Collins, 2013.

----. *Prodigal Summer*. New York: Harper Perennial, 2000.

Leopold, Aldo. *A Sand County Almanac: And Sketches Here and There*. Oxford University Press, 1949.

McCarthy, Cormac. *The Road*. Alfred A. Knopf, 2006.

Nixon, Rob. *Slow Violence and the Environmentalism of the Poor*. Harvard U P, 2013.

Oliver, Mary. *Wild Geese*.Bloodaxe Books Ltd, 2004.

Powers, Richard. *The Overstory*. New York: W. W. Norton & Company. 2018.

Thoreau, Henry David. *Walden; Or, Life in the Woods*. Boston: Ticknor & Fields, 1854

Chapter 14

Beaks of Dread : A study of Ecophobia and Environmental Crisis in "The Birds"

Garima Swami
Rohan Thomas Cherian

Abstract

"The Birds" is a short story written by Daphne du Maurier published in 1952. It is a horrifying analysis of ecophobia and environmental crisis. This paper will explore ecophobia and environmental crisis through an ecocritical reading of the short story by delving deeper into the narrative and revealing the anxieties resulting out of ecological disruptions and the broken relationship between the humans and the natural world. Through an analysis of the setting, characters, symbols and the narrative structure of the story, the paper aims to explore rich and dense ecological themes present in "The Birds". The setting of Cornish coast and the farmhouse under siege symbolically represents the vulnerability of humans, at the same time, the responses and reactions of the characters in the story presents the various attitudes towards environmental threats. The birds are the antagonistic force in the short story and embodies the destructive and malevolent side of the natural world when instigated.

Through an ecocritical reading of the story, the paper investigates the critique of anthropocentrism in the short story and highlights the need for an ecocentric approach. The short story also underlines ecological ethics, the moral responsibility of humanity towards environment and the growing concerns over its degradation and continuous exploitation. In addition to this, the prophetic commentary of the short story on present-day ecophobia reveals various anxieties surrounding loss of biodiversity, pollution, and changing climate. All in all, the short story is a cautionary tale of nature's revenge if left unchecked. The story urges to identify and accept the potential negative consequences of growing human intervention that disrupt ecology and advocates a harmonious existence along with all the non-human life forms.

Keywords: Ecophobia, environmental crisis, anxieties, climate change, avian attack, anthropocentric, ecocriticism.

"And the birds kept coming…" (Maurier 30) Daphne du Maurier's short story "The Birds" deals with the horrifying narrative of avian attack and explores the themes of ecophobia and environmental crisis. This classic story was also made into a film in 1963, directed by Alfred Hitchcock, which left a deep mark on the psyche of the audience with its chilling plot and unsettling imagery. "The Birds" serves as a critique of a frantic human relationship with the natural world.

"The Birds" delves into an alarming event of ordinary birds turning into potent threats and unleashing terror on the residents of the Cornish coast. The story not only focuses on the massive bird attacks but also serves as a symbolic representation of a more significant environmental crisis. It brings to light the psychological impact this ecological collapse has on individuals, also warning them of the potential threats of upsetting ecological equilibrium, illustrating the destructive power of nature and the deadly consequences of disrupting ecological balance.

Human relationship with nature has always been problematic as humans have always tried to assert themselves as superior to nature, exploiting its resources, slashing the forest, and enslaving the animals. Since time immemorial, literature across ages has explored this relationship and has shown how nature can be unpredictable and threatening if pushed to the very extent. In his 5th-century BC play, Aristophanes mocks the so-called superiority of humanity over nature and how much hatred they withheld for humankind:

CHORUS: Io! io! forward to the attack, throw yourselves upon the foe, spill his blood; take to your wings and surround them on all sides. Woe to them! let us get to work with our beaks, let us devour them. Nothing can save them from our wrath, neither the mountain forests, nor the clouds that float in the sky, nor the foaming deep. Come, peck, tear to ribbons. Where is the chief of the cohort? Let him engage the right wing. (Aristophanes)

Similarly, in George Orwell's 1945 novella *Animal Farm*, a group of farm animals who are cruelly treated by "the worthless parasitical human beings" (Orwell 28) decide to overthrow the masters, "only good human being is a dead one" (Orwell 44). These texts analyze the different ways in which animals react and fight against sustained oppression and violence.

This research paper explores the concept of Ecophobia- a term coined by an American journalist, George F. Will, in a 1988 *Chicago Sun* article titled "The Politics of Ecophobia," where he defines the term as "the fear that the planet is increasingly inhospitable." Later, the term was popularized by Simon C. Estok in his 1999 book, "The Ecophobia Hypothesis." He states:

It is a phobia that has largely been derieved from modernity's irrational fear of nature and hence has created an antagonist between humans and their environment. This antagonism in which humans sometimes view nature as an opponent, can be expressed toward natural physical geographies (mountains, windswept plains), animals (snakes, spiders, bears), extreme meteorological events (Shakespearean tempests, hurricanes in New Orleans, typhoons), bodily processes and products (microbes, bodily odors, menstruation, defecation), and biotic land-, air-, and seascapes" (Estok,1).

Ecophobia deals with the fear and anxiety associated with ecological threats, as showcased in "The Birds." It also provides insights into our responses to environmental catastrophes and ecological consciousness. The paper aims to explore the short story through the ecocritical lens and bring to light the complex relationship between humans and nature and their codependence. It serves as a powerful reminder of the prospective implications of ecological collapse and the urgency of acknowledging and understanding the ecological balance.

Ecocriticism, as a literary theory, offers an analytical lens through which we can examine texts that deal with themes related to the environment and their implications in literature. It emerged in the latter half of the twentieth century as a reaction against the Anthropocene, which Rangarajan, in his 2018 book *Ecocriticism*, defines as "a new era replacing Holocene in which human agency has become a significant geophysical force at par with natural forces, modifying the world's ecosystems with a greater rapidity than witnessed in any earlier period of human history." This idea opens the discourse of shifting the current flawed viewpoint of considering humans as the central agency and instead working towards prioritizing an ecocentric perspective. This allows the readers to examine and analyze ecological issues and their impact and probe questions on man's dominance over nature and the annihilation that follows.

Ecocriticism serves as the basis for analyzing the deep-rooted ecological concerns in Daphne du Maurier's "The Birds." The narrative explores the relentless avian attacks and the character's response to the ecological disruption, which can be further explored in terms of ecophobia. It delves into the themes of irrational fear, destructive and mysterious ways of nature, anxiety, and the never-ending fear of approaching death. The protagonist, Nat Hocken, desperately attempts to regain control over the bird's attacks and seeks to unfold answers to the mysterious forces of nature that work behind the deadly acts: "black winter descended in a single night" (Maurier 5).

As the story unfurls, the narrator Nat, a disabled II World War veteran, while plowing his land, notices some unusual happenings- "As the tractor traced it's path up and down the hill... the man upon it would be lost momentarily in the great cloud of wheeling, crying birds" (Maurier 1). The wheeling movement of the birds serves as a metaphor for mechanization and industrial advancement. This indicates a sharp reversal of things and shows nature gaining superiority over man. Another incident that explores this idea is when an unmade tractor driver tells Nat, "I could scarcely see what I was doing" (Maurier 1)—indicating the failure of humans to comprehend the consequences of globalization.

The story explores the drastic changes that nature exhibits, from being a source of solace to becoming a source of terror. One of the most striking features of ecophobia exhibited in the text is the sudden violent attacks of the birds. The story begins like just another day in the life of the protagonist, "Nat Hocken, because of the time of year, had been working in his garden" (Maurier 1). where the narrative is centered around humans, and nature takes a back seat. However, this ataraxic is dismantled when "Large flocks of birds were assembling on the roofs" (Maurier 10) and "The birds had been more restless than usual" (Maurier 1). Initially, Nat tries to associate this behavior with the changing climate; he states, "Winter is coming," and the birds are "Driven inland by the cold" (Maurier 8). Later, the birds start exhibiting unusual behavior, such as flapping their wings against the window shield and aggressively attacking humans. Even the sheer number of birds increases rapidly. There is not just one species that becomes aggressive but the whole of the bird flock: "Gulls," "starlings," "blackbirds," "sparrows," and "finches." (Maurier 3). "A multitude of birds" (Maurier 8). Which again indicated the abnormality of the situation and the panic and distress it created among the people. As time passes, the attacks become more frequent, aggressive, and coordinated, indicating that these avian attacks aren't natural and spontaneous but represent nature's malevolent potential.

The psychological impact on the characters also brings into light the growing sense of ecophobia. Nat is showcased as someone rational, practical, and observant, and he knows the ways of nature, as he has spent most of his life on the farm. He notices the large flocks of birds gathering around but dismisses the thought as a natural phenomenon. Nevertheless, as the story progresses and Nat himself is attacked in his own house, which is supposed to be the symbol of security and safety, it is then that he feels vulnerable and exposed. The birds, who are typically considered harmless and the embodiment of freedom, suddenly turn into uncontrollable weapons: "And the birds kept coming at him from the air, silent save for the beating wings. The terrible, fluttering wings" (Maurier 16). This instills a sense of fear, anxiety, and restlessness. He starts seeing these birds' not as individual characters but instead sees them as a collective force of wrath. "I am afraid. I am afraid of the birds" (Maurier 26). This shift in the perspective underscores the ecophobic idea of perceiving nature as an enemy. The ever-growing fear and psychosis encapsulate human behavior where they project the blame for these catastrophic events onto nature.

Another feature in the story is the inversion of the natural order. Throughout history, the narratives have always been Anthropocentric; man has always been projected as the center of the dominant force over the rest. It is firmly believed that humans are capable of controlling and dictating life on the planet. However, in "The Birds," the power dynamics are subverted. The avian attacks snatch away their sense of superiority and control from humans, leaving them vulnerable and defenseless. "A sort of frenzy had seized upon them" (Maurier 1). This reversal of roles creates the idea of existentialism among the masses as the characters understand that they are at the mercy of forces beyond their understanding, predictability, and control. This reversal of the natural order is a striking metaphor for the human race as the so-called safety walls that separate their order from chaos shatter.

The story's physical environment and setting further illustrate the theme of ecophobia. The isolated, cold, gloomy landscape of the English countryside in winter is a fitting backdrop for nature's grotesque and dark side. The harsh weather and barren land contribute to the hostile atmosphere, adding to the themes of vulnerability and isolation. The constant fear and anxiety of the bird's attack heightens this, making the outside natural world seem increasingly dangerous. "The sky was hard and leaden, and the brown hills that had gleamed in the sun the day before looked dark and bare now..." (Maurier 5). The sudden change of season from autumn to harsh winter also foreshadows the change in the natural characteristics of the birds. "The farm was lonely..The house was dark...The windows were black and opaque" (Maurier 27). The Hocken family's decision to seal the windows and doors symbolizes their isolation and an attempt to shut out the natural world and protect themselves from unexplained attacks. This heightened idea of seclusion and isolation intensifies the character's vulnerability and creates a sense of claustrophobia and dread.

Another striking aspect of ecophobia is the portrayal of the family structure as secluded from society as well as from nature. Hocken's family can be seen as the perfect example of this; they become increasingly distanced from the outside world. The radio, which serves as their only source of communication with the outside world, falls dead, leaving them stuck with their thoughts and fears without any outside scrutiny. This seclusion intensifies their fear and helplessness as they realize they are alone in this fight against nature. The physical barriers they create, be it shielding windows and gates or moving to the end of the countryside away from the crowds, become symbols of their separation from the natural world. This indicates their desperate and constant attempt at protecting themselves against the eerie forces of nature. The barrier also becomes a metaphor for the psychological and emotional distance that has developed between the human race and the natural world.

The descriptions of the environment as gloomy and dark represent the inner turmoil of the characters. The drastic weather changes, the unnatural silence, the rapidly growing number of birds, and the constant fear of death contribute to the overall idea of unease and impending doom. The birds' circular movement over the villagers' heads brings a sense of being watched: the uncertainty, uncontrollable attacks, lack of communication, and nature's unpredictability also fuel ecophobia.

The fictional apocalypse presented in "The Birds" mirrors real life environmental crises that have become a reality in contemporary times. Large number of birds are dying because of pollution, loss of habitat, and pandemics. It reminds us of the growing vulnerability of birds and interconnected ecosystems. The destruction caused by the birds in the short story can be seen as a metaphor depicting the negative consequences of human intervention in environment and its degradation. All environmental disruptions such as climate change and deforestation can be seen as mirroring the mass annihilation of birds in the short story.

The short story critiques anthropocentrism- a worldview which places humans at the center of creation- and this critique becomes very relevant especially in the context of environmental damage. The ultimate humbling of the characters (by the uprising of the birds) in "The Birds" who are initially seen as very confident in manipulating and exploiting nature is to be particularly noted. This clearly foregrounds the limitations in human comprehension and the negative consequences of their pride. The short story forces us to rethink the relationship between humans and nature, to accept and acknowledge the value of non-human lifeform.

The advocacy of ecological ethics which is central in this short story should also be noted. "The Birds" interrogates and challenges the moral responsibility of humans against the exploitation of the natural world for capitalistic gains and underlines boldly the severe ecological consequences that can arise out of such environmental disruptions due to ecological imbalance. The dimension of ecological ethics also mirrors contemporary debates around the efforts for conservation and sustainable development which highlights the importance and wellbeing of the natural world alongside humans.

In addition to this, the story also highlights ecophobia, the tendency of being anxious regarding the ecological threats which is contemporaneous. The depiction of a world under attack of the birds displays the growing sense of fear and unease because of environmental degradation and climate change. The characters in this story desperately try to survive amidst all the chaos and panic shows the real-life anxieties of the individuals in the contemporary world stricken with ecological disasters which is by large a product of the Anthropocene.

The story is relevant in the contemporary context and goes beyond fiction and should be seen as a warning for all the negative consequences of ecological exploitation and the importance of advocacy of environmental issues. The avian attack on the world in this short story should be seen as a revenge of the natural world for human exploitation of the natural world and an image of the increasing debts of humanity amassed due to unsustainable practices. Furthermore, the story has an open ending where the fate of the characters has been left uncertain which underscores the immediacy of finding solutions for the ecological damage and to create a world in harmony with the natural.

In conclusion, "The Birds" written by Daphne du Maurier turns out to be persistent study of ecophobia as well as ecological crisis. The terrifying narrative of the short story which depicts the avian antagonism explores the anxieties profoundly encircling the environmental disruption and degradation because of human intervention and greed. The setting of Cornish coast depicts anxiety resulting out of isolation and vulnerability in the face of natural adversities. The plot of avian attack on humanity is further symbolic of the nature's malevolent side that is overwhelming as well as catastrophic. All these elements of the story are woven around ecological themes that are very deeply reflecting the contemporary horrors of the twenty first century ecological concerns.

Works Cited:
Aristophanes.*The Birds*. Uncredited English translation. Project Gutenberg. www.gutenberg.org/files/3013/3013-h/3013-h.htm#link2H_4_0002. Accessed 4 July 2024.
Du Maurier, Daphne. *The Birds and other Stories.* Little Brown, 2012.
Estok, Simon C. "Ecomedia and Ecophobia."*Neohelicon*, vol. 43, 2016, pp. 127-145. doi.org/10.1007/s11059-016-0335-z.
Estok, Simon C. *The Ecophobia Hypothesis*. 1st ed., Routledge, 2018. doi.org/10.4324/9781315144689.
Orwell, George. *Animal Farm*. William Collins, 2021.

Rangarajan, Maithili. *Ecocriticism: Towards an Indian Perspective*. Pearson Education India, 2018.

Will, George F. "The Politics of Ecophobia."*Chicago Sun-Times*, Sun-Times News Group, 18 Sept. 1988, p. np.

Chapter 15

Eco linguistics

Mahima Gaur

Abstract

As a subfield of Linguistics, Ecolinguistics has become apparent as relatively interesting discipline in studying and evaluating the response of our Environment to any given Language.

This Article significantly co- relates the profound study done by the Norwegian-American Linguist Einar Haugen, the Ecological study of Language and how it is build and obtained.

Evolving in several directions, Ecolinguistics has used a variety of Linguistic tools to look into Language from the Ecological lexicon; thus aiming such issues as Bio- diversity, Sustainable Development, Climate change to Environmental justice.The Eco- centric Ideology implicates our Mother-Earth as a whole considering humans less recognizable. When Aldo Leopold coined the term, he stated in other words the relevance of all species including humans, which are inter- related in their growth proccedure.The History of Ecolinguistics can be traced to 19 70's, where it was developed as a socio- cultural, symbolic, and cognitive or Natural Ecology.In order to develop a crystal- clear understanding of Ecolinguistics it is essential to comprehend its relationship with Ecology.When the German Darwinist Ernst Haeckel first coined the concept of Ecology, he defined it as a complete science befriending Environment. Current studies done in "Distributed Language Perspective "the connection between Language and Ecology has been examined and probed in numerous ways.In other words, we can say that Ecolinguistics is a recently developed research area, which has been considered to creepe in as the most venerable branch of Linguistics with various approaches acknowledging a range of research questions. There is always an inaudible (silent) tete-a-tete between the Universeand Human souls.

Keywords: Ecology, Environment, Language, Humans, Relationship, Research.

Language can never stand in "Isolation" and transmission doesn't merely happen by manner of arrangements or succession of sounds....Language is an organized procedureand an integral, inseparable part of society and also in extricable from its terrain.

The fundamental notion here is that the practices which initiate languages form or work upon an ECOLINLINGUISTIC system where languages accumulate, increase, blend, differ; impart each other unanimously and collectively. This process is in interrelation with the environment. Language is susceptible to an exterior stimulant each single moment and it modifies to it quick. The biological similitude could be considered more relevant ---- in other words we can say that "Linguistic Ecology" has been now acknowledged as a discipline, not just an idiomatic expression. Just as Dialects voice any language sub- species too voice any Species. Einar Hangen in the general run of things is considered as the founding father of Language Ecology. According to him Language Ecology can we elucidated as the study of interactions between any given language and its milieu.

Ecology in other words appears to be a study of the natural science that establishes a connection among the living organisms, inclusive of humans and their physical environment.The focus here is twofold.

Firstly, they wish to cultivate Linguistic theories, which does deeper into contemplating that mortals not only form a civilized society as a whole but also form a substantial part of the wide reaching and wide-ranging ecosystems where life becomes pivot. Secondly, the next aim appears more practical revealing how Linguistics can be used to address social ecological affairs from atmospheric conditions and bio-diversity deprivation to environmental justice. Since the hypothesis of Ecology was applied to Language first and form most almost 50 years ago, the sphere of Eco Linguistics has taken a rapid growth as a flourishing branch of Linguistic. Einar Hangen's article "Ecology of Language" published in 1972 throws light upon the interactions between languages and multilingual surroundings. The biological understanding of Ecology in the study of language influenced Halliday's 1990 talk "New Ways of Meaning" the challenge to"Applied Linguistics". This recently developed sphere of eco linguistics has been broadly associated with Einar Hangen, the Norwegian American Linguist, who put in the metaphor of Ecology to language years ago. According to Hangen a society that uses language forms an environment including the social and cerebral surroundings of language as a whole but not the physical milieu.

He also set side by side the ecosystem between animals and plants in their environment. Ecolinguistics traverses from the part of language ---the life enduring connections of humans, the rest of the species and the tangible living world. In other words we can say, that just the way in which we endeavor and work upon diligently in order to rescue and save guard the endangered species we need language Ecology so as to preserve our endangered languages. Eco linguistics thus appears to be a thriving branch of linguistics. M.A.K.Halliday (1990) in his plenary address at the 10th AICA Congress,Greece said-- Language does not passively reflect reality; Language actively creates reality.Our reality is not something ready made and waiting to be meant- it has to be actively construed; and language evolved in the process of, and as the agency of, it's construal. An Architype of linguistic exploration came into view in the 1990s and took into consideration that language is implanted not only in the social factors or circumstances but also in the ecological surroundings too where all societies are embedded.

Let's have a look at the "Anthropocentrism" approach where the primary attention of linguistics is human language; how humans are upper and higher; how they have a substantial value and the privilege to exercise control over.The principles of Anthropocentrism also states that the other species must give way to humans and also that the worth of other species is determined and assessed by their serviceability to Humans.

This approach fundamentally is centered on human language the Linguistic Proficiency and accomplishment, as humans had a deep influence on societies of all kinds forming our bonding with the rest of the natural world. "Ecocentrism" is another term used by environmentalist and philosophers stating the relevance of all living beings and their invaluable contribution to the environment.

This philosophy believes that economic enlargement shouldn't be prioritized over safeguarding other species. Some areas of Mother Earth needs to be kept safe from human use and "non human animals" perspective needs to be demonstrated.

Ecocentrism in fact becomes inevitable for the sustainability of natural resources. It observes the impact of environmental wellbeing not only upon human species but also on other living species and abiotic elements. ALDO LEOPOLD has been ascribed as the initial Ecocentrism based on his writing in the late 1940's.

The Sustainable Development Goals (SDGs) are almost all associated with the environment. Eco linguistics isn't against constructing factories, electricity and developments but they wish to work for it through a sustainable way. SDG look about for a congenial life for one and all while preserving the environment for the coming generations.

The United Nations formulated the millennium development goals and attempted to achieve them from 2000 to 2015. Another key concept that has lately emerged with SDGs and eco linguistics is INTERSECTIONALITY. It talks about the overlapping of SDG s and social issues. Arran Stibby(2021) "Stories we Live By" talk about the stories which influence our thoughts and minds. STORIES here represent a different perspective of the people-" what we think what we do"

One story is IDEOLOGY for example for some people their value they feel is determined by money and possessions--this promotes an "Anthrocentric Ideology". Others believe that their values denote the way they help others, how they behave, interact and their talent and skill they possess. This belief may promote Ecocentric Ideology.

Another kind of story is a could be told as a Metaphor- Mother Earth can be an ecocentric encouraging environmental protection just as we may feel obligation to look after a mother's who raised us who bears so much without complaining and grudging.

Contrary to this an "Anthropocentric metaphor" could refer to the term "Harvest" which usually matches or juxtaposes with crops, also to the deed of butchering animals for food. The Harvest Metaphor appears "Antopocentric" as it disapproves the sentence (the thinking and feeling potential) of the animals through whom we get eggs, meat and other dairy products to build the unfair treatment not so much acceptable. Ecocentrictextual works focus on such major hallmarks of the real world.

The Ecolinguistics Analysis of "CIVIT COFFEE" well known in Indonesia as "KOPI LUWAK" too highlighted about the harm done to these innocent civets (mammals native to Africa and Asia) in order to make profit in producing coffee. The high priced Gourmet coffeeis prepared from the Civets waste as they are held captives and are compelled to feed on Coffee Beans in spite of it being not a normal part of their diet. As Ecological crisis is also a sort of communication, manifesting itself specifically in language, Ecolinguistics may justifiably be expected to play an important role in the mastering of the crisis.

"A vision and a conviction shared by most ecolinguistics is that research findings should contribute to sustaining diversity and the protection of animals" (Trampe 2018: 336)

Works Cited:

Bang, Jorgen and Wilhelm Trampe. *Aspects of an Ecological theory of Language*. Language Sciences. 2014. pp. 41-83-92

Kravchenko,Alexander. Two views on Language Ecology and Ecolinguistics.*Language Sciences.*2016 pp. 54. (102-113)

Nash, John. Is Ecolinguistics necessary? *Ecolinguistica: Revista brasileira de ecologiaelinguagem* (ECO-REBEL) 2 (2).2018. pp. 36-43.

Stibbe Arran. ed. Ecolinguistics and Globalization. In Nikolas Coupland, 2012.

Stibbe, Arran. "Ecolinguistics Language, Ecology and the Stories We Live By".*The Handbook of Language and Globalization*. Singapore: Wiley-Blackwell. pp. 406-425.

Chapter 16

Echoes of Progress: An Ecological Study of Arati Kumar Rao's Travel Narrative "Marginlands : Indian Landscapes on the Brink"

Shweta Kundu

Abstract

This paper delves into the intricate relationship between the ecocriticism, capitalism, and the evolving landscape and its effects on people and nature as depicted in the Marginlands (2023) by Arti Kumar Rao. In an era marked by environmental crises and rapid technological advancements, the concept of the Anthropocene captures the profound impact of human activities on the planet. Simultaneously, the relentless growth of capitalism has reshaped economic structures and intensified the commodification of nature and labour. This study aims to unravel the nuanced narratives that illuminate the precarious lives of individuals navigating the Anthropocene within a capitalist framework. Literature serves as a rich tapestry reflecting the complex relationships between humans, the environment, and the ever- evolving world. Drawing on ecocritical perspectives, the paper seeks to analyse the systemic tensions between environmental sustainability and the relentless pursuit of profit. Additionally, it examines how the development is affecting various landscapes in India such as the Ganges, the Thar Desert, the coast lines of the country, the Sundarbans and many more. The paper focuses on how people and environment negotiate the challenges posed by both the development and capitalism. This paper contributes to our understanding of the intersections between literature, environmental consciousness, and socio-economic transformations byanalysing the narrative through the ideas of Ramachandra Guha. By exploring the ways inwhich literature navigates the complexities of the capitalism, this study aims to foster criticaldialogue on sustainable futures.

Keywords: Ecocriticism, Capitalism, cultural materialism, development, nature.

All literary writings define the surroundings they are set in; thus, nature has always been an integral part of literature. But eco-criticism is a new area of study, which finds its origins in the environmental movements of the 1960s and 1970s, when people started understanding the impact that human activities such as deforestation, mining, and the use of chemicals, plastic, and fossil fuels have on the environment.

Life came out of nature, and thus humans are a part and product of nature. With the passage of time Man started considering that he is at centre and everything around him exists to aid him in his purpose. This placed Man above nature, which led to over-consumption of natural resources. Post industrial urbanization resulted in degradation of nature in all the spears, i.e., soil, air, water, animals and plants. The environmental degradation as a result has reached to a level that climate of the planet now depends on human activities, this is known as the Anthropocene. The *Cambridge Dictionary* defines Anthropocene epoch as "the most recent period in the earth's history, when human activities have a very important effect on the earth's environment and climate"

Many geologists believe that humans have altered the earth so much since the start of the industrial revolution that we are now living in a new epoch called the Anthropocene.

Rachel Carson's *Silent Spring* (1962) highlighted the threats posed to human health and natural systems by unregulated economic growth. Many environmental movements started taking place around the world after the 1960s, e.g., the Chipko Andolan and the Narmada BachaoAndolan in India, Chico Mandes's rubber-tapper movement in Brazil, and Wangari Matthai's tree-planting Campaign in Africa, and many more. The movements taking place around the world helps in making the environmental policies a bit more sensitive in many countries. Universities started running courses on environmental studies. According to Ramchandra Guha in *Environmentalism* (2000) "Elements of an environmental consciousness had, finally, begun to permeate the middle class." (xiv)

Cheryll Glotfelty has advocated for an ecocritical perspective that encourages a deeper connection with nature through literature. She posits that this perspective allows to appreciate the interplay between culture and the environment. By reading nature-oriented texts, helps in understanding the diverse ways in which literature portrays man's relationship with the natural world, whether as a source of inspiration, a means of reflection, or a catalyst for change.

In contrast to the serene vision of nature presented by Glotfelty, Harold Fromm introduces a more complex aspect of ecocriticism. Fromm challenges people to confront the darker aspects of our environmental history, addressing issues like pollution, exploitation, and the degradation of ecosystems. He encourages exploring literature that critically engages with the environmental issues and reflects the collective responsibility of human beings towards the state of the planet. Fromm believes acknowledging mistakes is the first step towards ecological redemption.

Cheryll Glotfelty defines ecocriticism as the study of the relationship between literature and the physical environment. A question may arise does nature requires a text-based theory to recognize ecological disasters and pollution as a serious issue? Pramod K. Nayar, in *Contemporary Literary and Cultural Theory* (2010), explains that the task of ecocriticism "is to see how theoretically informed readings of cultural texts can contribute not only to consciousness-raising but also look into the politics of development and the construction of 'nature'." because theory "is the analytic practice that shows us various contours of the real world" (241). Ecocriticism as a theory is more realistic as compared to other literary theories. Peter Barry in *Beginning Theory: An Introduction to Literary and Cultural Theory* (1995), says that Eco-critics "turn away from the 'social constructivism' and 'linguistic determinism' of dominant literary theories (with their emphasis on the linguistic and social construction of the external world) and instead emphasize eco-centric values of meticulous observation, collective ethical responsibility, and the claims of the world beyond ourselves." (270)

Travel writing as a genre provides a unique space for exploring human interactions with landscapes, cultures, and environment. Every travel account starts with a description of the non-human world of the place the author is referring. Therefore, it can be said that the knowledge about the non-human world and human civilization is deeply rooted in travel narratives. As Casey Blanton says, "close links between nature and travel writing that have alwaysexisted within the genre" (xiii) in the preface of *Travel Writings: The Self and the World (2002).*

Michael Cronin, in his book *Eco-Travel* (2022), points out that encounter between human and nature cannot be separated from the history of travel. Nature, in one form or another, is curled up with the story of human mobility. In order to create awareness, movement is necessary. Global environmental awareness is possible only when people visit places because there can be no observation, comparison or analysis without displacement. Travel writings provide a subtle medium to sensitize the readers because they are not monotonous and do not only contain monotonous facts. The world only becomes legible by a book. These travel writings play a dual role: description and classification. What readers cannot see for themselves, they can indirectly see through these travel accounts, illustrations or maps provided by the travelers. Global awareness requires global travelling. How readers view the places they are reading about depends on how travel writers choose to represent a place or a landscape. Cronin talks about Diana K. Davis's idea of the phenomenon is termed 'environmental imagery', whichmeans, "the constellation of ideas that groups of humans develop about a given landscape"(13). This can be understood by the example of travel writings composed by English travelers who reached Britain before or during the colonial period. These writings were the source behind the perception that the Empire formed about different places and nations on earth, such as in JosephConrad's *Heart of Darkness* (1902). In a similar fashion, these writings result in forming perceptions in the minds of readers. An ecologically aware writer has the capability to put forth his concerns in his works, which will lead to the development of eco-consciousness in his readers.

With the advent of industrial revolution, the industrial revolution, the phenomenon of capitalization, materialism, and utilitarianism came into existence. These realities have foregrounded human beings as very powerful. Human beings to meet their will and to extent their empire, they began to exploit nature and its several forms. The centrality of human beings amid nature has reduced the nature as an object of human desire. Human beings, to gain economic power, capital growth and the extension of the empire have exploited different dimensions of nature what is generally known as Anthropocene. Judith Butler calls it the 'condition of precarity'. Vlardimir Vernadsky in his article "Scientific Thought as a Geological Force" (1938) initially used the term Anthropocene. John Green in his *The Anthropocene Reviewed* (2021) has underlined the importance of the degrading effect of human endeavors on nature. The phenomenon of Anthropocene underlines and explores the conditions of ecosystems, climate change, loss of biodiversity etc.

The current geological age, viewed as the period during which human activity has been the driving force behind climate change and environmental degradation. Human activity is shapingthebiodiversity of the planet.The author Arti Kumar Rao travels to various parts of India, documenting her journey to the various vulnerable landscapes of the county. In an era marked by environmental crisis and rapid technological advancements, the concept of Anthropocene captures the profound impact of human activity. The relentless growth of capitalism has shaped the economic structures, and intensified the commodification of nature.

For example, the author says "in the boundless thar, deemed a wasteland by the authorities, miners bulldoze sand dunes guarding life-sustaining water."

We, humans, have stamped deserts as wastelands because of sand. But these places are fully functioning ecosystems. The sand dunes serve as protective guards for whatever small amount of water sources the place has. Mining and other such activities pose a great danger to even weather of the whole of north-west India, including Haryana, east Rajasthan, Delhi, and west Uttar Pradesh.

I would like to draw attention to the case of Aravalli hills. There are two parts of Rajasthan, one which is the desert and the other which is more like any other north Indian state, receive stable rainfall.Because of the Aravalli range, clouds just pass away from the dry part without raining. But what Aravalli does is clouds smash into the mountains and the other part of Rajasthan Haryana and Delhi receive rainfall because of it. The author brings attention to the vanishing Aravalli. We want marble for our home; therefore it is being mined for quite some centuries. Over the years, one can note difference in the height of the mountain too.

The case of corroding beaches of Kerala. The author visits many beaches and talks to the fishermen who live alone the coastlines, e.g. Shanghumukham (Tiruvantapuram) beach is the urge of being swallowed by the sea. Due to the increasing sea-levels many beaches around the world are bring engulfed by the sea. This world also effects the communities living on the coastline.

Due to natural and human induced climate change, India's most endangered landscape is being pushed to verge of destruction, the flora, the fauna, and the people who are dependent on forests for their living are bring effected.

Ramachandra Guha and Madhav Gadgil in *Ecology and Equity* point out that "India today is a veritable cauldron of social conflicts, many of which pertain directly to the control and use of natural resources." (2)

A person walking through India would immediately recognise the chronic shortage of natural resources faced by all the segments of Indian society. Ramchandra Guha and Madhav Gadgil in *Ecology and Equity* claim that

"fisherfolk are faced with the exhaustion of fish stock, shifting cultivators with the declining availability of forest land. Mat weavers are running short of reeds and peasants are short of dung with which tomanure their fields. Millions among the urban poor are shelter-less and without adequate water supply. Irrigated farmlands are tuning saline and whole coconut orchards are dying of disease.Paper mills are starved of their favourite raw material, bamboo, and textile mills are plagues by power cuts. City roads clogged with traffic and city air is full of noxious fumes. The ever-growing numbers of Indians, their exploding appetite conspired to ensure that all segments of society are in the midst of one resource crunch or another." (1-2)

The Sundarbans are the largest marsh of the world. This

area protects the people from the dangerous floods by reducing the impact of the floods. Arati Kumar Rao points out how life of fisher-men has changed due to loss of pray which was mainly the Hisla fish. She tells

"Everywhere I have gone. I have met Bengalis who would tell me of bygone times whne they could plunge their hands into the Meghna or the Podda rivers (the Ganga takes the name Padma in Bangladesh, which in Bengali is pronounced pod-da) and came up with shimmering 2.5-kilogram *ilishmaachh*...But increasingly such narratives are tinged with a forlorn nostalgia as this king fish disappears from its habitat." (106)

This has affected the lives of many fishermen. The author shares the experience of the fisher-men she met. They require specialised nets for the Hilsa fish which cost roughly $12,000 and boats which cost $15,000. They are living in debt because of such hight cost of investment and the decreasing amount of fish in the river. Some years back they would go out for an hour and get enough fish for the day but now it is impossible to find enough fish for every crewmember even in a whole day. (107)

In order to catch more fish these fishermen have to go deep into the forest to catch more fish. The author brings attention to the crab-catchers in the Sundarbans. Crab catching activities have increased in the mangrove forests of the Sundarbans. Earlier crabs were available on the outskirts of the forest but now due to increased hunters, many people have to row their boats deep in the forest where they got attacked by tigers. This is so frequent that the widows of the people who are attacked by tigers have been given a name "tiger-widow". She describes this as a sad situation when no-one is doing anything. The tribes are poor and the dangerous endeavour is their only chance at survival. The author narrates a story, one of many such incidents where a man named Nabin was pulled from the boat by a tiger, and this incident took place when he had gone deep into the forest to catch crabs (141). She also talks about a man named Asit Mandal who was attacked by a tiger while catching crabs, he was fortunate enough to be saved by his brother and nephew (146).

Communities have been living and thriving in this so-called wasteland for centuries, they have come up with ways to use the resources available to them and building things such as *khadeen* and *aagor*. This astonished Mahmud Shah in 1273 AD (25). There have been many government projects such as "Indira Gandhi Nahar Project (IGNP) is one of the most gigantic projects of the world aimed at de-desertify and transform desert wasteland into agriculturally productive area (39)". But the experience of the locals has not been satisfactory with the *nahars*. The water stinks with the smell of dead bodies of animals. They do not use the *nahar* water for drinking; they are dependent on the wells, *beris*, and other traditional sources for drinking water (40).

Talking about the Thar Desert the author says "to the untrained it is a wasteland: barren, arid, infertile, uncultivable" (24). In 1982-1988, supreme court of "India gave a landmark judgment against limestone quarrying in the lower Himalaya. The mines that hollowed out the Dehradun valley were declared illegal under the Forest Conservation Act" (38) this forced the government to find a new source of limestone, which "They found it in deserts north of Jaisalmer: high-quality limestone, low in silica, perfectly suited for the county's burgeoning steel industry. Bonus: no forest in the area for theSupreme Court to champion" (38).This also accompanied the National Wasteland Development Board's aim to bring "wastelands in the country into productive use through a massive programme of afforestation and tree plantations and for improving land productivity" (38). When the government started mining limestone, those mine mines emptied the *beris* and wells of the areas, which were a source of drinking water for the locals (41). The smaller *nahars* are dry and the area is truly turning into a wasteland because of lack of well-researched projects.

In the chapter "The Farakka Folly", the author talks about the numerous times since the British times when people have tried to tame the river Ganga and the river has pushed back all the attempts. It was until the construction of numerous dams, which obstructed the flow of the river. These affected lives of many communities living on the shore of the river. In the next chapter ("A Fleeting Flash of Fin"), the author talks about how the construction of dams has negatively affected the river and its life. In 2015 Nitish Kmar said "constructing more dams between Allahabad and Haldia will convert the Ganga into big ponds" (74). Construction of dams and other polluting agents such as factory waste have made the Ganga vulnerable. The flow of river has reduced, thus affecting life in the river. Gangetic dolphins' struggleto survive, in the river where it was an apex predator, because dams fragment the habitat and shipping also affects them largely.

The 2016 National Waterways Act identifies 106 rivers which will be converted into cargo-carrying waterways, because according to the administration it is more 'greener' than road traffic. But while passing the Act there were no discussions about the ecological impacts, or the impact it will have on the riverine life. Converting the river into waterway will require taking out sand (this process is called dredging) from the river bed time to time, so that boats can move without obstruction. Some species live on the river bed, "dredging disrupts and scoops out these breeding and feeding grounds endangering the survival of the species (74)". There has been a large decline in the population of the Gangetic dolphins because its habitat has been fragmented and also it has lost its food source to dredging.

The above stated examples are proof that the modern way of living is highly imbedded in consumerism and materialism. Climate change and environmental crisis are considered to be the most devastating global issues at present, chiefly caused by the anthropocentric activities in this post-globalization era. Industrialization and globalization are the pivotal triggers in developing the culture of consumerism across the world among human beings. The global environmental crisis is threatening the ecological balance and forcing the humans to examine the complex intersections where the environmental problems merge with the humanitarian crisis. Excessive exploitation of natural resources leading to the extinction of indigenous cultural values and practices is one of the outcomes of such intersectional complexity. Nature has been reduced to a means of fulfilling human desires and greed. Amitav Ghosh has even gone so far as to say that the carbon driven capitalist global economy of this human-centric civilization has deteriorated the environmental conditions to such an extent that even if no carbon emitting fossil fuels are to be used henceforth, still some consequences are bound to hit the human communities. These human instigated environmental devastations have detrimental effects leading to abnormal temperature rising, extreme weather condition, constant rising of sea levels causing inundation of coastal regions, abrupt wildfires and many other world-wide cataclysmic occurrences as well. The paper elucidates on environmental violence by state sponsored agendas and neocolonial enterprises, drawing on Arati Kumar Rao's portrayal of anthropogenic factors, subaltern migration, climate change, ecological disruptions, and environment refugees.

Conclusion

Industrialism, capitalism and consumerism have exceeded their stay. Human activities are centred on only economic growth. This economy centred mindset has driven the earth to a point of destruction. The governments all over the world need to consider the ecological impacts of any projects and acts they pass. Vast and detailed researches are required in order to study how will a particular project effect the biodiversity of the area and how will it effect the people living in those areas. The people living in the ecologically sensitive area are the ones worst affected by any disruption in their habitat. Human need to understand that the earth belongs to every form of life equally. Human activities should be planned in such manners that they do not harm any other life form. Human activities have put their own survival at risk. This rear has been breaking heat records every day. In a couple of years, the heat will be above human survivability levels. Man needs to be sensitive towards the environment, even if he does not want to think about other living things and the earth itself, for his own good.

Works Cited:

Rao, A Kumar. *Marginlands: Indian Landscapes on the Brink*. Picador India, 2023, New Delhi.

Carson, R. *Silent Spring*. Penguin Books, 2000, London.

Cronin, M. *Eco-Travel: journeying in the Age of Anthropocene*. eds. Nandini Das and Tim Youngs, Cambridge University Press, 2022.

Green, J. *The Anthropocene Reviewed: Essays on a Human-Centered Planet*. Dutton Penguin, 2001.

Guha, R. *Environmentalism: A Global History*. Penguin Books, 2000.

Guha, R. and Madhav Gadgil.*Ecology and Equity: the use and abuse of nature in contemporary India*. Penguin Books, 1995.

Chapter 17

Ecological Cognition along with Green Metacognition essential for Green politics and Eco politics

Anita John

Abstract

Alok Shukla, a 43-year-old environmentalist, emerged as a beacon of hope for the preservation of Chhattisgarh's lungs, the Hasdeo forests, winning the prestigious Goldman Environmental Prize. His achievement brought to light a transformative perspective on the necessity of green politics. Shukla's endeavors elucidated that safeguarding the environment transcends mere confrontations with governmental and corporate entities involved in coal mining and deforestation; it embodies a quest for genuine democracy. The pursuit of green politics initiatives encompass a spectrum of actions, from protecting natural ecosystems to promoting renewable energy sources, advocating for conservation measures, mitigating climate change impacts, promoting social equity, transitioning to a green economy, reforming political systems, fostering global cooperation, conducting mass education and awareness campaigns, and maximizing community engagement.

In essence, green metacognition integrates environmental awareness with metacognitive skills, enabling individuals to reflect on their thinking processes and apply cognitive strategies to address environmental challenges effectively. Encouraging introspection, critical evaluation of environmental information, sustainable planning and implementation, collaborative problem-solving, and grassroots activism are integral to nurturing green metacognition. Leaders such as Jacinda Ardern, Angela Merkel, Emmanuel Macron, Justin Trudeau, Xi Jinping, Greta Thunberg, and

Narendra Modi have demonstrated green metacognition through their commitment to environmental sustainability and advocacy for green initiatives at national and international levels.

A 43-year-old environmentalist, Alok Shukla, the crusader to save the lungs of Chhattisgarh, the Hasdeo forests who won the Goldman Environmental prize has given a completely new perspective to the need of GREEN POLITICS. Having a safe environment to live in is a part of the constitutional right to life.He made the tribal's understand that Hasdeo forest protection movement is not just a fight with the government and corporations involved in coal mine rigging and deforestation, but a fight to attain true democracy. This is a fight for every farmer who would have to bear the long term effects of climate change on impacting monsoon cycle. It is a fight of every environmentalist working for wildlife conservation. Only when every citizen is able to rise from the geographical boundaries of regions,cross cultural boundaries and make every environmental movement as a Jan Andolan , mass movement, will we be able to bring mass awakening for our constitutional, legalrights, and the need for a green planet for the future.

"Green Parties in a Post-Growth Society: New Politics and Regional Development" by Michael O'Neill, published in 2015, explores the role of green political parties in promoting sustainable development within the context of a post-growth society. The book delves into the evolving political landscape where traditional models of economic growth are being questioned in favor of more sustainable and equitable alternative.

Sustainability in a local context involves not only environmental practices such as energy conservation, but also policy efforts to involve communities, develop organizational capacity, and encourage widespread adoption.Sustainability leadership is the promotion of a variety of practices, over time, by a broad array of actors including council members, citizens, state legislators, and others—that is, the type of social change leadership defined by Van Wart in *Dynamics of Leadership*. However, the key role of public administrators in local sustainability has largely been ignored in the literature. Using a national database from U.S. cities, this study provides an organizational-change explanation of the important sub roles of administrators in local sustainability. It finds that administrators can have a substantial function in sustainability leadership by engaging citizens, enhancing technical expertise, mobilizing financial resources, and developing managerial execution capacity for sustainability. Effective administrators help overcome dispersed public perspectives, organizational constraints, and technical challenges in local sustainability, which can result in better organizational performance of sustainability policies.

Green politics initiatives encompass a broad spectrum of movements, policies, and actions dedicated to advancing environmental sustainability, social justice, and ecological responsibility. Here's an outline of some fundamental aspects of green politics initiatives:

1. **Environmental Protection**: At the heart of green politics lies the commitment to safeguarding the environment. This encompasses endeavors to tackle climate change, advocate for sustainable development practices, safeguard biodiversity, diminish pollution, and conserve natural resources.

2. **Transition to Renewable Energy**: Green politics advocates for shifting from fossil fuels to renewable energy sources like solar, wind, hydroelectric, and geothermal power. This transition aims to curtail greenhouse gas emissions and reduce dependence on finite resources.

3. **Conservation Practices**: Conservation initiatives prioritize the preservation of natural habitats, protection of endangered species, and promotion of sustainable land use practices. This includes establishing protected areas,

implementing wildlife conservation programs, and endorsing sustainable agriculture and forestry practices.

4. **Climate Change Mitigation**: Green politics underscores the pressing need to combat climate change by slashing carbon emissions and adapting to its repercussions. This involves advocating for policies such as carbon pricing, emissions regulations, energy efficiency measures, and international agreements such as the Paris Agreement.

5. **Pursuit of Social Justice**: Green politics intersects with social justice concerns, recognizing that environmental degradation disproportionately affects marginalized communities. Initiatives in this realm aim to combat environmental racism, address economic inequality, and rectify the unequal distribution of environmental advantages and burdens.

6. **Transition to a Green Economy**: Green politics advocates for transitioning to a green economy that prioritizes sustainability, equity, and well-being over GDP growth and profit maximization. This encompasses initiatives like investing in green technologies, generating green jobs, and encouraging sustainable consumption and production practices.

7. **Political Reform**: Green politics pushes for political reform to dismantle systemic barriers to environmental and social progress. This may entail campaign finance reform, electoral reform, and the promotion of participatory democracy and grassroots activism.

8. **Global Collaboration**: Recognizing the global nature of environmental challenges, green politics stresses the significance of international cooperation and diplomacy. This entails collaborative efforts with other nations to tackle issues like climate change, biodiversity loss, and environmental pollution.

9. **Education and Awareness Campaigns**: Green politics initiatives strive to raise public awareness about

environmental issues and empower individuals to take action. This includes educational programs, public outreach campaigns, and endeavors to promote environmental literacy and civic engagement.

10. **Community Engagement Maximization**: Green politics places value on community involvement and grassroots activism as pivotal drivers of social and environmental change. Initiatives in this domain concentrate on empowering local communities to engage in decision-making processes, implement sustainable solutions, and advocate for their interests.

These initiatives are often championed by political parties, advocacy groups, non-governmental organizations (NGOs), and grassroots movements dedicated to advancing environmental sustainability and social justice. Only when green metacognition is included in all national and international school curricula to sensitize children from young age will we be able to produce responsible citizens, conscientious politicians, administrators, and alert media in every nation.

"Ecological cognition" amalgamates elements of environmental consciousness ("green") with metacognition, which pertains to the capacity to contemplate and manage one's own thought processes. Essentially, ecological cognition entails pondering how our cognitive faculties can be harnessed to tackle environmental challenges and advance sustainability.

Here are several instances to elucidate the notion of ecological cognition:

1. **Evaluating Personal Environmental Impact**: Ecological cognition involves individuals introspecting on their behaviors and consumption patterns to comprehend their environmental footprint. This may entail critically assessing daily routines like energy usage, transportation preferences, and waste generation, and contemplating how these routines could be adjusted to mitigate environmental harm.

2. **Scrutinizing Environmental Information**: Ecological cognition also encompasses critically analyzing information pertaining to environmental issues. This entails scrutinizing information sources, evaluating the accuracy and reliability of data, and being cognizant of potential biases or misinformation. Through engaging in metacognitive processes, individuals can make more judicious decisions regarding environmental matters and potential solutions.

3. **Strategizing and Executing Sustainable Practices**: Ecological cognition extends to devising and implementing sustainable practices. This involves establishing objectives to diminish one's environmental impact, formulating strategies to attain those objectives, and reflecting on progress over time. For instance, an individual practicing ecological cognition might set a target to decrease household energy consumption, devise a plan to achieve this objective (such as installing energy-efficient appliances or adjusting thermostat settings), and regularly evaluate their progress and make adaptations as necessary.

4. **Collaborative Troubleshooting**: Ecological cognition can also entail collaborative problem-solving and decision-making processes. This could involve engaging in dialogues with others to pinpoint environmental challenges, brainstorming potential solutions, and reflecting on the efficacy of different approaches. By collaborating and leveraging collective metacognitive abilities, groups can devise innovative solutions to intricate environmental dilemmas.

In summary, ecological cognition underscores the significance of reflective contemplation and self-regulation within the realm of environmental consciousness and sustainability. By employing metacognitive skills to address environmental issues, individuals and communities can make more deliberate and impactful decisions to foster a healthier planet.

World leaders who have shown Green Metacognition
Jacinda Ardern (New Zealand):

Ardern has shown green metacognition through her government's commitment to addressing climate change. New Zealand passed the Zero Carbon Act in 2019, which sets a target of zero net carbon emissions by 2050 ·and establishes a framework for emissions reduction. Ardern's government has also banned new offshore oil and gas exploration permits as part of efforts to transition towards reneable energy sources.

Angela Merkel (Germany):

Merkel has demonstrated green metacognition through her leadership on environmental policies in Germany and the European Union. Germany has set ambitious targets for renewable energy deployment, with a goal of generating 65% of its electricity from renewable sources by 2030. Merkel has also been instrumental in shaping EU climate policies, including the European Green Deal, which aims to make the EU carbon-neutral by 2050 One of the longest standing **global leaders in sustainability**, former Chancellor of Germany Angela Merkel was a picture-perfect example of what leadership for sustainability should look like. Serving Germany from 2005-2021, she oversaw Germany's transition to renewable energy and pledged to phase out both coal-fired and nuclear power plants. In 2019, the German government announced a plan to achieve net-zero greenhouse gas emissions by 2050.Merkel has also been an active participant in international climate negotiations, including the United Nations Climate Change Conferences. In 2015, she played a crucial role in brokering the Paris Agreement. For her climate conscious efforts, Merkel has received numerous awards and accolades, including the UN's Champions of the Earth award and *TIME* magazine's Person of the Year award in 2015.

Emmanuel Macron (France)

Macron has shown green metacognition through his government's emphasis on environmental issues and sustainability. France has implemented measures to promote renewable energy; including increasing the share of renewables in the energy mix and phasing out coal-fired power plants. Macron has also supported initiatives such as the Paris Agreement and has called for stronger international action to address climate change. Serving as the President of France since 2017, Emmanuel Macron is an outspoken advocate for climate action, both domestically and internationally, having described "climate change as the biggest issue we are facing". Macron has introduced a number of measures aimed at reducing France's greenhouse gas emissions and promoting renewable energy, including a new climate plan to reduce France's reliance on nuclear power and increase domestic renewable energy generation to 40% by 2030. He's also been a leading voice in international climate negotiations and a vocal supporter of the Paris Agreement. He's also a champion of biodiversity protection through legal protection of wild regions in France and his revolutionary concept of biodiversity credits (in the same vein as climate credits) was introduced at COP27.For his environmental leadership, Macron has received numerous awards and accolades, including the United Nations' Champions of the Earth award and the Global Citizen Award for World Leader.

Justin Trudeau (Canada)

Trudeau has demonstrated green metacognition through his government's commitment to environmental protection and sustainable development. Canada has implemented a nationwide carbon pricing system, invested in clean energy technologies, and pledged to achieve net-zero emissions by 2050. Trudeau has also emphasized the importance of indigenous knowledge and community involvement in environmental decision-making.

Xi Jinping (China)

Jinping has shown green metacognition through his government's recognition of the importance of environmental sustainability. China has implemented ambitious plans to reduce air and water pollution, increase renewable energy deployment, and achieve carbon neutrality by 2060. Jinping has also emphasized the need for green development and ecological conservation as priorities for China's future. Jinping, as the President of China, has pledged to prioritize environmental protection and sustainable development. China has committed to reaching peak carbon emissions by 2030 and achieving carbon neutrality by 2060. Jinping's government has implemented various measures to promote renewable energy and reduce air and water pollution.

Greta Thunberg (Sweden)

While not a political leader in the traditional sense, Greta Thunberg has had a significant impact on global environmental politics. As a young climate activist, she has inspired millions of people around the world to take action on climate change and has spoken at various international forums, urging political leaders to prioritize environmental issues.

Narendra Modi (India)

Prime Minister Narendra Modi of India has demonstrated a commitment to environmental sustainability and green initiatives through various policies and initiatives. Here are some ways in which he has shown green metacognition:

Renewable Energy Targets: Modi has set ambitious targets for renewable energy generation in India. The country aims to achieve 175 gigawatts (GW) of renewable energy capacity by 2022 and has further extended this goal to 450 GW by 2030. This includes targets for solar, wind, hydro, and other renewable energy sources, demonstrating a recognition of the importance of transitioning to cleaner energy sources.

International Climate Leadership: Modi has played a prominent role in international climate negotiations and has positioned India as a leader in the global fight against climate change. India was a key player in the negotiation of the Paris Agreement in 2015, and Modi has reiterated India's commitment to the agreement and to achieving its climate goals.

Clean India Mission (Swachh Bharat Abhiyan): The Clean India Mission, launched by Modi in 2014, aims to address sanitation and cleanliness issues across India. This includes initiatives to improve waste management, promote sanitation practices, and reduce pollution. The mission reflects an understanding of the linkages between environmental cleanliness, public health, and quality of life.

International Solar Alliance (ISA): Modi launched the International Solar Alliance in 2015 with the aim of promoting solar energy deployment globally. The alliance brings together countries that are rich in solar resources to collaborate on solar energy projects, research, and capacity building. By championing solar energy on the global stage, Modi has shown a commitment to renewable energy and climate action.

Afforestation Initiatives: Modi has emphasized the importance of afforestation and reforestation in combating climate change and environmental degradation. Initiatives such as the Green India Mission and the National Afforestation Programme aims to increase forest cover, restore degraded land, and enhance biodiversity. These efforts reflect an understanding of the role of forests in carbon sequestration and ecosystem services.

Electric Mobility and Clean Transportation: The Indian government under Modi has introduced various policies and incentives to promote electric mobility and reduce vehicular emissions. Initiatives such as the Faster Adoption and Manufacturing of Hybrid and Electric Vehicles (FAME) scheme aim to incentivize the adoption of electric vehicles and support the development of charging infrastructure.

While there may be criticisms or areas for improvement in Modi's environmental policies, these examples demonstrate a recognition of the importance of environmental sustainability and a commitment to green initiatives at the national and international levels.This world actually needs more green visionaries, with more green metacognition, more green sensitivity like theRaimond de Hullu, a Dutch architect,whose brain child is OASIS (Organization for the Advancement of Sustainable Internet Standards), His visionary approach to architecture and urban design, reflects his vision of a holistic and interdisciplinary approach to architecture and urban design, drawing on principles of sustainability, innovation, and social responsibility to create spaces that are not only aesthetically pleasing but also environmentally responsible, socially inclusive, and resilient to the challenges of the 21st century.

Works Cited:
Shruti Sonal.What is vikas,and at what cost do we want it, asks , 'green nobel' winner, an interview of Alok Shukla, , times of India, Jaipur,May 5,2024.
O'Neill, Michael. Green Parties in a Post-Growth Society: New Politics and Regional Development. Ashgate, 28 Dec. 2015.
Van Wart,M. Dynamics of leadership in Public Service: Theory and Practice: April 12.2012.
Kraft, Michael E., and Daniel J. Fiorino. Green Parties and Politics in the United States.Routledge, 27 Feb. 2015.
 Mulvaney, Dustin (Ed.). Green Politics: An A-to-Z Guide. SAGE Publications, Inc., 3 Feb.2011.
Bomberg, Elizabeth, John Peterson, and Richard Corbett. Green Parties and Politics in the.European Union. Routledge, 28 Oct. 1998.

Cato, Molly Scott. Green Political Economy: Integrating Ecology and Economy. Routledge, 10 Oct. 2013. Wall, Derek. The No-Nonsense Guide to Green Politics. New Internationalist, 1 Aug. 2010.
An interview of Raimond de Hullu on https://unitedinbeauty.wordpress.com. August11, 2015.

Chapter 18

Teaching and Environment Pedagogy: An Indian Perspective

Gargi Singh
Nitesh Singh

Abstract

Ecocriticism is the study of the relationship between humans and non-humans in cultural history, and how this relationship is portrayed in cultural productions. Culture is an essential part of Human Development and it is within this culture that the Education system is incorporated. This system is a part of the larger Ecological framework as proposed by Urie Bronfenbrenner. The contribution of various Indian Educationists and their education philosophies have immensely contributed to impact the thought process of children regarding environment. Every perspective presented in the paper focusses on a unique dimension of connecting real education with environment. In extension to the philosophical dimensions various programs at National, state, NGO's and school level have been pivotal in portraying the pedagogical practices in teaching and environment which are highlighted as the best practices for the same. These practices are highlighted in the different systems of the Ecological framework. The efforts for amalgamating teaching with environment across Indian context are immense; the need of the hour is to acknowledge the best practices and place in efforts to enhance them further.

Keywords: Ecological, Environment, Culture, Educationist

Introduction

Greg Garrard defines ecocriticism as a critical analysis of environmental issues in literature or culture. He says that ecocriticism is the study of the relationship between humans and non-humans in cultural history, and how this relationship is portrayed in cultural productions. Culture is an essential part of Human Development.Human development sees an individual developing within a system, wherein each system contributes towards the development of a thought process in the growing child. The culture we are a part of influences various systems we are a part of. The ecological system theory developed by Urie Bronfenbrenner sees a child growing amidst five systems. The connect between the human and the Non-Human is established within these developing systems and the child.

On the basis of the ecological theory the current paper tries to bring attention towardsthe Indianeducation system and the various approaches within this system that have been constructively engaged to promote the overall well-being of a child by emphasizing on the elements of nature and its contribution towards development of an individual.Since centuries Indian gurukul systems had been one of the strongest systems that promoted the overall well being and development of a child in connection with nature and environment. The works of various Indian writers and thinkers indicate a relation between the environment and humans. The works of GijubhaiBadheka, tarabai Modak, J Krishnamoorty and many more have been benchmarks to emphasize the coexistence of Humans and the Nature. It is noteworthy that their work in education had been related with the early years of children, in order to attain a perspective of that the human, the natural—can coexist, cooperate, and flourish in the biosphere. This system of education can be very well connected with the ecological system theory developed by Urie Bronfenbrenner that sees a child growing amidst various ecological systems, in order to develop as a conscious citizen towards the environment.

The current Research paper aims to highlight on three

key dimensions-

1. The Ecological Systems Theory: A Developmental Perspective aligned with the developing thought processes of an individual

2. Contributions of Indian Thinkers and Writers towards valuing environment in Teaching

3. Best practicesin India to enhance in students an environment connect and sensitivity

The Ecological Systems Theory: A Developmental Perspective aligned with the developing thought processes of an individual

Urie Bronfenbrenner's theory defines complex "layers" of environment, these layers are also called systems wherein each has an effect on a child's development. This theory looks at a child's development within the context of the system of relationships that form his or her environment. This theory has recently been renamed "bioecological systems theory" to emphasize that a child's own biology is a primary environment fueling her/his development. The interaction between factors in the child's maturing biology, his immediate family/community environment, and the societal landscape fuels and steers his development. Changes or conflict in any one layer will ripple throughout other layers. To study a child's development then, we must look not only at the child and her immediate environment, but also at the interaction of the larger environment as well.

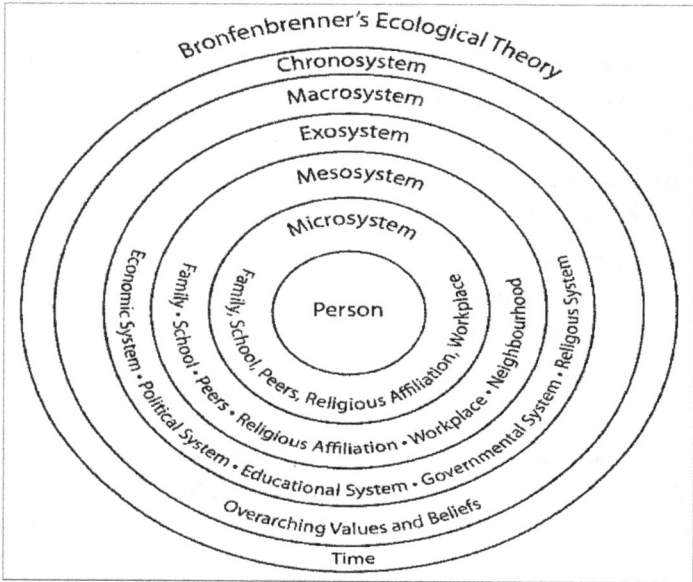

An adapted illustrated model of a Bronfenbrenner's
Ecological Theory (Adapted from Berger, 2007).

Insight into the Various Systems of Theory

The microsystem – this is the layer closest to the child
and contains the structures with which the child has
directcontact. The microsystem encompasses the relationships andinteractions a child has with her immediate-
surroundings (Berk, 2000). Structures in the microsystem
include family, school, neighborhood, or child care
environments. At this level, relationships have impact in two
directions - both away from the child and toward thechild.
For example, a child's parents may affect his beliefs and
behavior; however, the child also affects the behaviorand
beliefs of the parent. Bronfenbrenner calls these bi-
directional influences, and he shows how they occur among
alllevels of environment. The interaction of structures within
a layer and interactions of structures between layers is keyto
this theory. At the microsystem level, bi-directional

208

influences are strongest and have the greatest impact on thechild. However, interactions at outer levels can still affect the inner structures.

The mesosystem: this layer provides the connection between the structures of the child's microsystem (Berk, 2000).Examples: the connection between the child's teacher and his parents.

The exosystem: this layer defines the larger social system in which the child does not function directly. Thestructures in this layer affect the child's development by interacting with some structure in her microsystem (Berk, 2000). Parent workplace schedules or community-based family resources are examples. The child may not bedirectly involved at this level, but he does feel the positive or negative force involved with the interaction with hisown system.

The macrosystem: this layer may be considered the outermost layer in the child's environment. While not being aspecific framework, this layer is comprised of cultural values, customs, and laws (Berk, 2000). The effects of largerprinciples defined by the macrosystem have a cascading influence throughout the interactions of all other layers. Forexample, if it is the belief of the culture that parents should be solely responsible for raising their children, thatculture is less likely to provide resources to help parents. This, in turn, affects the structures in which the parentsfunction. The parents' ability or inability to carry out that responsibility toward their child within the context of thechild's microsystem is likewise affected.

The chronosystem: this system encompasses the dimension of time as it relates to a child's environments. Elementswithin this system can be either external, such as the timing of a parent's death, or internal, such as the physiologicalchanges that occur with the aging of a child. As children get older, they may react differently to environmentalchanges and may be more able to determine more how that change will influence them.

In a nutshell, Bronfenbrenner's view is that a child's development is significantly affected by the complex world that envelops her/him whether it be the minutest of the conversations s/he has with her/his playmates, or the social and economic life-circumstances into which s/he is born. l. For instance, a child's eco-sociological model would consider the components of green-space, food quality and source, outdoor play, exposure to toxins, and ecological connection in addition to the familial relations, societal norms, and other social influencers.

The work further discussed will help the readers to connect with the different layers. The contributions of various Indian thinkers towards valuing environment has been a part of the exosystem of the child , however has impacted the micros system wherein multiple interactions of the child at school and home have been impacted.

Contributions of Indian Thinkers and Writers towards valuing environment in Teaching

Education is one of the major medium to apply the thought or idea in practice. Multiple Indian thinkers and writers have been pivotal in valuing education with a special connect with environment. These Indian thinkers emphasized on various educational philosophies, however the current paper examines the ideas they proposed for environment and its importance in teaching.

Gijubhai Badheka

GijubhaiBadheka worked extensively in southern Gujarat. In 1920 Gijubhai set up his first Balmandir, Dakshinamoorti at Bhavnagar in Gujarat. He was influenced by Maria Montessorie, an educationist and thinker from Italy and liberally used the educational philosophies of Frobell, Dalton and others. Though he borrowed ideas from the west, he systematically oriented these thoughts to suit Indian conditions. His system of education was indigenous in nature and suited to the Indian socio-cultural fabric. He emphasized on the space where children have freedom to learn in a 'free' and 'natural' environment, especially in the formative years. He published extensive literature for teachers and parents to promote his ideas regarding Education.

Jiddu Krishnamurti

Krishnamurtigave a concrete form to his thought on education by his experiments.His educationalphilosophy is popularly known as 'Right Education' or 'Right Kind of Education'. Krishnamurtidiscusses about the right environment, about right functions of education, right curriculum, rightmethods of teaching, right teachers and right school which collectively makes Krishnamurti's RightEducation. He reflects his educational thought in many of his books from which 'Education andSignificance of Life', 'On Education', 'Life Ahead' and Letters to the School (Vol.1 & Vol. 2) areforemost.

He has presented an integrated curriculum to ensure the complete or holistic development of the child. He was very much concerned about environment therefore he advocated the study of environment with other subjects. In his educational institutes'environmental studies' has its existence as a separate subject.He gave much importance to the nature, the surrounding of which we all are the parts.He advocated preserving nature, the birds, animals, reptiles, insects etc. and spending time withnature in order to be sensitive and respectful towards nature. Now the policy makers also realizethe importance of same and recommended to introduce "Organic Living" and "Environmental Education" in the curriculumand also suggested to develop "respect for environment" in allstudents.

Tarabai Modak

Padmabhooshan Shrimati Tarabai Modak was a pioneer in the field of preschool ofeducation. Tarabai pioneered the concept of balwadi- a centre for preschool children.

Shestarted two types of balwadis at Bordi - Central Balwadis and AnganBalwadis.Tarabai stressed that theteachers should make their own play material from locally available materials. Thethings that could not be made by teachers were made by local artisans.Tarabai also initiated the concept of the Meadow School where teachers went to themeadows to teach the children who could not leave their cattle.The Gram Bal Shiksha Kendra at Kosbad, which under Tarabai's leadership began the programme of preschool education for the tribal children of Kosbad Mills, now runs acomplex of educational institutions ranging from a balwadi to a high school, traininginstitutions for teachers at different levels and a workshop for preparing educationalmaterials. The trainees of Kosbad, after receiving training in the institutions, are sentto villages to set up anganwadis devise play material from locally available materialand mobilize community support.

Anutai Wagh

Anutai Wagh worked closely with Tarabai Modak. While Tarabai initiated theconcept of the meadow school, it was Anutai Wagh who developed and carried thisconcept further. She made a major contribution by Indianizing Montessori materials, using stones, leaves, pebbles etc. available in the environment.   Again connecting the individual towards the environment they belong to.

Rabindranath Tagore

Tagore was a naturalist, believing in immediate and direct contact with nature as ameans of education. He said that "Children with thefreshness of their senses come directly to an intimacy with this world. This is a greatgift they have ... and must never lose their power of immediate communication withit... We should have the gift to be natural with nature and human with human society."Learning through the environment: Tagore stressed teaching through environment.To the preschooler, he said, teaching should be done when they are on 'naturewalks' or 'on trek'. "If possible I would recommend children to carry thenotebooks and to go on writing while they are on trek", he said.

Overall all these educational philosophies greatly emphasized on experiential learning and its importance in the context of the environment. To a great extent all these ideas have been amalgamated and incorporated in the National Education policy 2020 and National curriculum Framework 2023.

Best practices in India to enhance in students an environment connect and sensitivity

This section of paper attempts to showcase some of the best practices in teaching and environment pedagogical innovations and implementation.

Policy

The National Education Policy (NEP) 2020 aims to increase environmental awareness, encourage practical action, and equip students with the knowledge and skills to protect the planet. Environmental education in Indian school curriculum aims to help students understand the environment and its natural resources, and to inspire them to take action to create a sustainable future.The NEP also recognizes the role of educators in integrating sustainability principles into the curriculum.

Pedagogical Enhancement in Teaching Learning Processes

Azim Premji Foundation through their Voluntary Teacher Forum (VTF) worked on teaching-learning process by analysing the Tamil Text books. They further integrated environmental themes with language teaching and ensured meaningful experiential learning with the help of various aspects of nature and moving from the known to the unknown with the support of events from daily life practices, which made the students' understanding better. Homeroom teachers were able to integrate nature-based lessons and activities by combining subjects, like language-EVS lessons, and Tamil-English. The teaching-learning process, including the classroom practices, became so much more effective when we integrated nature-based experiences along with languages and maths to increase ecological consciousness. More effective when we integrate nature-based experiences along with languages and maths, to increase ecological consciousness.

In a study where Indian students showed more willingness to act in a pro-environmental manner in comparison to European and Australian equivalents, it was found that one of the important factors that contributed to their pro-environmental attitude was the presence of Eco-clubs, environmental displays and environmentally orientated assemblies in their schools which were focused on imparting non-formal environmental education to the students (Chhokar et al., 2011).

In a study conducted on schools in Kerala, it was found that a special programme named SEED (Student Empowerment for Environmental Development), aimed at creating environmental awareness among students, was introduced by a leading newspaper of the state in association with a major bank and it was very effective in creating environmental awareness amongst school students (T. Ram and Pereira, 2014).

Another study showedthat the presence of a National Park near the school did not make much difference in the knowledge of students regarding wildlife conservation, but conducting regular awareness programs focused on wildlife conservation such as lectures, nature trails, camps, wildlife movie screening, game shows, and provision of educational material greatly improved theknowledge of students about conservation (Kidwai, 2018).A research involving students of VIII and XI standard found that field-based educational programs, such as field trips are very importantteaching tool in EE as they help in improving the relationship of students with their localenvironment. These programs develop a sense of curiosity, compassion and willingness in studentsand provide them with an opportunity to explore and engage with their environment as well ascreate a positive attitude towards biodiversity conservation (Ramadoss and Poyya Moli 2012).

According to research by Ramadoss and PoyyaMoli (2011)active biodiversity education programs conducted in urban and suburban schools werefound to be effective in enhancing the knowledge, interest and skills of students related to theprotection and conservation of local biodiversity and natural resources.

Patil (2006) in a review of research studies on methods of teaching in EE referred to studies by Indubala and Kidwai, which concluded that video films and fields trips as a medium of instruction were found to be effective in teaching EE. She found that Sen in his study concluded that encouraging classroom environment, method and quality of instruction and feedback methodology impacted the learning outcomes in students. Further, she referred to the studies of Sunnetha, Tomar and Modak, who respectively found multidisciplinary approach; activity-based instruction and EE club activities to help develop a positive attitude in students towards the environment (Patil, 2006).

Hanley et al. (2019), in their research highlighted a special kind of exchange program conducted between few public schools in Kentucky and private schools in eastern India. It developed a yearlong curriculum with online modules combined with field research opportunities on theavailability, quality and usage of water. The highlights of the research indicated various aspects wherein

- Student creativity and cooperation was enhanced.
- It supported students understanding on water-related issues at the global level as well as issuesparticular to their region and made a connection between water and

culture.

Teacher capacity building for teaching Environment Education

According to Ravindranath (2007), to promote Environment Education in India the department of education has been involved in extensive programs at National and State levels, even NGO's have been enthusiastically engaged in this direction. Efforts have been made to incorporateenvironmental concepts into the teaching of other disciplines, provide teachers with pre-serviceand in-service training to acquaint them with the concepts as well as various pedagogicalapproaches involved and create and distribute high standard resource materials related to environment education. Various types training has been provided to teachers to teach EE in schools and Centre forEnvironmental Education (CEE) has played an important role in conducting various environmentaleducation programs.

Development of Resource centres

Centre for Environmental Education (CEE) has created regional centres which helped schools, students andeducators by acting as resource centres for them (Almeida and Cutter-Mackenzie, 2011). In addition, toprovide educators with a resource on environmental activities, NCERT with the help of Centre forEnvironmental Education, Ahmedabad (CEE) published a handbook for teachers entitled "Joy oflearning" which aims to make EE a joyful learning experience for learners (Gopal and Anand,2006).

Other Programs

CEE runs outreach of two key national Environmental Sustainable Development programmes targetingschool students: the Paryavaran Mitra (PM) 'friend of the environment' programme and theMinistry of Environment, Forest and Climate Change, India,MOEFCC's National

Green Corp programme (NGC), Bangay (2016). Both the programmes are based on differentapproaches: NGC is an action-based initiative for secondary students which encouragescommunity involvement through extra-curricular activities focusing on key sustainability issuessuch as water and energy conservation, biodiversity protection, resource and waste managementand land use planning. Whereas PM is based on the whole-school approach and works towardsincorporating sustainability concepts in the curricula of VI to VIII grade. The activities andresource material related to PM fall under the pedagogic framework of Explore, Discover, Think,Act and Share; covering five key themes: water and sanitation, energy, biodiversity and greening,waste management and culture & heritage.Further, Roberts (2009) found that NGC was able to bring environmental awareness and behaviour change in students.

All the pedagogical practices that have been mentioned are functional at all the systems of the ecological framework, eventually imbibing in the children a sense of belonging and responsibility to reestablish the connect between the human and the non-human.

Conclusion

The efforts made across the five systems of Urie Bronfenbrenner are well reflected through the article. The need of the hour is to revisit the good practices and enhance the perspectives of all the children through more educational pedagogies that become the concrete pillars to support the cognitive patterns of the children to experience the angle of coexistence between humans and the environment.

Works Cited:

Anand, V.J. "Krishnamurti's Philosophy of Education". International Journal of Research in all Subjects in Multi Languages. I.F.6.156 Vol. 8, Issue: 8, August: 2020 (IJRSML) ISSN: 2321 – 2853

Berger, K. S. (2007). The developing person through the life span. New York: Worth Publishers.

Berk, L.E. (2000). Child Development (5th ed.). Boston: Allyn and Bacon. 23-38Moving "eco" back into socio-ecological models: A proposal to reorient ecological literacy into human developmental models and school systemsDecember 2011Human Ecology Review 18(2):167-173December 201118(2):167-173. Nick Stanger

Integrating Environmental awareness with academic subjects. 2022. https://azimpremjiuniversity.edu.in

Early childhood care and education. TarabaiModak. https://earlychildcareeducation.wordpress.com/about/philosophers/tarabai-modak/.

Thriveni C. "Rabindranath Tagore's Philosophy on Indian Education". (2022) International Journal of Home Science.https://www.homesciencejournal.com (accessed May 19, 2024).

Ravindranath, M. J. (2007). Environmental education in teacher education in India: Experiences and challenges in the United Nation's Decade of Education for Sustainable Development. Journal of Education for Teaching, 33(2), 191–206. https://doi.org/10.1080/02607470701259481

Almeida, S., & Cutter-Mackenzie, A. (2011). "The Historical, Present and Future ness of Environmental Education in India". Australian Journal of Environmental Education, 27(1), 122–133. https://doi.org/10.1017/S0814062600000124

Kidwai, Z. (2018). Role of wildlife and environmental awareness in developing conservation aptitude among students around Corbett National Park, Uttarakhand, India.

11(1), 14.

Ramadoss, A., &Poyya Moli, G. (2011). Biodiversity Conservation through Environmental Education for Sustainable Development—A Case Study from Puducherry, India. International Electronic Journal of Environmental Education, 1(2), 0

Patil, A. (2006). The development and implementation of a teacher education model in environmental science education for indian certificate of secondary education (ICSE) schools (Order No. 3237093). Available from ProQuest Dissertations & Theses Global. (305342835). Retrieved from http://ezproxy.library.yorku.ca/login?url=https://searchproqu estcom.ezproxy.library.yorku.ca/docview/305342835?accou ntid=15182

Bangay, C. (2016). Protecting the future: The role of school education in sustainable development – an Indian case study. International Journal of Development Education and Global Learning, 8(1), 5–19. https://doi.org/10.18546/IJDEGL.8.1.02

Roberts, N. S. (2009). Impacts of the National Green Corps Program (Eco-Clubs) on students in India and their participation in environmental education activities. Environmental Education Research, 15(4), 443–464. https://doi.org/10.1080/13504620902994127

Hanley, C., Freeman, R. L., Fryar, A. E., Sherman, A. R., & Edwards, E. (2019). Water in India and Kentucky: Developing an Online Curriculum with Field Experiences for High School Classes in Diverse Settings. Journal of Contemporary Water Research & Education, 168(1), 78–92. https://doi.org/10.1111/j.1936-704X.2019.03322.x

Gopal, G. V., & Anand, V. V. (2006). Environmental Education in school Curriculum an overall perspective. 11 https://egyankosh.ac.in/bitstream/123456789/34220/1/Unit-2.pdf

Chapter 19

Ecopoetics as a Medium of Environmental Communication in Indian Films

Anoopama Yadav

Abstract

The late twentieth century has awakened to a new menace: ecological disaster. The most important environmental problems that humankind faces as a whole are nuclear war, depletion of valuable natural resources, population explosion, sharp increase in productivity of exploitative technology, conquest of space with the main motive of using it as a garbage dump, pollution, and extinction of species, among others. In such a context, ecocriticism theory has begun to address the issue as a part of academic discourse. The gap between man and nature has been increasing by heaps and bounds in the modern world of science and technology. Therefore, bringing about a balance between man and nature and ecology has been a dire need of today's time.

The exploitation of nature for man's unsatiable cravings has found resonance in cinematic portrayals. Cinema within an ecological slant helps us comprehend the ways in which culture has destroyed nature. The number of Indian films that feature environmental wildlife or climate change in their messaging is on the rise. Films about the environment and climate issues have a deep impact on human behavior. Indian cinema is mainly known for environment-oriented films. Nowadays, film makers are producing films to raise awareness about environmental issues.

This research paper offers how films based on ecocriticism and ecofeminism can lead mankind to a balance between man and nature. Depletion of natural resources, human deeds that harm the ecological balance and their adverse effect on our society will be explored.

Keywords: film, ecocriticism, ecofeminism, environment, ecology, awareness.

Ecocriticism is the latest and newest type of theory in criticism that has evolved in the 21st century. Modern scientists are very worried about the very existence of the earth and its resources. Modern science and technology have created dangers for the future generation of mankind. The breaking of the layers of ozone due to much carbon dioxide and too much consumption of natural gas, crude oil, etc. has made us think seriously about how we can protect the Earth and the environment in order to survive ourselves and our future generations. Ecocriticism is also known as *greenstudies*. It is popular in *ecopoetics*. It is also referred to as *environmentalliterarycriticism*. Ecocriticism deals with how environmental issues, cultural issues concerning the environment, and attitudes are presented and analyzed. One of the main goals of ecocriticism is to study how individuals in society behave and react in relation to nature and ecological aspects. David Arnold and Ramchandra Guha's *Nature, Culture, Imperialism* (1995) have been remarkable works in the environmental history of India and Southeast Asia. Vandana Shiva in *StayingAlive* (1988) and Guha and Juan Martinez-Alier (*VarietiesofEnvironmentalism*, 1998) have studied the development and ecological problems of Third World countries.

The Indian films call attention to complex environmental problems and the lives and subsistence affected by such issues. The films deal with human-wildlife disputes and environmental issues. These days, the filmmakers who proceed towards such complex issues are confident about the role of anticlimactic environmental films that considerately grasp the trope to bring consciousness and encourage action among audiences. *Fukrey* 3 (2023) portrays a water shortage, an event quite common during the summer in many Indian cities. A scene depicting a water tanker being surrounded by screaming, shouting hundreds of people waiting desperately to get their shareis set in an alleyway in Delhi. This scene depicting a water shortage in Delhi was seen as a welcome trend in bringing up a real environmental issue in a commercial target film. In another movie, *TheArchies* (Nov. 2023), the protagonists were shown fighting to save a park. *Kedarnath* (2018) portrayed the impact of the 2013 flash floods in Uttarakhand. Lakhs of people were uprooted and cut off from others. Many died being taken away by the flood. The livelihood of lakhs of people was devastated. The story of *Lakadbagha* (Jan. 2023) revolves around hyenas being rescued from wildlife trafficking. In the film *Sherdil: ThePilibhitSaga* (2022), a sarpanch with a desire to gain solatium plans to go into the forest to be killed by a tiger. The filmmakers motive lies to highlight whatever is happening to the people. To convey a message and encompass entertainment, the target audience will be covered. A recent study by researchers at FLAME University, Pune, examined how nature, environment, and climate have been featured in Indian films since the 1940s. It was found that there are hundreds of Indian films that feature nature, wildlife, and the environment, including popular films such as *MotherIndia, Pather Panchali,* and one of the biggest commercial hits of 1971, *HaathiMeraSaathi.* At that time, these films were viewed entirely from a societal perspective.

The documentary film *NotJustRoads,* directed by Nitin Bathla and Klearjos Eduardo Papanicolaou, was part of the 2021 edition of the *All Living Things Environmental Film Festival* (ALTEFF). The documentary revolves around the development of the Dwarka Expressway in Delhi, which was first contemplated in 2007 to relieve traffic congestion and secure better connectivity. The narrative uses a combination of elegance and descriptive anthropology to communicate the stories of humans and non-humans whose lives are entwined with the big road being built. The road covers land with many ecological commons initially inhabited by villagers, herders, and the working class. Through this film, the makers have interrogated and examined the development that comes with environmental and social violence. The depictions of shabby houses, building workers laying the roads, and herdsmen left with no way to take their cattle, farmers with diminishing agriculture fields, resolute salesmen trying to sell properties, bothered environmentalists trying to safeguard the biodiversity, combined with the sound of machines at work, reformers expressing opposition to saving Aravalli Park, and the bizzare music of cricket, make the film a captivating watch. *Not Just Roads* proposes to build cross-mindedness among all the parties and bring consciousness to what happens when intensive capitalism imposes violence on the environment. Filmmakers should focus on producing captivating happenings that carry audiences into the world of their environmental films. A strong narrative structure, immersive visuals, sound, and the use of emotion may support such transportation (Morris et al., 2019; Ratcliff & Sun, 2020).

The Oscar-winning best documentary, *Elephant Whisperers,* features climate change, wildlife, biodiversity, and the environment. Director Kartiki Gonsalves has showcased an Indian couple who devote their lives to caring for an orphan baby elephant named Raghu, forging a family like no other. *Elephant whisperers* create more awareness, empathy, and connection to elephants and also to other living beings that we share our spaces with. It depicts the sacred bond between man and animal while also looking into elephants as a species and how intelligent and beautiful they are. The film focuses on indigenous people and their way of life. *Shoot That Leopard,* directed by Sohail Jafri, goes around a human-leopard dispute in a Himalayan mountain forest. The protagonist, Ashwani Kumar, shoots the leopards with his camera and showcases them in the habitats around Shimla to spread consciousness among people. Lakhpat Singh Rawat kills a leopard with his gun. He is an official hunter for the forest department. He looks at his work as community service. Filmmakers also need to be aware of the various identities that make up their audience and choose characters for subjects that are relatable and empathetic. They should note that people more readily adopt the behavior of those they feel are similar to themselves (Bandura, 2009). The film also presents the opinions of wildlife experts and researchers, who describe the human-wildlife dispute as mainly a conflict between people. It is more about human administration than animal management. *Your Tiger, Our Forest,* directed by Ishan Sharma, is a documentary film that talks about Brahmapuri, Maharashtra, and a hotbed for human-tiger conflicts.

Agriculture lands are located close to the forest, and the villagers depend on the forest for resources. Placing the local community on the same platform as the forest department and the wildlife scientist is crucial for putting an end to human-wildlife conflict. Films can bring about discussion and awareness, but grass-roots action is what will bring about change. In Third World countries, the preservation of wilderness makes little sense where there is a shortage of land for the poor. Ramchandra Guha (1989), a renowned thinker and historian, talks about the notions of development in the Third World based on Western models of modernity. Environmental concepts about conservation derived from the West and the ancient social and cultural practices of local areas are denied. Guha and Martinez-Alier developed the idea of an 'environmentalism of the poor' (1998). They proposed that environmentalism in poorer nations cannot be separated from the issues of sources of income, dissemination of resources, and social justice. The poor tribals in the jungles sustain themselves by cutting wood for fuel. To assert that this is deforestation and should be made illegal is to disregard the very basic inequality of the social structure. Environment justice movements like India's Chipko and Narmada Bachao are about the preservation of ecosystems that help the poorer sections of society sustain themselves.

The film *Sherni,* directed by Amit Masurkar, explores different contours of ecofeminism. This movement came into existence in the latter half of the twentieth century. Ecofeminism calls for prompt action to end all oppression. It views the world as divided into two groups: the privileged and the oppressed. The privileged group involves upper- or middle-class humans, technologically advanced males, and the oppressed group is poor, working-class, non-human animals, undeveloped nature, and females. The ecofeminists link stereotyping, discrimination, factionalism, and prejudice against another species as the main oppressors on earth. They argue that men focus on rights and women on responsibilities. This makes the woman more environment-friendly, for her point of view towards 'utilisation' of nature in a more responsible way. Ecofeminism ties the two movements of feminism and environmentalism together and pinpoints male dominance and a patriarchal societal structure as the fundamental causes of taking advantage of and abuse of both women and nature.

In the film *Sherni*, Amit Masurkar has projected the empowerment of women by putting stress on the ideals of ecofeminism effectively through the plot. The protagonist, Vidya Vincent, is played by Vidya Balan, who is deputed as a Divisional Forest Officer. She faces a crisis due to tigress T12, who is terrorizing the dwellers in that village. The surrounding area around the village is covered by forest. People are dependent on firewood for fuel and green pasture for the cattle. Hassan Noorani, played by Vijay Raj, is a professor of entomology. He endeavors to educate members of the constituency regarding the coexistence of tigers and the villagers. Vidya Vincent believes in saving the livelihood and lives of villagers without killing the tigress T12. But the ruling and opposition parties foment the agenda of killing the tigress for political gains. Vidya and Noorani, along with the forest officers and the women in the village, are shown as empathetic towards the tigress T12. They support the perspective that carnivorous animals never intrinsically look to hunt and kill humans; rather, the need for survival compels them to travel across the territory inhabited by humans. A vital role is played by forest officer Vidya Vincent in spotting the tigress and scrutinizing the psychology of the tigress through sitting in different government meetings. She has an austere belief in saving the lives of villagers without killing the tigress. Filmmakers should embrace the potential for environmental films to offer meaningful experiences to their audience, exploring profound concepts and displaying the complexity and vastness of natural environments (Oliver et al., 2018; Raney et al., 2020).

Sherni explorers the parallel between the subduing and exploitation of the powerless, that is, the population of the village, and the oppression of the tigress T12. Vidya and her team discover that T12 has given birth, and for sustenance, she will wander near the villages to hunt down cattle. She is made to hold back in her job of protecting the tigress by the politicians, the poacher, and the senior forest officer whom she once aspired to become. Through this off-centered representation of an eco-feminist heroine, Amit Masurkar introduces a new edge to feminist Bollywood cinema in *Sherni*—the interrelation between the nurturing aptness of women and nature.

The main resistance of the ecofeminist order and the masculine indifference for nature appear in the rivalry between poacher Pintu, played by Sharat Saxena and Vidya. Male politicians and Pintu planned to take advantage of the situation to assert their power. Pintu declares his masculinity by hunting down the tigress. Noorani rightly points out that Pintu wishes for another trophy by killing the tigress; this way he can assert his power against nature. The killing or injuring of animals is illegal under sections 428 and 429 of the Indian Penal Code, but most Indians torturing animals to death for business or for fun in India do so without being punished. French feminist *Francoised'Eubonne*, who coined the term ecofeminism, proposed that the movements for gender equality and ecology are related, as the disempowering and ill treatment of women by people of color and the environment are all carried out or continued through patriarchal dominance. This film remains an extraordinary milestone in terms of women working in opposition to the patriarchal social structure.

The film explores the conflict between humans and non-humans, raises awareness about the conservation of wildlife, and is critically commended as a well-researched document-tary film depicting environmental concerns with the narrative of saving a tigress untwisted in the political, social, and bureaucratic entangle of the society dwelling in the Indian forests. The theme of the film centers on the deliberate devastation caused by the tigress T12, the reason being the increasing infiltration of villagers into the forest for animal fodder, agriculture, human settlements, mining industry, and road infrastructure. The film depicts the dissemination of humans at the expense of non-humans, thereby leading to the encroachment of forest areas and jeopardizing species of wildlife. It is interesting and fascinating for the audience's visual literacy. The female protagonist is presented as a modern woman resisting conventional image by the nature of her work as a female forest officer, which is largely shown as a male-dominated realm, and by her personal life, wherein she puts duties in her career above the duties of marriage and motherhood. Nevertheless, her maternal feelings are triggered when she comes across the fact of the tiger cubs petting her against the male hunter Pintu, which reveals the patriarchal nature of the forest society that considers the repression and control of nature and puts no importance on the unfairness against nature and the environment. Nature and women are both regarded as marginalized. Therefore, women relate to nature as their inherent sisters are seen to be more enterprising in matters of nature protection. Film, as a popular medium, has different narrative techniques to highlight and focus attention on aspects of ecocriticism and ecofeminism.

Environmental films have become a fully developed visual genre in recent years. Their efficacy as a means of enthusiastic discussion about intricate environmental issues results from the resilience and charisma of the medium and the positive changes in the methods of storytelling. Nowadays, film makers scrutinize ways in which the stories might bring out the need for reflective thoughts, self-actualization, and ideas within viewers through a combination of story, visual, sound, and facts provided. The filmmakers are expressing their interest in a new world of environmentalism with new ideas. Some ideas and concepts are not critical but suggestive. They are exhibiting films from every stage and trying to portray the confrontations of everyday life, which is something to be cheered for. With the latest equipment and new storytelling styles, the environment and wildlife cinema are appealing to more people than ever before, and it's riveting to see the developments. These filmmakers have tried to explore beyond the issues and unfold varied solutions in their fields.

Works Cited:

https://books.google.com/books/alid=04qzEAAAQBAJ&sou
rce=kp_cc
https://doi.org/10.1080/089494668.2022.2129258
https://feminismindia.com/2021/06/22/sherni-review-vidya-
balan-ecofeminism/
https://feminisminindia.com/2021/06/22/sherni-review-
vidya-balan-ecofeminism/
https://india.mongabay.com/2021/11/films-that-offer-a-
space-for-discussion-on-complex-environmental-issues/
https://india.mongabay.com/2024/02/hindi-cinema-
embraces-environmental-narratives/?amp=1
https://www.newindianexpress.com/magazine/2021/jun/27/s
herni-movie-review-a-pitch-perfect-roar-2321258.html
https://www.onelittlestep.in/5-bollywood-movies-on-
environmental-issues/
https://www.shethepeople.tv/filmtheatre/sherni-trailer-
review-vidya-balan-film/
A.A. Raney, M.B., Oliver& A. Bartsch, "Eudaimonia as media effect." In M.B. Oliver, A.A. Raney & J. Bryant (Eds.), *Media effects: Advances in theory and research*, Routledge, 2020, pp 258-274.
A. Bandura, "Social cognitive theory of mass communication." In J. Bryant & M, B. Oliver (Eds.), *Media effects: Advances in theory and research* , 3rd ed., Routledge, 2009, pp 94-124.
B.S.Morris,P.Chrysochou, J.D.Christensen, J.L.Orquin, J.A.Barraza, P.Zak, & P.Mitkidis,"Stories vs. facts: Triggering emotion and action -taking on climate change."*Climate Change*, 154(1-2), 2019, pp 19-36.
C.L. Ratcliff, & Y. Sun, "Overcoming resistance through narratives: Findings from a meta-analytic review."*Human Communication Research*, 2020, 46(4),pp. 412-443.
M.B.Oliver,A.A.Raney,M.D.Slater,M.Appel,T.Hartmann,A.
Bartsch,F.M.Schneider,S.H.Janicke

Bowles,N.Kramer,M.L.Mares,P.Vorderer,D.Rieger,K.R.Dal e& E.Das, "Self-transcendent media experiences:Taking meaningful media to a higher level." *Journal of Communication*, 68(2), 2018, pp. 380-389.

P.K. Nayar, *Contemporary literary and cultural theory: From structuralism to ecocriticism.* Pearson Education India, 2010, pp. 248-249.

P.K. Nayar,*Literary Theory Today*,Asia Book Club,New Delhi,2002,pp. 290-294.

Chapter 20

Environmental Ethics of Aarsh System in Vedic Literature

Ashutosh Pareek

Abstract

This study delves into the intrinsic relationship between Vedic Culture, the world's oldest literature &culture, and the environment, shedding light on the environmental ethics embedded in ancient civilizations and assessing our contemporary adherence to these principles. Throughout human history, the environment has been integral to our existence, providing essential elements like clean air and water. The concept of Panch Mahabhutas &Ditties is most relevant to our ecological awareness.

This research underscores the enduring relevance of environmental ethics within Hinduism and highlights the potential of ancient wisdom to inform contemporary environmental stewardship. Thispaper will describe the rich tapestry of Vedic literature to uncover insights into humanity's relationship with nature, ecological principles, and environmental sustainability which may be called in one word as ecological ethics. Drawing upon ancient Indian texts such as the Vedas, Upanishads and other philosophical treatises, the paper explores the reverence for nature, ecological consciousness and environmental ethics embedded within these ancient scriptures. Through a comprehensive analysis, it elucidates the ecological wisdom and relevance of Vedic literature in contemporary environmental discourse, highlighting its potential contribution to shaping sustainable practices and fostering a deeper connection with the natural world.

Keywords: Ecology, Environmental ethics, Vedic methodology, Aarsha System, Balanced development,

Sustainable Growth, Vedic Vision, Rita, Panch Mahabhutas.

1. Introduction

Vedic philosophy which is also called Aarsh system derives infinite creativity, actions and power from universal laws of Nature. Twentieth century has witnessed increasing focus on growth and accumulation of wealth at the cost of society resulting in many socio-economic, political and environmental problems.

In Vedic philosophy, core function of business is to create wealth for 'Wellbeing of all stakeholders'. Sustainable growth comes by earning money following 'Values'. Key to success lies in results in higher performances. The long-term interests of an organisation are best served by adopting an integrated approach to maximise the Global Product.

Aarsh System, the system revealed by Sages, often described as a way of life, stands out as one of the earliest and most scientifically inclined belief systems. Central to Hindu philosophy is the notion that nature is a divine gift, with human life intricately linked to the health of the environment. In Vedic theology, natural elements such as Air, Water, Sun, Earth and Fire are revered as manifestations of the divine, worthy of worship.

The Vedas emphasize the importance of respecting and preserving nature, even in eras when environmental conservation was not a mainstream concern. These texts advocate for ecologically benign rituals and practices, suggesting that adhering to them could offer solutions to modern environmental challenges.

The Vedic period represents a pivotal era in Indian history characterized by profound philosophical and spiritual inquiry. Central to Vedic thought is the interconnectedness of all life forms and the reverence for nature as a divine manifestation. This paper aims to examine the ecological ethos embedded within Vedic literature, offering insights into ancient environmental wisdom and its implications for modern ecological discourse.

About 1.97 billion years ago, when the present cosmos came to existence, four ancient sages namely Agni, Vayu, Aditya and Angira received the complete knowledge of 'God', 'Soul' and Atharva-Veda. This knowledge is pure and stored in the Cosmic Records. Millions of sages have got access to the cosmic knowledge reservoir and shared it for the benefit of global society.

Vedic philosophy provides many clues for sustainable growth of all. For example quoting hymns of Rig-Veda, Dayananda Sarasvati (1872) wrote about an aeroplane having trio-merits of flying into the sky, streaming on water and moving on road. It happened thirty years before manufacturing of first air-craft of present era. He explained that I have seen many hymns in Veda to get in-depth knowledge about it; but a glimpse is enough for the wise men. However, little efforts have been made to integrate the search of scientific knowledge with Vedic studies since then.

Through this research paper, a deeper understanding of nature, ecocriticism, and environmental ecology in Vedic literature is elucidated, offering valuable insights into ancient environmental wisdom and its implications for contemporary sustainability efforts.

2. Conceptual Framework

This section provides a theoretical framework for understanding nature, ecocriticism, and environmental ecology within the context of Vedic literature. It delineates the key principles and philosophical underpinnings that inform Vedic perspectives on the natural world, including the notions of Dharma (righteous duty), Karma (action and consequence), and the interconnectedness of all living beings.

The Rig-Vedic hymns portray the world as a place where human beings are expected to enjoy life. Rig-Veda explains the 'cosmic order' stating that physical as well as moral laws govern the entire universe and that no transgression of these laws is allowed.Vedic philosophy identifies four objectives to be sought in human life namely, Value system, Money, Desires and Salvation. These should be followed in such a way that Value system leads to attainment of money, money leads to fulfilment of desires and finally desires leading toLeading Organisation. These four principles are called : 1. Value System (Dharma), 2. Money (Artha), 3. Desires (Kama), 4. Salvation (Moksha).

Vedic philosophy emphasizes that Values are the basis of entire universe. Values constitute those actions, which were upright in the past, upright today and will remain upright in the future. Following hymn from ancient book, 'Mahabharata' explains essence of Value system (Dharma) stating: "O men! Essence of Ethics (Dharma) lies in living together on the Earth like brothers and prosper by using the immense resources of the world. It will eliminate all the ills & sorrows and lead to attainment of cosmic peace for all." Values based system empowers every member of the organisation to take decisions as long as it doesn't harm others. However, every action which may adversely impact others should be based on Values.

3. Environmental approach in Aarsh System:

Here, the paper explores specific passages from the Vedas, Upanishads, and other Vedic scriptures that reflect ecological consciousness and reverence for nature. It examines hymns dedicated to various elements of the natural world, such as Agni (fire), Varuna (water), Vayu (wind), and Prithvi (earth), elucidating the symbiotic relationship between humans and the environment as depicted in Vedic literature.

N. J. Lockyer has declared: "The Vedas, in fact, is the oldest book in which we can study the first beginnings of our language and of everything which is embodied in all the languages under the sun."The Vedas deal with knowledge, the knowledge of all sorts. They cover knowledge both physical and spiritual. Especially the Vedic views revolve around the concept of nature and life.In recent days, environmental science and ecology are disciplines of modern science under which study of environment and its constituents is done with minute details. As Science, they are established in 20th century, but their origin can be seen long back in the Vedic and ancient Sanskrit literature.

4. Environmental Ethics and Sustainability

The concepts of environment differ from age to age, since it depends upon the condition, prevalent at that particular time. In this paper, an effort is made to find out the awareness of ancient Indian people about the environment. As Sanskrit literature is so wide we refer here mainly to Vedic texts, particularly the Vedic Samhitas. The Environment (Protection) Act, 1986 defines the environment as follows: 'Environment includes water, air and land and the inter-relationship which exists among and between water, air and land and human beings, other living creatures, plants, microorganisms and property.'From the above definition, it can be briefly said that environment consists of two components namely biotic (living organisms) and abiotic (non-living materials) factors. The living organisms can be grouped into three types - those living mainly on land, in water and in air. The non-living materials of the environment are land, air, water, property etc.

According to one indigenous theory established in the Upanishads, the universe consists of five basic elementsviz. - 1. Earth or land, 2. Water, 3. Light or luster, 4. Air, and 5. Ether. The nature has maintained a status of balance between and among these constituents or elements and living creatures. A disturbance in percentage of any constituent of the environment beyond certain limits disturbs the natural balance and any change in the natural balance causes lots of problems to the living creatures in the universe. Different constituents of the environment exist with set relationships with one another. The relation of human being with environment is very natural as he cannot live without it. Fromthe very beginning of creation he wants to know about it for self-protection and benefit.

According to Aarsh System Environment is the whole of Divinity, Cosmic order, Nature and division. We can make strong collaboration with all of these elements. A better understanding creates a better vision to our ecological phenomena.

Divinity to Nature: Attributes assigned to deities fit in their natural formsand activities, as Soma is green, fire is bright, air is fast movingand sun is dispenser of darkness. The characteristics of theseforces described in the verses prove that Vedic seers were mastersof natural science.A famous geologist S.R.N. Murthy has written on the earthsciences in the Vedas. He has somehow a different opinion aboutVedic gods and hence states, 'the natural geological aspects havebeen described as Indra, Agni, Vayu, Varun, Usas etc.

Cosmic Order 'Rita' and Varuna: In the Vedas, the order ofthe Universe is called '*Rita.*' Rita reduces chaos to cosmos, andgives order and integration to matter. It also gives symmetryand harmony in the environment.According to H.W.Wallis 'Theprinciple of the order of the world, of the regularity of cosmicphenomena, was conceived by the *Rishis*to have existed as aprinciple before the manifestation of any phenomena. Thephenomena of the world are shifting and changeable, but theprinciple regulating the periodical recurrence of phenomena isconstant; fresh phenomena are continually reproduced, but theprinciple of order remains the same; the principle, therefore,existed already when the earliest phenomena appeared.'

Division of Universe: The universe consists of three intertwined webs, *Prithivi, Antariksha* and *Dyau.* Vedic scientists divided even the length in three calling them upper, medium and lower. The tripartite division of the universe into three regions- *Prithivi*, the earth, *Antariksha*, the aerial or intermediate region which is between heaven and earth, and *Dyau*, the heaven or sky is very well established in the Vedic literature. A verse from the Yajurveda states that the division of universe was done on a subtle level, and not on gross level.The Vedic sages had the capability of looking at such a subtle level, which is beyond the reaches of modern science. Here; in reference to environmental study, we regard the division of the universe as the most important concept of the Vedas.

In the Atharvaveda, the earth is described in one hymn of 63 verses. This famous hymn called as *Bhumisukta* or *Prithivisukta* indicates the environmental consciousness of Vedic seers. The seers appear to have advanced understanding of the earth through this hymn. The earth is described then as being present in the middle of the oceans (sedimentary rocks) and as one having magical movements. The hymn talks about different energies which are generated from the form of the earth.'O *Prithivi*! thy centre, thy navel, all forces that have issued from thy body- Set us amid those forces; breathe upon us.Mantra also says that the Earth is our mother and we are the sons & daughters of the Mother Earth.'

Water is essential to all forms of life. According to Rigveda the water as a part of human environment occurs in five forms: 1. Rain water (*Divyah*) 2. Natural Spring (*Sravanti*) 3. Wells and canals (*Khanitrimah*) 4. Lakes (*Svayamjah*) 5. Rivers (*Samudrarthah*)

Chandogya Upanishad describes about qualitiesof water - 'The water is the source of joy and for living a healthy life. Itis the immediate cause of all organic beings such as vegetation, insects,worms, birds, animals, men etc. Even the mountains, the earth, theatmosphere and heavenly bodies are water concretized.'the cycle ofwater is describedfrom ocean waters reach to sky and from skycome back to earth.Rainwaters are glorified. The rain-cloud isdepicted as *Parjanya* God.

Yajurveda says, '*Vayu* has penetrating brightness.' The meaning of *Vayu* is made clear in Shatapatha Brahmana in the following Mantra, 'Sun and rest of universe is woven in string.What is that string that is *Vayu*.' This verse clearly shows that here*Vayu* cannot mean air alone.Rigveda mentions- 'O Air! You are our father, the protector. Air hasmedicinal values.'Let wind blow in the form of medicine and bringme welfare and happiness.'

Medicated air is the international physicianthat annihilates pollution and imparts health and hilarity, life andliveliness to people of the world. Hilly areas are full of medicated airconsisting of herbal elements. Another verse describes characteristics of air - 'The air is the soul of all deities. It exists in all as life-breath. Itcan move everywhere. We cannot see it. Only one can hear its sound.We pray to air God'Ancient Indians, therefore, emphasized that theunpolluted, pure air is source of good health, happiness and long life.Vayu god is prayed to blow with its medicinal qualities.

Akash is an important particle of the environment. Modern environmentalists discuss sound or noise pollution.There is a relation between ether and sound. The sound waves movein sky at various frequencies. Scientist could see the sky which existsonly in the vicinity of earth, but *Taittirya* Upanishad throws light ontwo types of ether *i.e.*one inside the body and the other outside thebody. The ether inside the body is regarded as the seat of mind. Aninteresting advice to the mankind is found in the Yajurveda-'Do notdestroy anything of the sky and do not pollute the sky. Do not destroyanything of *Antariksha*.'

'sanaM'is the ethical part of our environment. The mind is most powerful and unsteady. Although the study of mind does not appear directly under the contents of modern environmental science but in reference to cultural environmental consciousness of Vedic seers, we find many ideas discussed in Vedic literature on the pollution of mind and its precautions.Considering the havoc that the polluted minds may create, our ancient sages prayed for a noble mind free from bad ideas. The logicians recognize *Manas* as one of the nine basic substances in the universe.

The '*Yajna*' is regarded as an important concept of Vedic philosophy and religion. In broader sense it is the part of Vedic environmental science. Yajurveda and Rigveda describe it as the 'navel (nucleus) of the whole world.'It hints that *Yajna* is regarded as a source of nourishment and life for the world, just as navel is for the child. Vedas speak highly of '*Yajna*.' Through it, seers were able to understand the true meaning of the *Mantras*. Yajna created all sorts of knowledge.

It is considered as the noblest action. In simple words, *Yajna* signify the theory of give and take. The sacrifice simply has three aspects: *Dravya* (material), *Devata* (deity) and *Dana* (giving).When some material is offered to a deity with adoration, then it becomes *Yajna*. Pleasing deity returns desired material in some different forms to the devotee. This *Yajna* is going on in the universesince beginning of the creation and almost everywhere for productionand, also for keeping maintenance in the world. Even the creation ofuniverse is explained as *Yajna* in the *Purusha Sukta*.

Thus, the conceptof *Yajna* seems to be a major principle of ancient environmental science.In environment all elements are inter-related, and affect eachother. Sun is drawing water from ocean through rays. Earth gets rainfrom sky and grows plants. Plants produce food for living beings. Thewhole process of nature is nothing but a sort of *Yajna*. This is essentialfor maintenance of environmental constituents. The view that *Yajna*cleans atmosphere through its medicinal smoke, and provideslongevity, breath, vision etc., is established in Yajurveda. Few scholarshave attempted to study the scientific nature of the Vedic *Yajnas*. Undoubtedly, they have never been simple religious rituals, but have avery minute scientific foundation based on fundamental principles.According to Vedic thought, *Yajna* is beneficial to both individual andthe community. *Yajna* helps in minimizing air pollution, in increasingcrop yield, in protecting plants from diseases, as well as in providinga disease-free, pure and energized environment for all, offering peaceand happiness of mind. Moreover, *Yajna* serves as a bridge betweendesire and fulfillment.

5. Contemporary Relevance and Implications

The paper discusses the contemporary relevance of Vedic ecological wisdom in the face of global environmental challenges such as climate change, deforestation, and biodiversity loss. It explores how insights from Vedic literature can inform sustainable practices, promote environmental stewardship, and inspire a deeper appreciation for the interconnectedness of life

In modern Sanskrit, the word *Paryavarana* is used for environment, meaning 'that which encircles us', which is all around in our surroundings. But in the Atharvaveda words equivalent to this sense are used; such as Vritavrita, Abhivarah,Avritah, Parivrita etc. Vedic view on environment is well-defined in one verse of the Atharvaveda where three coverings of our surroundings are referred as Chandansi: 'Wise utilize three elements variously which are varied, visible and full of qualities. These are water, air and plants or herbs. They exist in the world from the very beginning. They are called as Chandansi meaning 'coverings available everywhere.' It proves the knowledge of Vedic seers about the basic elements of environment.

Modern Indian Scientists are astonished and also feelproud of our ancestors for their knowledge and views aboutenvironment. Ancient seers knew about various aspects ofenvironment, about cosmic order, and also about the importance ofco-ordination between all natural powers for universal peace andharmony. When they pray for peace at all levels in the *'Shanti Mantra'*they side by side express theirbelief about the importance ofcoordination and interrelationship among all natural powers andregions. The prayer says that not only regions, waters, plants trees,natural energies but all creatures should live in harmony and peace.Peace should remain everywhere. The *mantra* takes about the concordwith the universes peace of sky, peace of mid-region, peace of earth,peace of waters, peace of plants, peace of trees, peace of all-gods,peace of Brahman, peace of universe, peace of peace; "May that peacecome to me!"

6. Conclusion

To conclude, this research paper underscores the profound ecological wisdom embedded within Vedic literature and its relevance for contemporary environmental discourse. It advocates for a holistic integration of Vedic principles with modern environmental practices, emphasizing the importance of cultivating a deeper spiritual connection with nature to address pressing ecological challenges and foster a more sustainable future.

It is clear that the Vedic vision to live in harmony withenvironment was not merely physical but was far wider and muchcomprehensive. The Vedic people desired to live a life of hundredyears and this wish can be fulfilled only when environment will beunpolluted, clean and peaceful.

The Vedic sages felt the greatness of these forces. They adored these activities. They appreciated these forces. They worshiped and prayed them due to regard, surprise and fear. They realized instinctively that action, movement, creation, change and destruction in nature are the results of forces beyond men's control. And thus they attributed divinity to nature.

The knowledge of Vedic sciences is meant to save the humanbeings from falling into an utter darkness of ignorance. The unity indiversity is the message of Vedic physical and metaphysical sciences.Essence of the environmental studies in the Vedas can be put here byquoting a partial *Mantra* of the Ishavasyopanishad 'One should enjoywith renouncing or giving up others part.Vedic message is clearthat environment belongs to all living beings, so it needs protectionby all, for the welfare of all'. Thus the study proves the origin ofenvironmental studies from the Vedas.The famous Kalyan mantra gives a great thought for the welfare of everyone.The mantra says that may all beings be happy, may all beings be healthy. May all beings experience auspiciousness. Lets no one suffer.

These mantras reflect the reverence for nature and ecological consciousness found in Vedic literature. They celebrate the interconnectedness of all life forms and emphasize the importance of living in harmony with the environment.

Works Cited:

1. Dayananda Saraswati (1872); Atharva Veda 8-2-21; Yajur Veda 30-18; Bhagwad Gita 8-17 to 19.
2. Rig Veda 10-130-4 to 7; 8-100-10, 11.
3. Mahanam Upnishada 17.6; Manu Smiriti, 1-108.
4. N. J. Lockyer, The dawn of Astronomy, Massachusetts, Institute of Technology, p. 432.
5. A.R. Panchamukhi, Socio-economic Ideas in Ancient Indian Literature, Rashtriya Sanskrit Sansthan, Delhi, 1998, p.467.
6. इमानि पञ्चभूतानिपृथिवीआपज्योतींषि। : आकाश : वायु Aitareya Upanishad 3.3.
7. S.R.N. Murthy, Vedic View of the Earth, O.K. Printworld, New Delhi, 1997, p.12.

8. H.W. Wallis, the Cosmology of the Rigveda, Cosmo Publications, 1999, pp.94-95.
9. Yajurveda 7.5.
10. S.R.N. Murthy, Vedic View of the Earth, D.K, Printworld, Delhi, 1997, p.87.
11. यत्तेमध्यंपृथिविय्च्चनभ्यंयास्तऊर्जस्तन्व:संबभूवु:।
    तासुनोधेह्वभिन:पवस्वमाताभूमि:पुत्रोअहंपृथिव्या:पर्जन्य:पितासउन:पिपर्तु
    ॥ Atharvaveda 12.1.12.; RTH Griffith, The Hymns of theAtharvaveda, D.K.Publishers, Delhi, 1995AD ,P 95.
12. या आपो दिव्या उत वा स्रवन्ति खनित्रिमा उत वा या: स्वयंजा। समुद्रार्था :
    : या: शुचायपावकास्ता आपो देविरिह मामनन्तु॥ Rigveda 7.49.2.
13. Chandogya Upanishad 7.10.1.
14. अप:समुद्राद् दिवमुद्वहन्ति दिवस्पृथिवीमधि ये सृजन्ति।Atharvaveda, 4.27.4.
15. Raja Ram Mohan Roy, Vedic Physics, Scientific Origin of Hinduism, Golden Egg Publishing, Toronto, 1999, p. 84; Jaiminiya Bra. 1.192; Yajurveda 1.24; Shatapatha Bra. 8.7.3.10.
16. उत वात पितासि न:। Rigveda 10.186.2.
17. आ वा वाहि भेषजम्। Ibid, 1.37.2.
18. वात आ वातु भेषजं शम्भु मयोभु नो हृदे। Ibid 10.186.1.
19. आत्मा देवानां भुवनस्य गर्भो यथावशं चरति देव एष। घोषा इदस्य : शृण्वरि े न रूपं तस्मै वाताय हविषा विधेम॥ Ibid 10.168.4.
20. स य एषो अन्तर्हृदय आकाशा। सुवरित्यसौ।: Taittiriya Upanshad 1.6.1; 1.5.1.
21. द्यां मा लेखीरन्तरिक्षं मा हिंसी:: Yajurveda 5.43.
22. Nandita Singhavi, Vedon Me Paryavarana, Sonali Publications, Jaipur, 2004, pp. 313- 356.
23. Tarkasamgrahah 2.
24. अयं यज्ञो विश्वस्य भुवनस्य नाभि: Yajurveda13.62; अयं यज्ञो भुवनस्य नाभि: Rigveda 1.164.35.

25. यज्ञेन वाचः वदवीयमायन्। Rigveda 10.71.3.

26. तस्माद् यज्ञात् सर्वहुतः ऋचः सामानि जज्ञिरे। Ibid, 10,90.9.

27. यज्ञो वै श्रेष्ठतमं कर्म। Shatapatha Brahmana. 1.7.1.5.

28. आयुर्यज्ञेन कल्पताम्। प्राणा यज्ञेन कल्पताम्। चक्षुर्यज्ञेन कलपताम्। Yajurveda 9.21.

29. M.L.Gupta, The Cosmic Yajna, Samhita Books Jaipur, 1999, pp.46-47.

30. वृतावृता Atharvaveda 12.1.52.7.

31. अभीवारः Ibid. 1.32.4.

32. आवृता Ibid .10.1.30.

33. परीवृता :Ibid. 10.8.31.

34. त्रीणि छन्दांसि कवयो वि येतिरे पुरूरूपं दर्शतं विश्वचक्षणम्।

   आपो वाता ओषधयस्तान्येकस्मिन् भुवनार्पितानि॥ Ibid 18.1.17.

35. द्यौ :शान्तिरोषधय :पृथिवी शान्तिराप:शान्तिरन्तरिक्षं शान्ति : शान्तिर्ब्रह्म :शान्तिर्विश्वेदेवा :।वनस्पतय:शान्ति शान्ति:सर्व शान्ति:, शान्तिरेव शान्तिमा शान्तिरेधि॥ सा :Yajurveda 36.1; Atharvaveda 19.9.94; A.C.Bose, The Call of the Vedas,Bhartiya Vidya Bhavan, Mumbai,1999, p.281.

36. तच्चक्षुर्देवहितं पुरस्ताच्छुक्रमुच्चरत्।पश्येम शरदः शतंजीवेम शरदः , शृणुयाम शर,शतंशतंप्र ब्रवाम शरदः शतमदीनाः स्याम शरदः शतं भूयश्च , शतात्॥ शरदः Atharvaveda 19.67.1.

37. ईशावास्यमिदं सर्वं यत्किञ्च जगत्यां जगत्।तेन त्यक्तेन भुञ्जीथा मा गृधः कस्यस्विद्धनम्॥ Iishavasyopanishad,1.

38. "सर्वेभवन्तुसुखिनः, सर्वेसन्तुनिरामयाः। सर्वेभद्राणिपश्यन्तु, माकश्चिद्दुःखभाग्भवेत्॥"[1] This mantra is not in Vedas. But this is famous with some variation in Garuda Purana 2.35.51, Bhavishya Purana 3.2.35.14.

Chapter 21

Ecocriticism - A Peep into the Bioscope

Aarya Palawat

Abstract

'Ecocriticism' as a term is still debated and evolving due to the recent wide interest of philosophers, litterateurs and filmographers. Ecocriticism in cinema examines how films represent environmental issues and the natural world. This approach analyzes how movies reflect, reinforce, or challenge societal attitudes toward nature and ecological concerns. By focusing on themes such as environmental degradation, climate change, and human interaction with the natural world, ecocriticism in cinema explores how visual storytelling can influence and reflect ecological awareness.

This paper explores the key aspects of ecocriticism in films that include the portrayal of landscapes, the depiction of human-nature relationships, and the impact of cinematic narratives on viewers' environmental consciousness. It highlights environmental destruction or present alternative visions of harmonious coexistence with nature. This article also critiques industrialization and consumerism, offering insights into how cultural artefacts shape and are shaped by ecological contexts. Through this lens, ecocriticism help reveal how films engage with ecological themes, potentially inspiring audiences to consider their own environmental impact and the broader implications of their actions. By examining cinematic representations of the environment, scholars and viewers alike gain a deeper understanding of the cultural and ethical dimensions of environmental issues.

Keywords: Ecocriticism, Eco cinema, Nature, World, Destruction

As a plot or subplot, nature has always found place in various human arts; sometimes a shade in a painting reflects the artist's emotion, and sometimes the mingling of two roses shows the union of two bodies. We have been making art that reflects the many sides of the environment for as long as we have known nature. Films that talk about nature and show its many shades, whether trees, animals, or climate change and its consequences for different beings, are not new to us. They are watched through the ecocritical lens.

While most of us relate this term to the modern dystopian disaster cinema, which clearly takes us to the end of this world, ecocriticism talks about the process, the minute details, the struggles of humans with nature, and the bond and connection that they share. Eco cinema not only aims to raise awareness about environmental issues but also employs innovative techniques and visual aesthetics to deepen viewers' understanding of ecological concerns and humanity's role within the natural world, making it a rich field for both artistic expression and critical discussion.

One such film is Alejandro G. Iñárritu's *The Revenant*, which is not just about conflicts among tribes, betrayal, unyielding perseverance to survive a harsh environment, and avenging but has a strong ecocritical connotation. Iñárritu has used cinema, a potent medium of cultural representation and communication, to address environmental issues. In this masterpiece, land stands witness to the conquest and subjugation, where postcolonialism and ecocriticism converge. The exploitation of the environment, considering it mute and lifeless, and utter disregard of the indigenous communities and landscape with an aim of profit maximization in capitalist enterprise recurs in The Revenant.

In *The Revenant*, the natural environment has been highlighted in its truest form possible, and to achieve this purpose, the director Alejandro Gonzalez Iñárritu's has shot the movie in natural light. Nature in the film is so vibrant and alive that it almost achieves a sense of mysticism. This setting has opened the avenue to probe the relationship between man and nature in multiple layers of inquiry. 'The Revenant' means one who has returned from the dead. Though, the film gives superhuman grit and perseverance to the protagonist Hugh Glass to survive the harsh environmental conditions after being mauled within an inch of his life by a grizzly bear and subsequently abandoned by his fellow mountain men. It looks like the movie preaches man, blinded by greed of consumption and colonization and on the verge of his own death by harming the environment, to desperately try to save himself. Anthropocentric greed has been established early on in the film when the antagonist Fitzgerald, an embodiment of the colonial master with attributes of exploitation, selfishness, lack of conscience, and cunning, declares to the other fur trappers appointed by the Rocky Mountain Fur Company to amass "thirty pelt bales" instead of "fifteen pelt bales."

In this film, we see how nature makes and break a human, how it provides raw material for development, and how experiences and conditions mould and refine these traits, leading to the diverse range of human outcomes. We see how Hugh survives an unforgiving winter and snowstorm and how a dead horse saves his life. In order to save himself, he merges into nature, surrenders to it, and finds ways to survive, and in his quest for survival, he cuts open the gut of the carcass and removes the insides. He then squeezes himself into its abdominal cavity and gives himself the gift of life. Once the weather gets better, he gathers a bit of strength; he comes out of the carcass and caresses it out of gratitude. In a tremendous act of cinematography and amazing execution, the glistening sunrays of a new morning are shown greeting Hugh Glass through leaves drenched in fresh morning dew. It shows how a vibrant and lively nature, a witness to Hugh's relentlessness in the face of all odds, gives him a ray of hope, a new energy to continue his fight for survival.

The Revenant shows us how Mother Nature always opens a window, but one has to be able to see it. The dead horse becomes a site of conflicting ideas: mother nature's life-giving quality at times even at the cost of her life, just as a woman brings a new life in this world and, at times, dies in the process; man's inseparability from and dependence on nature; as well as man's taming and using of non-human objects for his own selfish interest. It also points out men's unethical dwelling and lack of concern not only for the environment but also for each other, as a severely injured Hugh was left alone to die by his fellow men. In the course of the film, we also see a physically and emotionally damaged Hugh Glass put a flower on the mouth of his son's dead body. The little flower, in this context, reflects man's embeddedness in the natural environment. The human body, irrespective of gender, race, and class, is created from nature and returns to nature. At the end of the movie, we see Glass's wife as a goddess of nature who is pleased with Glass's journey, his newly found wisdom, and lets justice lay in the hands of the Creator and his respect for the natural environment. New materialist concepts of matter turning them into a living reality abound in the movie. It also uses a terrific survival story in the wilderness to show nature in its unbound glory, and it also opens a space for showing how a human being can be receptive to nature's boons and, in the process, unveils the meaning of existence. Depicting that when time comes nature will put an end to exploitation of all sorts. While receiving the Oscar for *The Revenant*, Leonardo di Caprio ended his speech with the words, "Let us not take this planet for granted; I do not take tonight for granted."

The world of Eco cinema is vast; one filmmaker who continuously includes ecocritical analyses into his films is South Korean writer and director Bong Joon-Ho. He beautifully merges several angles of analysis and creates sharp and beautiful films that are as enriching for the eyes as they are for the mind. While all of his films have political commentary in them, one that stands out in terms of ecocritical thought is *The Host*.

It is about a monster who rises from the Han River in Seoul after an American company completely disregards safety protocols and dumps heaps of chemicals down the drain. The film is based on an incident when the American military dumped a big amount of formaldehyde down the drains in Seoul, and just as shown in the film, this led to big protests. This film combines several political commentaries, with ecocriticism in the context of anti-imperialism being the biggest one. The monster in *The Host* is the recurring entity, like the colonizer and imperialist influence. Ecocriticism in the context of imperialism is a layer that is often disregarded in art. In contemporary as well as historical ecocritical films, the line between protagonists and antagonists, known as eco-heroes and eco-villains, has been very blurred. In all the other films, dystopian realities are presented with very little context, leaving us with a disastrous world with no answers as to how protagonists ended up in the situation and how they're going to get out of it. But *The Host* rejects that from its very start, as we are told from the beginning that the disasters we are about to witness are a result of a specific company's choices, and this realization, in combination with the history it's based on, sets the tone for the film in regards to protagonists and especially antagonists.

Another such cinematic experience is Ang Lee's *Life of Pi*, which is based on Yann Martel's novel with the same name. The movie depicts the beauty that grows between human and non-human environments. It encompasses rich and pictorial seascape, marine life, dolphins, birds, albatrosses, Wilson's petrels, a short-tailed shearwater, masked boobies, vivid descriptions of weather, rain, storms, blasts, thunder, lightning, and a carnivorous island—a floating organism of algae of leviathan proportions—and how the order of this ecosystem in and on the sea is destroyed by man who pours tons of waste on the seashores surrounding big towns and capitals. The director shows conception of interconnectedness through the natural cycle of the 'food chain'. The hyena eats the zebra and the orangutan on the lifeboat, and in turn she is eaten by Richard Parker, the tiger. Mr. Pi spends 227 days with a ferocious tiger on a rough and stormy ocean and a carnivorous island without water to drink and food to eat but somehow learns to survive in an adverse environment. His many challenges underscore man's integration with nature.

Pi, traveling by a ship named Tsimtsum to Canada with his family and a few zoo animals, realized in the middle of nowhere that the ship was sinking. He found the situation as 'unbelievable as the moon catching fire'. Soon, he was alone and orphaned in the lap of the Pacific Ocean, hanging to an oar; an adult tiger in front of him sharks beneath him. He was guggling between life and death in the lifeboat, and along with him were Richard Parker (a tiger), a zebra, a hyena, and the Orange Juice, a female orangutan. In order to survive, Pi draws a separate territory for himself and Richard Parker very intelligently. He finds ways not to let the tiger enter his territory, and soon both Pi and Richard Parker live on different kinds of sea life for their survival.

After a long, long hardship, Pi happens to see a freshwater pond. He reaches an island that is six or seven miles in diameter. This island is not a normal piece of land, a small hand mass rooted to the floor of the ocean, but is rather a free floating organism, a ball of algae of leviathan proportions. On this strange island, Pi sees trees growing directly out of vegetation without any soil. Pi and Richard Parker stay here for some time, sleeping in their boat and exploring the island during the day. Pi discovers a huge colony of meerkats who sleep in the trees and freshwater ponds. One day, Pi finds human teeth in a tree's fruit and discovers that the island eats people. He and Richard Parker head back out to sea and finally reach a Mexican beach. There Richard Parker runs off, and villagers take Pi to the hospital.

There is always beauty, splendour, and the presence of opposites such as smoothness and roughness—a sea of tranquillity and tumultuousness in the ocean—but Pi learns to merge and adjust himself even in an antagonistic atmosphere. In fact, what appear to be opposites in nature is nothing but different facets of nature. It's a man's duty to learn to adjust himself to them to live happily and peacefully.

Motion pictures are capable of reaching the most number of people, especially in the modern era of technology. They influence a large number of audiences and have the reach to gradually bring about a positive change by depicting the follies of human existence. It is a potent medium of representation of cultures, history, natural environment, human psyche, life, and beyond. Films like *The Revenant*, *The Host*, and *The Life of Pi* provoke several thoughts in the minds of their spectators while laying the most emphasis on the natural environment, which the films' cinematography captures exceptionally. The most intriguing part of these films is that their respective plots are thoroughly ecocentric and speak of environmental concerns without stating them directly but by exploring complex webs of relationships among human beings, the material world, and the natural world. They intervene with the themes of history, love for family, and the astonishing range of human willpower, but all of these are related to and situated within the living and breathing natural world, which watches everything as an overarching and omnipresent spirit.

Various viewpoints and ideas are allowed to corelate seamlessly as the films do not directly address ecological issues but delves deeper into the reasons of environmental destruction, that is, the unbridled pleonexia of imperialism and holds up the mirror to human beings, warning them of their own coming doom resulting from greed. They also penetrate deeper into human consciousness and impels the audience to think. They speak of exploitation at many levels but never show environmental exploitation directly. Rather, they use cinematography to give a broader picture of nature where the exploitation takes place. They use glimpses, scenes, metaphors, and dialogues loaded with meaning to show human lust for consumption.

All these are terrific survival stories in the wilderness to show nature in its vivid glory and also open a space for showing how a human being can be receptive to nature's boons and, in the process, unveil the meaning of existence. Such wisdom gleaned from nature is enough to put an end to exploitation of all sorts. Apart from the breathtaking cinematography, story, and presentation, these films also tell us the realms of time and place do not bound that ecocriticism. It is, was, and will always be a global issue, concerning all the races, times, and geographical locations. Hope is vital for any movement; the idea that there is a better world waiting for us as long as we're ready to build it and fight for it is what keeps us as a society and as a world going.

Work Cited:
*The Revenant,*directed by Alejandro G. Iñárritu
*The Host,*directed by Bong Joon- Ho
*Life of Pie,*directed by Ang Lee
https://youtu.be/AOoP56eXtzM?si=bbb1bb_fNF7Y4P2R
https://youtu.be/XD9X2obq1WQ?si=JaUKVnz9ySBZSL_v
https://youtu.be/LqnC020GJWE?si=q17nUDGKTPPg8C3Y
https://youtu.be/y75p0Ocxg0A?si=RxethamPQUkUGjD6

List of Contributors

1. Aarya Palawat, Dialogue Writer in Films and Serials.
2. Ambika Gahlot, Assistant Professor, Department of English, Regional Institute of Education, NCERT Ajmer.
3. Anita John, Department of Political Science, Mayo College Girls' School, Ajmer.
4. Dr. Anoopama Yadav, Assistant Professor of English, Maharaja Agrasen College for Women, Jhajjar, Haryana.
5. Dr. Ashutosh Pareek, Associate Professor, Department of Sanskrit, SPC Government College, Ajmer, Rajasthan.
6. Dr. Gargi Singh, PGT Psychology, Mayo College Girls' School, Ajmer.
7. Garima Swami, Research Scholar, University of Rajasthan, Jaipur. Rajasthan.
8. Dr. Karthika V P, Assistant Professor, Department of English, Government College, Daman.
9. Mahima Gaur, Associate Professor, Department of English, SPC Government College, Ajmer, Rajasthan.
10. Dr. Neelofar Kohri, Assistant Professor, Department of English, Government M.S. College for Women, Bikaner. Rajasthan.
11. Nitesh Singh, Delhi World Public School, Ajmer.
12. Dr. Pooja Khanna, Professor, Department of English, Aditi Mahavidyalaya, University of Delhi.
13. Dr. Poonam Rani Gupta, Professor, Dept. of English, Baikunthi Devi Kanya Mahavidyalaya, Agra, Uttar Pradesh.
14. Dr. Rishika Verma, Assistant Professor, Department of Philosophy, School of Humanities and Social Sciences, Hemavati Nandan Bahuguna Garhwal University, Srinagar (Garhwal), Uttarakhand.

15. Rohan Thomas Cherian, Assistant Professor, Department of English, St. Xavier's College Jaipur. Rajasthan.
16. Dr. Sanjana Sharma, Professor, Department of English, S.P.C. Government College, Ajmer (Rajasthan).
17. Dr. Sanju Choudhary, Assistant Professor, Department of English, University of Rajasthan, Jaipur. Rajasthan.
18. Dr. Shruti Dubey, Aviation English Instructor, Chimes Aviation Academy, Sagar, Madhya Pradesh.
19. Dr. Shruti Soni, Assistant Professor & Head of School of Life Long Learning, Anand International College of Engineering, Jaipur, Rajasthan.
20. Shweta Kundu, Research Scholar, Department of English, Banasthali, Rajasthan.
21. Dr. Smriti Srivastava, Assistant Professor, Department of English, Government College, Daman. DNH & Daman & Diu.
22. Dr. Sunita Dhankhar Professor, Department of English, Aditi Mahavidyalaya, University of Delhi.
23. Dr. Tamishra Swain, Assistant Professor, Dept. of English and MELs, Banasthali Vidyapeeth, Rajasthan.
24. Dr.Vrinda. R. Chanth Assistant Professor, Department of English, Government College, Daman. DNH & Daman & Diu.

www.ingramcontent.com/pod-product-compliance
Lightning Source LLC
Chambersburg PA
CBHW050213270326
41914CB00003BA/395